D0064720

SPEAKING SILENCES

STILLNESS AND VOICE
IN MODERN THOUGHT
AND JEWISH TRADITION

SPEAKING
SILENCES

STILLNESS AND VOICE
IN MODERN THOUGHT
AND JEWISH TRADITION

———

Andrew Vogel Ettin

UNIVERSITY PRESS OF VIRGINIA
Charlottesville and London

THE UNIVERSITY PRESS OF VIRGINIA
Copyright © 1994 by the Rector and Visitors
of the University of Virginia

First published 1994

Library of Congress Cataloging-in-Publication Data
Ettin, Andrew V., 1943–
    Speaking silences : stillness and voice in modern thought and
Jewish tradition / Andrew Vogel Ettin.
        p.   cm.
    Includes bibliographical references and index.
    ISBN 0–8139–1509–0
    1. Silence—Religious aspects—Judaism.   2. Spiritual life—
Judaism.   3. Silence.   I. Title.
BM723.E43   1994
296.3—dc20   94–9178
                                                                CIP

Printed in the United States of America

For My Family

its stories told

and untold

Contents

A Note on Texts

Wherever practical, I have consulted the original-language texts and provided my own translations, as indicated in the endnotes. Occasionally I have revised unnecessary gender-specific language in translations of traditional religious texts.

Transliterations follow generally accepted systems, with the usual exceptions for familiar names and terms.

Acknowledgments

One acknowledgment must be general: Although I did not always have a good answer at hand, I am nonetheless grateful to the many people from varying backgrounds who reacted with interest to the mention of the topic of this study and asked to know more. Their responses encouraged me both to continue and to write with the interests of specialists from several disciplines and nonspecialists in mind.

Much of the writing of this book took place during the summer of 1992, during a National Endowment for the Humanities seminar at Yale University directed by Benjamin Harshav. I am grateful to the NEH and to Professor Harshav for that opportunity. Benjamin and Barbara Harshav were encouraging, helpful in providing texts, and attentive to errors. I am also grateful to my co-participants for their questions, suggestions, and interest along the way; Alan Tansman, Marina Raskin, Sam Kassow, and Sonja Hedgepeth assisted with particular references. The cordiality of Sonja, Marina, Evelyn Avery, Sally Ann Drucker, Kerstin Hoge, and Natania Rosenfeld balanced the summer's work with the pleasures of friendship.

Rabbi James Ponet and the Egalitarian Minyan at Yale cordially provided great spiritual warmth on Shabbat mornings. Jane Snaider's hospitality buoyed the start of a new venture; Ginger Clarkson and Mark Ryan generously offered the beautiful, light, calm environment of their home in which to live and work.

Colleagues in the Wake Forest Humanities Clubs, especially David Levy and Gregory Pritchard, helped with insightful questions, as did the anonymous readers for the University Press of Virginia. I appreciate the readers' promptness and attentiveness to the text.

I am deeply grateful to Susan Leonard, who found time from a busy practice to talk with me over lunches about the theological issues raised in this book.

Among my family, I particularly want to thank Carole, knowing that I do not thank her often enough, and Anna, a God-wrestler.

28 June 1993

9 Tamuz 5753

Excerpts from Bella Akhmadulina, *The Garden: New and Selected Poems*, bilingual ed., trans. F. D. Reeve. © Henry Holt & Co.

Excerpts from A. R. Ammons, *Collected Poems*. © W. W. Norton & Co.

Excerpts from Maya Angelou, *I Know Why the Caged Bird Sings*. © Maya Angelou, 1969.

Excerpts from *Borderlands/La Frontera: The New Mestiza*, © 1987 by Gloria Anzaldúa. Reprinted with permission from Aunt Lute Books (415) 558–8116.

Excerpts from Ingeborg Bachmann, *Werke*. © R. Piper Kg Verlag, 1978.

Excerpts from Sarah Zweig Betsky, ed., *Onions and Cucumbers and Plums*. © 1981 Sarah Zweig Betsky.

John Cage, reprinted from *Silence*, pp. 22–23. © 1961 by John Cage, Wesleyan University Press, by permission of the University Press of New England.

Excerpts from Paul Celan, *Lichtzwang*. © 1970 Suhrkamp Verlag.

Excerpts from *But What: Selected Poems*, by Judith Herzberg and translated by Shirley Kaufman. *Field* Translation Series no. 13, 1988 (© Oberlin College Press).

Excerpts from *An Interrupted Life* by Etty Hillesum. English translation (©) 1983 by Jonathan Cape Ltd., copyright (©) 1981 by Haan Uniboek b.v., Bussum. Reprinted by permission of Pantheon Books, a division of Random House, Inc.

Excerpts from Irving Howe, Ruth Wisse, and Khone Schmeruk, eds., *The Penguin Book of Modern Yiddish Verse*. © Penguin USA.

Excerpts from Irena Klepfisz, *A Few Words in the Mother Tongue*. © 1990 by Irena Klepfisz. Reprinted by permission of the publisher, The Eighth Mountain Press: Portland, OR, 1990.

Excerpts from Primo Levi, *Ad ora incerta*. © Garzanti Editore, 1984.

Excerpts from Adrienne Rich, *The Fact of a Doorframe*, W. W. Norton & Co. © 1984 Adrienne Rich.

Excerpts from *Out of Silence: Selected Poems* by Muriel Rukeyser, edited by

Kate Daniels (TriQuarterly Books / Northwestern University Press, 1992). ©
1992 by William L. Rukeyser.

Excerpts from Gerald Stern, "Behaving Like a Jew," from his *Leaving Another Kingdom: Selected Poems by Gerald Stern*. Copyright © 1990 by Gerald
Stern. Reprinted by permission of HarperCollins Publishers, Inc.

Excerpts from Georg Trakl, *Dichtung und Briefe*. © 1969 Otto Müller
Verlag.

Excerpts from Hana Wirth-Nesher, "Between Native Tongue and Mother
Language in *Call It Sleep*," *Prooftexts* 10 (1990). Reprinted by permission of
The Johns Hopkins University Press.

To the Reader

To write about silence—even more, to speak about silence—may seem paradoxical; to write or speak about speech as well may seem solipsistic. Yet both are compelling, and not merely to the person engaged in the activity. Someone who is known to write is likely to be asked, probably with discomforting frequency and often at dismaying times, what one is working on. Surprisingly, the simple reply, "Silence," usually provokes a request to talk about it. Why do we want to know about silence, and why can't we let it be? Groping to answer such questions has led this writer to probe the links between silence and utterance.

Problems in communication may have become a cliché, but the matter is not trivial. The issues involved are theological, philosophical, psychological, and even political as much as literary. We in Western societies inherit a tradition associating cosmic creation and human prophecy with speech, but we also live in a world in which our contacts with both (as Emerson and Dickinson lamented) come through the words spoken directly ages ago by a seeming-distant God to human beings long gone. In our age we listen hopefully to what sounds very much like a vast wordlessness in which at times something may seem to be communicated, and some of us contend with language in an effort to fit it to what we believe we have grasped. No wonder that theoreticians in our century have so concerned themselves with language, silence, and the possibility of dialogue. Theologians (Buber, for one), psychoanalysts (Freud and Lacan), philosophers (Wittgenstein and Levinas), literary critics (Bakhtin)—simply to mention these names among many is to recall the breadth and even obsessiveness with which utterance and stillness have been probed. No wonder that societies around the world seem fixated on the media, for the vehicles of public communication have themselves become absorbing topics; no wonder that the search for "intelligent life" in outer space has concentrated on a quest for radio transmissions.

Such diversity of disciplines suggests that the issues dealt with in this study embrace a broad range of human concerns. Although most of the texts to be discussed come from areas of literature and religion, I hope that readers who do not specialize in either field and those who may not be professional academics will find that this book speaks to them thoughtfully about issues of interest in language they can understand. For reasons explained below, much material derives from the rich body of traditional Jewish writings and practices. I have attempted to present these in ways accessible to readers unfamiliar with that tradition, while also striving to address even those more knowledgeable.

Examples have been chosen for their potential to help in defining or exploring the issues, a purpose that seems best served by disregarding questions of canonicity as well as the limits of particular artistic genres or periods. Some writers will be cited frequently, but this book does not attempt a systematic analysis of any particular writer's ideas about the meanings of language or silence. Throughout, the guiding principles have concerned understanding how silence and utterance relate to one another and why each is important to us.

Introduction

SILENCE AND SPEECH differ obviously from one another, but they are not strangers to each other. Too often regarded simply as antithetical, silence and speech should be understood as inseparable partners in an eternal conversation. Each teaches about acts of creation. We learn about giving shape to this world in which we live, and we learn about shaping the artistic forms through which we represent and attempt to comprehend experience.

This study attempts to find how both the awareness of silence and the struggle to articulate something amid silence take shape within the form as well as the thematics of art. That is, we will consider not only—and not primarily— what the artist says about silence and the challenges of creation but also the textual details through which ideas and attitudes about these themes become manifest as elements in artistic style and techniques, the ways in which the impression of the stamp appears in the wax of the text. More ambitiously, because the dichotomies of silence and language express polarities within art and within life, we will seek to recognize how oppositions between silence and language shape our comprehension of what is blessed and what is cursed, the functions of silence and speech in creating and destroying.

Although it engages both topics, this book represents neither a study of the theory of creation nor a study of the Holocaust. The issue is not exclusively Jewish, although the principal subinquiry will concern how the Jewish tradition engages and is engaged by the topic. The biblical tradition underpinning much of modern Western culture begins with the Jewish exploration of how the process of creation unfolds, and that tradition posits creation through speaking. Jewish mystical writings exemplify the broader mystical tradition associating silence with pure understanding of deepest truth, however. Jewish history also attests to a continuing need to respond—be it through protest, lament, or complexly nuanced speechlessness—to the divisions and destructions, the exiles and exterminations that have been inseparable from experience from the beginning of creation itself. Exile at the very least arouses awareness of linguistic differences and the implications attendant on using different languages. Jews have been intimately acquainted with exile throughout history, but the experiences of exile are not unique to Jews. Sander Gilman has expressed the idea that "adapting to a new language, as did African blacks in slavery, the Irish following Cromwell, or the Jews in the Diaspora, means at least a period in which the novelty of the language makes a sensitive speaker aware of the hidden agenda of Otherness present in the language to be adopted. Such a moment of conscious disparity is also present in the tensions that exist between class-determined linguistic differences."[1] These issues are no more time-bound, unfortunately, than ethnically circumscribed. Yesterday's newspaper reports that in areas of Slovakia with a predominantly ethnic Hungarian population, Hungarian-language signs have been removed by the new government; in parts of the United States, requiring public signs in Spanish is as controversial as English signs in Quebec; and acceptance of ethnic languages in schools remains volatile around the globe.

Just below the surface of the text of this book lies another level of discourse about criticism and culture. Other writings about silence and language preserve category distinctions that seem unhelpful and even obstructive. Those writing from literary and artistic contexts ignore the theologians and philosophers, who, in turn, may cite works of art for examples but virtually disregard the insights of Cage the composer and of Olsen and Malraux the fiction-writers. This study consciously attempts to talk across that barrier between the sacred and the secular.

This work also attempts to open a dialogue that will render more permeable the boundaries of Jewish studies. That puts the issue rather starkly but perhaps not unfairly. Works dealing with Jewish texts tend to be segregated into an academic Pale of Settlement. With infrequent exceptions, they are read only by those whose interests center on Judaica, and they are often devoted to Jewish writings only.[2]

Concentrating on meanings relevant within the culture and context of the Jewish environment certainly requires no defense. Persuasive historical and conceptual reasons could be advanced as to why that is the most appropriate context in which to deal with Jewish writings and ideas. Particularly in chapters 2, 3, and 8 but also elsewhere throughout the book, we too will focus on understanding how the issues of silence and language are shaped through the special characteristics of Jewish language, stylistics, and history. The reader not especially concerned with Jewish matters should find that these expositions do not seem like the domestic tales of someone else's family; rather, the discussion should be like listening to devotees expound on a subject native to us all, even though we may not be intimately acquainted with their particular branch of it. In other words, this study is informed by Jewish writing but not exclusively concentrated on it.

Wordlessness is not a vacuum. Those who have written about the conditions broadly gathered under the term *silence* have different situations in mind, and they have differing outlooks on those situations. Tillie Olsen struggled against the external and internal obstacles she encountered as a creative writer, but she also contested the other obstacles before her as a woman writing and as a working-class mother striving for opportunities to write. Her experiences led her to hear in the many varieties of authors' silences the stifled creative voices of artists contending with themselves, their medium, or their society, particularly the muzzled voices of women writers striving first to find a way to speak and then to be heard.[3]

The composer John Cage, in almost dialectic opposition to Olsen, wrote of silence not simply as a musician's resource but as an opportunity to discern the usually obscured sounds that are inseparable from our physical lives. Involved himself in a larger aesthetic program undercutting the familiar distinctions between art and life, Cage composed some of his music using what we generally consider noise, disorganization, and random sounds occurring during what ordinarily would pass for silence. Within the natural phenomenon that we take to be silence, he discerned audible suggestions that the distinction between sound and silence is both illusory and irrelevant.[4]

André Malraux, humanist, former Marxist idealist, World War II resistance fighter, writer, art critic, and for a time France's minister of culture, applied the metaphor of "the voices of silence" to the eloquence of the visual arts but in a particular way reflective of his background. To Malraux, works of art communicate through their form and materials a record of their historical and social settings; they become silent witnesses to the ways in which broad cultural contexts and individual insights condition human experiences and possibilities.[5]

Without referring to Malraux's work but standing in opposition to its optimistic humanism, Ihab Hassan (in a book very much of its historical moment, 1966) suggested that literature itself was heading toward a silent ending in "anti-literature." Writing seemed increasingly obsessed, he suggested, with language's futility. This "literature of silence" he found paradigmatically embodied in two stylistic and ideological extremes. At one extreme lay the entropic silence within Samuel Beckett's obliteration of the word in despair of ever articulating "the Unnameable." Far off, at the other extreme in the works of Henry Miller (a writer seemingly devoid of silences), one could infer a postorgiastic silence following desperate efforts at making language live the body's experience. On one end, Hassan claimed, waited the "cosmic consciousness" that would "by-pass language," as Marshall McLuhan envisioned, while on the other was the spiritual salvation achieved through unshackled language, an idea typified by Norman O. Brown's conviction that because "the fall is into language," the way to redemption "is speaking with tongues . . . prelapsarian language . . . words with nothing to them."[6]

Moral and political issues are addressed more directly by the literary and social critic George Steiner. Raised attuned to Jewish experience (unlike Olsen, who also is Jewish), Steiner writes with the burdened consciousness of his personal past as a French-born Jew of Viennese ancestry who escaped the Holocaust because his family moved to the United States in 1940. Although sympathetic to Marxism's social and historical perspectives on art, Steiner's writing (unlike Malraux's) is troubled by the biographical and historical meanings of silences as responses to historical events, particularly to the Holocaust. Whether in the form of the painfully noble silence of writers who concluded that art could only be silent after one had known the unspeakable (as Theodor Adorno had asserted, "No poetry after Auschwitz") or the shamefully ignoble silence of those who did not speak out before, during, or after the horrors, silences as well as speech tell their tales of consciousness and conscience.[7]

Steiner's essays consider the morality of silence but do not engage the specifically theological context embodied in expressly religious texts. André Neher, from his standpoint as a Jewish philosopher and biblical interpreter who hid in France during World War II and later made his home in Jerusalem, probed the ambiguous theology and hermeneutics of silence through language and action in (primarily) the Hebrew Bible. Neher's subtle discourse examines the silence before creation and at the core of wisdom—God's silence about the divine nature and purposes, divine and human silences in the ongoing conversation between I and Thou as recorded in the text of the Hebrew Bible and rabbinic commentaries on that text, including the theological questions about silence posed by the modern *ḥurban*, the destruction that has been termed the Holocaust.[8] Like his friend Elie Wiesel, whose work he also discusses, Neher strives with passion both to confront human silence and to comprehend divine silence during the *Shoah*.[9]

By contrast, another modern philosopher, Max Picard, a German-speaking Swiss Catholic who faced the issues between (as the title of one of his books expressed it) "Hitler and ourselves," regarded silence as positive. Multiple in its manifestations, the silence of which he writes is joined mystically to the processes of creation and creativity, to spiritual renovation, and to prayer. Picard's silence (*Schweigen*, in his German original) seems more akin to mystical stillness. Silence, he believes, is the antidote to the noisy turmoil of disharmony and war distracting us from our spiritual focus, crowding out the inner space in which we would know our own mind rather than being subsumed into the collective swirl. Picard argues that it was not silent complicity but frenzied commotion that allowed Hitler's successes. Amid the bustle of modern, machine-age living, Picard suggests, it became harder for human beings to listen to themselves, their hearts, their thoughts, their consciences, their quiet but consistent communications from the divine and eternal. People could not often discern "the thin still voice" (1 Kings 19:12, *kol d'mamah dakah*) or what rabbinic tradition elsewhere terms the *bat kol,* the "daughter of the voice" of God.[10]

Focusing on the Jewish tradition of using language to speak to and about God, David Wolpe has pondered the terms of spiritual relationship with a God who "works through words but dwells in silence." Wolpe's study is shaped not only by his scholarly familiarity with midrash but also by his commitments to tradition and spiritual counseling as a Conservative rabbi, and his work receives emotional energy from his own love of language and from the impelling experience of his mother's inability to speak following a stroke. Although principally exploring the significance of words in Jewish theology, Wolpe also examines the silent language of feelings not uttered as well as the unexpressible mystery of God that human beings experience as silence.[11] Although not refuting the contention, Wolpe's book refines the claims of another scholar, José Faur, who has written that "Jewish mysticism is silence at its best" and that "silence is the ideal typology of the Jewish sage."[12] Such concepts of the importance of silence in the Jewish spiritual tradition derive not only from thematic statements in biblical and rabbinic texts but also from the life experiences of sages and mystics, who might include two of the most compelling figures of the nineteenth-century Hasidic movement, the enigmatic storyteller Rabbi Nachman of Bratslav and the mysteriously withdrawn Rabbi Menachem Mendel of Kotzk. Each, through what he left unsaid, made language's limitations discomfittingly clear, and the Kotzker particularly troubled faith by glimpses of inner torments unsolaced, as if he had heard God's silence and felt that it was silence toward him.[13]

Although not himself a theoretician essaying this topic, Elie Wiesel deserves mention in this company. Particularly in *Night* and his later novel, *The Testament,* and in the pages he wrote about the same time on the Hasidic rabbis from Worke, Wiesel has struggled to understand silence's baffling contradictions. "The silence of the victim is one thing, that of the killer, another. And that of the spectator, still another. There is creative silence, there is murderous silence. To a perceptive human being the universe is never silent—but there exists a universe of silence, and only perceptive human beings are aware of it."[14] Those toward whom he most often seems drawn are the ones who know that God is silent and who challenge that muteness with their own silences, their defiance of a God less righteous than God's own teachings and less faithful than God's own martyrs, challenge it with silent eloquence and silent tears, defying God also to dwell in silence.

As this brief survey suggests, silence has not bred silence. Fittingly, it has not bred dialogue either. Aside from the rare cross-reference, none of these writers takes note of the works of any of the others. They have, furthermore, variously named that to which they have listened, not always with great taxonomic interest in nuances of lexical distinctions. The result is less a problem in vocabulary than in refining conceptual distinctions or in making them. Theoreticians should not be blamed, however, for resisting the balkanization of terminology, for it may not be easy or always useful to draw lines separating phenomena that resemble one another and form parts of one network of terminological interrelationship. To suggest an analogy, although good clinical and political reasons exist to distinguish between suppression and repression, these two conditions may manifest themselves so similarly and be so symbiotically related that insisting on rigorously differentiating between them may prevent us from recognizing their connection. So with the language designating silences. In English and French alike, *silence* seems to be the defining term, although the situation to which it refers might warrant the word *stillness* instead, and sometimes *muteness* seems to be the issue. German writers have available and sometimes seem to preserve distinctions among such related terms as *Schweigen* (silence, including being silenced or silencing oneself), *Stille* (stillness), and *Schprachlosigkeit* (speechlessness). Hebrew similarly allows distinctions among *sheket* (silence), *dumiyah* (stillness), and *sh'tikah* (quietness), to cite just some of the relevant terms.[15] Usage, however, tends to obscure rather than solidify those differences over time. Therefore, it does not seem appropriate to insist on rigorously differentiating among such related terms, except insofar as some particular context suggests.

If, as seems to be true, each of these theoretical studies has been monologic (no matter how many texts each has spoken of or how many varieties of silence), the effect has been like so many separate voices narrating their own tales of an enigma. This may be inevitable, though ironically so, as one attempts to mediate (to whatever degree mediation is possible) between speaking and being silent. Between these two, of course, there is no middle ground but rather a boundary that we constantly cross and re-cross. Picard was surely correct up to a point, at least in a literary context. (The historical and ethical interpretations will remain, of course, more problematic, more the food for argumentation.) To know what it is that we have to say, we require the silence in which we step away from the fray, attentive to finely tuning our own receptors, listening carefully for what we can hear in the voices around us and in the stillness of understanding and listening to ourselves attempting to articulate with greater or lesser precision what our own voices can say, trying to find our words, trying to shape our voices. Beyond that point, however, the dual impulses to hear and speak require that we engage as fully with the language connecting us with others as with the silence connecting us with our inward self and what we perceive as eternity.

With what (as the Talmud might ask) could this be compared? Some apartment buildings still have one of the security devices of the early electronic age, a buzzer-speaker system. A caller rings the apartment bell from the building lobby. The resident goes to a call box in the apartment, switches the little microphone and speaker to "Talk" and asks the visitor's identity. The visitor responds at the lobby's call box and can be heard in the apartment if the resident has moved the switch from the "Talk" to the "Listen" position. To let the visitor into the building, the resident presses another button, which will disengage the front-door lock, typically with a raucous buzz. Subtle timing is necessary at both ends of the communication because neither party can see the other. The person replying in the lobby often starts talking too soon or the resident switches too late, or perhaps the other way around because the visitor is disoriented by hearing a voice rather than the buzzer.

It seems difficult to remember that at a given time one must either fully listen or fully talk. Perhaps the difficulty lies in our rarely doing anything with such total singleness of attention. To listen fully is perhaps harder than its opposite. Indeed, only remarkable and memorable individuals are capable of turning to others with the full direction of their attention, as if listening to that person at that moment is of the utmost significance. Listening with such intensity to wherever the silences occur may be even more difficult. First we must notice them as worth listening to and then we must learn how to listen. Then we must learn how to speak about what we have heard.

While Jewish theologians have explored the richness and painfulness of divine silences, they have also recognized the divine gift and human responsibilities of speech. Rabbi Arthur Green correctly observes about the Genesis story's effect on "the formation of the Jewish psyche. . . . We are a civilization of language, one that bears endless respect and affection for the written or spoken word."[16] Green's context is the biblical and rabbinic interpretive tradition. Societal influence is also significant, however, as Gilman noted: "Writing plays a central role in defining Jews against the preconceptions of the world in which they find themselves. . . . They therefore are at pains to constantly stress their ability to understand, to write, on levels more complex, more esoteric, more general, and more true than do those treating them as 'inarticulate Jews.' "[17] Commenting on the working-class occupations of some of the most notable Yiddish-American poets, Benjamin Harshav captures their attitude: "Being proletarian and poor was a transitory stage, a temporary necessity brought about by the hard course of history, while aristocracy of the mind, ambition to achieve the highest intellectual standards, was inherent in being

Jewish or—as they would insist—in being human."[18] The second and third chapters of this book will examine the religious and social significances of silence and speech in Jewish tradition.

The omission of the definite article—not *the* Jewish tradition—is deliberate. For reasons explored later, even some knowledgeable Jews have reacted to the topic of this book with startled bemusement. Recognizing even instinctively that we are a civilization of language, they think of Jews as verbal or as noisy in groups; they recall the outpouring of benedictions and prayers at home as well as in the synagogue that is inseparable from Jewish religious life; they recall generations of professional or amateur storytellers, neighbors, homilists, poets, disputants, activists, cantors, shoppers, scholars, orators, actors, translators, musicians, legal authorities, prophets, and tradespeople using any number of languages with apparently neither social nor philosophical anxiety about speech or attraction toward stillness. They ask, "Is there silence in Jewish tradition?" Perhaps a book such as this one inherently risks distortion: concentrating on what a particular tradition contributes to our grasp of a phenomenon, we may seemingly imply the tradition is obsessed with the issue. Much of Jewish tradition accepts the right to secular or sacred words in uncomplicated confidence and even joy. "Eternal God," we traditionally quote from Psalm 51 thrice daily, "open my lips, that my mouth may declare your glory."

This study demonstrates that Judaism also embraces stillness and that some Jewish thinkers have cherished it. Wiesel and certain of the Hasidim do find it chilling and spiritually haunting, but Wolpe and Franz Rosenzweig, one of the greatest Jewish philosophers of the early twentieth century, believe that speech's higher function consists of leading us to perfect understanding or spiritual oneness with God that is to be experienced through silence. Within the course of its religious thought, Judaism has pondered and variously measured the power and limits of orality along with the beauty and the fearfulness of silence.

Still, notwithstanding the specifically—but, as Harshav cautions, not exclusively—Jewish resonances of these issues, there seems some potential value inherent in observing how Jewish and non-Jewish texts might converse with one another, even if one preserves (as this study attempts) the particularities of the Jewish linguistic and cultural milieus. The works discussed in this book deliberately cross these categorical distinctions.

What does this great enigma of silence hold? We will attempt in chapter 4 to understand that form of silence that is like the divine mind before genesis.

Contemplating the openness of possibility, the creator enjoys the total freedom of indeterminateness and potentiality. This gives way to the silence of contemplative realization, the mind entering the process of genesis, making connections that are theoretical and still remain to be actualized. Through speech, God brings the world into being. Another way to understand that is to say that through language, the creator creates. The psychoanalyst Jacques Lacan developed a secular version of this idea: "It is the world of words which creates the world of things [*le monde des mots qui crée le monde des choses*]—the things originally confused in the *hic et nunc* of the all-in-the-process-of becoming [*tout en devenir*]. . . . Man speaks therefore, but it is because the symbol has made him man."[19]

Although such ideas invest the word with tremendous power, they also suggest that the word is an outward extension of the divine or the eternal, which implies that if there is true silence, then it is with God and it is God. But God is not only silence, though God may be silent. Arthur Green has caught the essence of the Jewish mystical sense of the relationships between silence and speech and between speech and creation in these terms: "The oneness of silence becomes the multiplicity of words or things, both referred to as *devarim* in Hebrew. . . . Once the well of that silence is plumbed, the gush of *devarim*, of constant creation through language, never ceases. Were the flow of divine speech to be halted even for an instant, some hold, the entire cosmos would return to nothingness."[20]

This makes a paradoxical situation for human beings, for we become like God when we use words to bring something new into being, and yet the essence of the divine is unreachable in words because it resides behind all words. Further, our own attempts at articulation will be imperfect representations of experience; God alone knows no gap between language and reality, word and deed. For us, words are not things; although we may use words, we are not at all sure that we are making anything by doing so. Indeed, we may even become aware of the paradox that we who use words—at least sometimes make with words, seem at times even to make words—are ourselves creatures of words. By the divine word we were brought to be, and we are made human through language's legacy. To quote Lacan again,

Symbols in fact envelop the life of man in a network so total that they join together, before he comes into the world, those who are going to engender him, . . . so total that they bring to his birth, along with the gifts of the stars, if not with the gifts of the fairy spirits, the design of his destiny; so total that they give the words which will make him faithful or renegade, the law of the acts which will follow him right to the very place where he *is* not yet and beyond his death itself; and so total that through them his end finds its meaning in the last judgment where the *verbe* absolves his being or condemns it.[21]

Understandably, once silence is broken by speech or threatened by it, our negotiations of both speech and silence become problematic and ridden by anxieties. Either we feel overcome by a network of language in which each utterance is overdetermined or we are doomed to ultimate failure in attempting to create rather than just to fabricate, and even our attempt risks intruding upon the divine prerogative of creation (chapter 5). The varieties of silence, both positive and negative, reflect these inherent tensions. One can think, for instance, of the silence granted by complete trust and the silence resorted to out of wary suspicion; the silence of peace and the dead silence of devastation; the silence of piety before the awesome, perplexity before the ineffable, horror before the unspeakable. We remember the meaning of being silenced, through repression (for instance, "the love that dares not speak its name") and oppression. We know the experience of being too overwhelmed for words, of not knowing what to say.

Yet for each of these manifestations of silence, a counterpart just as positive or negative can be found in language, for we have been expelled from the garden of perfect unity with language and exiled into a world where we live, as exiles, with and through the medium of the word (chapters 6 and 7), at times exiled as a culture from the esteem and the discourse of the larger culture in which we dwell (chapter 8). In a sermon on Rosh Hashanah, the Jewish New Year, when the repeated blasts of the shofar (ram's horn) is the most notable ceremonial feature, Rabbi Sue Levi Elwell cited the importance of "listening" while acknowledging the corresponding significance of uttering:

Might we be able, maybe for the first time, to listen to our own voices and hear our own truths? For when we can hear our own breathing, our own heartbeats, the sound of our own blood pulsing through our veins, then we can begin to hear the essential humanity of those around us. Their cries, and moans, and laughter, will no longer be muted by the cacophony of our daily lives. If we listen, carefully and deliberately, we may, in the words of theologian Nelle

Morton, "hear others into speech." Will we hear those around us who have been silent and silenced? . . . Will we hear those who call for justice?[22]

Listening and speaking forth are not merely two separate enterprises. One makes the other possible by making a place for it. So "cries, and moans, and laughter" can be "muted" by life's "cacophony." Silence must exist for speech to come into being, and too much noise drowns out communication.

True, through language we construct communities, be they the one human community separating us from other animals, the particular speech community of those who share our language and verbal culture, or the multivoiced community of texts varied in accents and styles audible in what Bakhtin called "the dialogic imagination." Still, through language we also disconnect ourselves from the biological continuum of life-forms, from the speakers of other languages in which we are profoundly deaf and mute, from the still, small presence at the inner core of being that we may call God (and in so calling it, render it yet more complicated and controversial). When we define ourselves and struggle for our own integrity as human beings, the rights to speech and to silence are equally essential. Amid oppression, both language and silence are potential means to integrity and means of self-defense—tools and weapons (chapter 9). To speak or speak out, to remain silent or hidden—among all human rights and privileges these seem the most personal. Of course they should: we are made in the divine image.

2

Speaking of Silences

ALL OF US who have stared at a blank page or screen, wanting to write, needing to write, yet reluctant to put down the first word, have looked into the visage of silence. Words, like sodden dead leaves, fail to rise, or they swirl in the mind but defy forming into sentences. As soon as the sentences appear, they disintegrate, as we hear them form, vapid, self-evident, or false. Then they stop. Thought blows dryly through the rock city of Petra, deserted and barren. No locks can be rattled, but we are sure that the words are all there, behind the silence, within the silence.

Speech itself may be locked inside, even when we suffer on physiological impairment. Hélène Cixous asserts, "Every woman has known the torture of beginning to speak aloud, heart beating as if to break, occasionally falling into loss of language, ground and language slipping out from under her, because for women speaking—even just opening her mouth—in public is something rash, a transgression."[1] Certainly, women's use of language, any language, is laden with anxieties that have arisen through centuries of men's monopolization of the public word. Yet without denigrating these particular consequences of cultural inequities between men and women, we can believe that men, educated and uneducated alike, have also known such fears as they

13

face language. Even Milton—who more apt than Milton to embody male authority over language?—in his greatest work acknowledged his dependency on a power he could not command: "If answerable style I can obtain / Of my celestial patroness." His *if* holds volumes. "So fail not thou, who thee implores."[2] Fear of being left to one's own inadequacies is the shadow of Damocles's sword. The difficulty of addressing the public does not always stem from deficient self-confidence or excessive shyness; neither does resistance to using the telephone. They may derive from our finding words intractable. Is it our personal capabilities that we distrust, or the medium of language? How early do we learn that the eloquence we hear within us comes out as tin?

Everyone who amid the clamor and clatter of a normal life has tried to create anything has been in contact with the need for silence. Set aside even the confounding claims of what we must do for a living and how we negotiate our days with those amongst whom we make our lives. Assume food in the kitchen, ready to be eaten, all the laundry clean and properly put away, the checks and birthday card in the mail. Assume a clean, well-lighted place, a room of one's own, five hundred pounds a week. Assume all of this, and yet a knock on the door or the intrusion without a knock, the ringing telephone or kitchen timer, children left too long to their own entertainments, construction work down the block, or the insistent pulsation of rock music throbbing two doors away— all fragment our phrases before we can get from introductory clause to subject, and similes deflate as if slashed with an axe. We grope toward understanding, toward a form of speech, lying just beyond our verbal reach, if only we could attain the still place where we could hear the inner language and shape the outer language. Coleridge attributed the unfinished state of his visionary "Kubla Khan" to his being interrupted by the unexpected arrival of someone known to literary history only as "the man from Porlock." How many of us would thankfully have a "Kubla Khan" left to show after such an interruption? Would we all not wish that the man from Porlock had lost our address?

Such disruptions threaten creativity under the most privileged of circumstances. The artist we have just imagined enjoys literacy and health and home—a "normal" life, for the world's Westernized middle classes, a life about which most of the world's population now and throughout history could at best fantasize. Most of us who nourish some aspect of our beings by creating or enjoying the fruits of others' creativity can assume that commotion at the door is not the sound of rioting gangs or the state's killers breaking in, that thundering outside does not mean the bombardment is getting closer, that the screaming we cannot elude does not come from anyone we cherish. Under the other circumstances, when mere existence must be scraped for at the margins of survival, both will and conscience struggle with the antinomies of silence and speech, so bound as each is to life's contention against death. Looking at creativity undertaken on such terms, a critic should be silent.

Still, even in the most privileged of circumstances, silence beckons, and it appalls. Believing that it is the lode wherein everything beyond the ordinary verbiage in which we daily traffic lies hidden, we feel sure that it is complexly eloquent and profound. Though James Merrill has cannily described time as "Ever that Everest among concepts," when we step through the doorway of silence we venture into the expanse of space or the expanse of death, into all those mysteries that words have been unable to open fully to us. We become conscious of existing within a web of emotions or thoughts so interconnected that our powers seem completely absorbed by the task of contemplating them, mutely. For all sound might be understood as what occurs within a vast sweep of seeming silence. Taken separately, every word is but the crack of a piece of fruit broken off a tree amid what Mandelshtam called the "endless song / of the deep forest's silence" (*nemolčnogo napeva / glubokoj tishiny lesnoj*).[3] Metaphysically, silence may evoke the wistfully supposed unity before the human "fall . . . into language" or the awesome fate of all: "after the last judgment, the silence." It may even be the longed-for liberator that will free us from the ancient tyranny of verbiage and reason, from "the evil-smelling old Logos," the messiah that will fulfill a weary world's invocation for organic peace, "Come in silence, and say nothing."[4]

People who hear and therefore live amid sound notice silence so infrequently that it can feel monumentally weighty with power in those rare moments when we become cognizant of it. At such times we are likely to become aware of duration as well, as if the absence of sound has slipped us into another dimension. Concertgoers, through some collective act of willpower and unwritten social contract, generally avoid producing noises during fifteen minutes or more of a symphonic movement, yet as soon as the music pauses between movements the break will be filled with the cacophony of people all over the auditorium who at that moment feel that they must cough. Is it plausible that so many have suppressed for so long a powerful physiological impulse? Surely much of that coughing arises from a different sort of discomfort, not purely physiological, caused by the sheer presence of silence. Ask worshipers how long the "moment of silence" has lasted at a religious ceremony and they will almost always overestimate it, often considerably. That is not only because our inner sense of time is poorly refined but also because a short period of silence seems to last for a relatively long time. We do not know what to do with that duration, apparently outside time's flow simply because it exists in silence.

Amid silence, time may seem to have stopped, not merely in reverie but in a complete hiatus of process. The following poem by the early-twentieth-century Austrian writer Georg Trakl (representing a gentler experience of silence than we usually find in his often-tormented work) is especially notable because each stanza uses a different word for the phenomenon of silence: the noun *Schweigen* in the first, the adverb *sprachlos* in the second, and the adjective *stillen* in the third. The variety expresses the pervasiveness and subtle shadings through which silence becomes manifest.

> Das Unbewegten Odem. Ein Tiergesicht
> Erstarrt vor Bläue, ihrer Heiligkeit.
> Gewaltig ist das Schweigen im Stein;
>
> Die Maske eines nächtlichen Vogels. Sanfter Dreiklang
> Verklingt in einem. Elai! Dein Antlitz
> Beugt sich sprachlos über bläuliche Wasser.
>
> O! ihr stillen Spiegel der Wahrheit.
> An des Einsamen elfenbeinerner Schläfe
> Erscheint der Abglanz gefallener Engel.

> Breath of the Motionless. An animal-face
> stiffens with blueness, its sacredness.
> Mighty is the silence in stone;
>
> the mask of a nightbird. A soft triad
> fades to a tone. Elai! Your visage
> bends mutely over the azure water.
>
> O! you still mirrors of truth.
> On the solitary one's ivory temple
> gleams the reflection of a fallen angel.[5]

The reader familiar with English poetry may be reminded of "silence and slow time," the foster parents of Keats's Grecian urn. The effect in Trakl is synaesthesic and universal. Not the timeless urn but fleeting life seems held, like Sleeping Beauty's court, as if turned to living stone, fallen yet perfect. The only sound, that soft melodic triad, dissolves into a single tone (skillfully evoked through Trakl's phonemic sequence, *Drei*klang, *ver*kling*t, einem*). Motionlessness and silence join in turning all breathing things into masks, transforming the temporal. The poem implies that not only motion but also sound typifies the transitory. Silence is the stilling touch of the eternal.

Silence can feel just as potent when it is the last recourse of those pushed to the limit, those for whom words and thoughts alike can only collect a coating of dust behind drawn shades. The portentous turbulent silence between Senta and the Dutchman in Wagner's opera, *The Flying Dutchman,* seems to bind them palpably to each other. During a long passage in which, seeing one another for the first time, the two characters stand without moving or singing, the orchestra articulates unspoken swirls of feeling within each of them and between them, eloquence indifferent to words. Their mutual silence is all the more momentous because it is preceded by a stunning shriek from Senta at the moment when she first sees this man, whose picture has already claimed her devotion. Her outcry virtually compresses all verbal articulation into one explosive instant so that we hear simultaneously in it the ultimate reduction of language (into a mere phoneme) and the ultimate expressive limit of language (fully saying what the speaker feels). After Senta's *Geschrei,* silence alone seems appropriate from the human throat.

Under duress, silence may be the final resort. Elie Wiesel's character, Grisha, the mysteriously mute son of a murdered Yiddish poet (one of Stalin's silenced victims) eventually reveals the cause of his affliction. Questioned insidiously about his life by someone who might be an informer, Grisha thinks that by his answers he is being robbed of his personal identity along with his memories. "The more I spoke, the less I existed; he robbed me of what I cherished most. . . . One more month and I would have forgotten everything." Then it was that the "miracle"—or perhaps, he thinks, "accident"—occurred, when after locking his jaws so as not to speak he opens with a sudden spasm and, biting down, severs his tongue. He knows that his silence is different from that of his father, a man who retained it under torture, yielded it eventually to the seduction of writing, and at last fell mute to the killer's gun before he could finish his tale. Possessing the father's purloined manuscript saves Grisha from his likely fate, "silence and ashes."[6] Yet silence saves him.

On the other side of stillness, Samuel Beckett, a modern master at exploring silences, used the particular resources of television and two actors (originally, Jack MacGowran and Sean Phillips) to create an emotionally complex drama, "Eh Joe," in which the camera follows the seedy Joe around his room as he responds only through the emotions on his face to the woman's voice talking to him inside his mind—she is never seen, he is never heard. Yet the voice-over narration by itself cannot carry the drama. Joe's speechlessness changes meanings as his expressions alter and beads of sweat form in reaction to the prodding, probing inner voice. His self-centered remoteness from other people emerges through his muteness, eloquently accompanying the facial exposure of his coarse smugness, barrenness, and haunted misery.

An example from another medium demonstrates how a related form of silence communicates the essence of an emotional state. By means of stillness, one of modern ballet's great artists, Lynn Seymour, created a memorable moment in Kenneth Macmillan's choreography of *Romeo and Juliet:* Seymour's Juliet, in love with Romeo but commanded to marry Paris, reacts to her mother's and nurse's rejection of her protests by simply sitting motionless on her bed. The dancer, who contributed this idea to the choreography, explained her insight in an interview, "What am I thinking there? Nothing. Nothing as Juliet and nothing as me. If you're in a predicament like that, it's very hard to think. . . . It's just like squeezing yourself together."[7] Although Seymour's inspiration seems to have originated principally from psychological rather than choreographic acumen, as an artist she directed it through dance's formalistic implications. In a medium defined by movement, stillness poignantly expresses not knowing where to turn.

Perhaps in looking from any one of these expressions of silence to its dichotomous opposite, we are drawn to admit how puzzling and ambiguous are silences's meanings. Silence speaks with two voices, each capable of a range of inflections and tonalities. Paradoxically, silence expresses creative energy being stored, as in a battery, and also creativity suppressed, silenced. Perhaps it is a phantom: there really is no silence, because within the seeming silence lies the white noise of our own meanings. Consider an illustration of that ambiguity. The final frames of the classic movie *Queen Christina* focus on Greta Garbo's face. Garbo, as the queen sailing from Sweden to self-imposed seclusion after her lover's assassination, stands solitary at the ship's prow, staring silently into her future. That ending sequence, with the camera closing in on Garbo's splendid, masklike visage, has proven for moviegoers one of the most vividly recalled experiences of the actress's dramatic power. Her expression has been interpreted variously as epitomizing noble resignation, suppressed mourning, nostalgic recollection, or an exquisitely nuanced synthesis of complexly related emotions like regret, remembrance, and self-assurance. The director, Rouben Mamoulian, asked some years later for the key to this sensitively wrought moment, explained what he had sought from his star. After several takes had failed to register exactly the right emotion, he recalled, "I told her to think of absolutely nothing at all." That vacancy became the empty receptacle into which viewers have poured their own interpretations. This anecdote illustrates how the voice of silence speaks powerfully but equivocally: those who have listened to it have heard what their experiences and temperaments have prepared them to hear.

Let us make one essential distinction. Works of artistic creativity and of spiritual creativity use silences and anxieties about interrupting silences as formal and thematic elements within their works, and it is with these that we shall be primarily concerned. Silence or its lack is also a condition of the artist's life experience, however. Writers, those who try to write, and especially those who want to write but strive in vain are fixated on silence and the anxiety of breaking from it into speech. Similar words could be written of artists in any discipline. But there are so many silences. Public speech, in whatever form it takes, requires the privilege of access. So Gray acknowledged when the country churchyard stimulated him to ponder the destiny of a "mute inglorious Milton." Whitman felt that he, as poet and prophet, was the conduit by which others could become articulate and heard: "through me many long dumb voices . . . of the interminable generations of prisoners and slaves, . . . forbidden voices."[8] Among the silences of the dumb and forbidden voices, Virginia Woolf recalled in *A Room of One's Own* that of a hypothetical Judith Shakespeare, whose unwritten biography Woolf feelingly reconstructed to make us notice the absence of her unwritten plays, the silence of her stilled voice. Yet we remember that art also needs silence. Tillie Olsen, for instance, contrasts "natural silences, that necessary time for renewal, lying fallow, gestation, in the natural cycle of creation" (about which she chooses not to write) with those smothering silences whose forms she traces in her book, silences that she calls "unnatural; the unnatural thwarting of what struggles to come into being, but cannot."[9]

Even here, though, the term *unnatural* turns problematic. Certainly the countless talents frustrated by practical hardships and by any of the various bloody or icy forms of societal suppression and indifference have fallen mute because they have been unnaturally trammeled down. On the other hand, the "thwarting" of creativity that elicits grieving and rage from Melville and Conrad in passages that Olsen quotes seems pitiably and terrifyingly natural. What writer does not recognize how the frustrated will beats against intractable language or a locked imagination? Against this form of repression there can be no solidarity, no affirmative action outside of ourselves.

Worse, the inner silence of repression and the natural silences of fallowness and gestation may appear very much like one another, much as Spenser's Duessa plausibly masquerades as Una. The quiet regenerative time is essential. Yet the satisfaction of having written may be almost inseparable from the anxiety about whether one will be able to write again. When the artist withdraws into the essential stillness, like the epic hero enjoying a respite in some pastoral retreat, it seems hard to be certain whether one is finding temporary refreshment in cooling shades or rather being swallowed up by the shadows.

We cannot sensibly separate stillness and creative energy or silence and the word any more than we can pull apart shuttle and loom. Whatever happens in the silence before creation, in the gathered stillness, it is out of that silence that we create. Our creating devours the silence that has made creation possible. Paradoxically, the silence must end for the creating to begin, and that creation also concerns what occurred in the silence. But when we are in its midst, the silence has nothing direct to say to us about its nature: so like hollowness, so like a deep well quietly filling with dark waters, so like the soothing sleep that plunged steadfast Palinurus into the enveloping sea. How, we wonder, can we escape from it, put into articulated form what we experience in it, if indeed we are fortunate enough to experience anything at all? Or will it hold us instead?

Because the process by which we are able to create is so mysterious, we seem to rediscover continually the paradox expressed by Edmond Jabès, "Making a book could mean exchanging the *void of writing* for *writing the void*."[10] Jabès suggests that the two, the writing and the void, somehow survive together, although in changeable relationships. It is as if words are the writer's chisel and hammer, silence the stone the writer must chip away without completely obliterating. The text, the form, will show the double presence of the hand that has worked on the material and the material that remains, in some sense intact and yet obviously altered. We learn to live with, or perhaps against, that silence. Eventually, we may comprehend it as our constant and longer-lived companion, strange confidante, perilous comrade. The poet Eugenio Montale, tracing the ways of the eel through its sinuous and resourceful probing of aquatic depths, at last grasped that to understand its habits means to acknowledge it as "*sorella*."[11] We, knowing silence, may also have to call her "sister."

Silence and language do not oppose one another in some simple dialectic in which unequivocal moral valences accompany each term. They cross one another in the fabric of our thought and become the texture of our being. They can no more be opposed to one another than warp can rival weft. Writing is possible because of the blank page; speaking is possible because of silence. Even when we have to compete to get a word in edgewise, hush someone else, or outshout a rival, we know that we can be heard only when there is airspace for our words, much as written words need space around the letters to be legible. Language requires silence around it. The silence allows us to distinguish the unsaid along with the said, permits us to notice what is absent even as we attend to what is present.[12] Consequently, we ask who speaks and of what? What dwells within the silence, what hedges it in, and what is said when that silence is broken? Where is the witness whose testimony will corroborate? What does speech contribute to our lies and our self-deceptions, and what does silence offer?

Textual memories disturb easy formulations: the biblical Jacob's duplicitous voice conniving the blessing of his father, Isaac, Cordelia's principled silence rejecting the blessing of her father, Lear—do they not seem either pragmatically or ethically problematic? The demurral of Melville's Bartleby, whose persistent "I prefer not to" is less a refusal of a request than a refusal to engage the other person, draws the most meager verbal veil in front of a silence deep, pained, and ultimately enveloping but impenetrably enigmatic. If, furthermore, we are persuaded that "language is the dwelling-place of being," it is chilling to recall that the famous philosopher who framed that idea not only leaped eagerly and early to Nazi Party membership and its attendant rewards of academic power as rector of Freiburg University, but also that after the war he constructed a moat of silence around his Nazi-era activities. Therefore, if language is the dwelling place of being, surely Heidegger's silence must testify eloquently to a void in his being.[13]

Breaking into speech—whether in praise, lamentation, complaint, invitation, or indeed any of the many moods that will move us, articulately or not, to give voice—is a way of intruding our own presence into the fact of another presence. (Perhaps the writers who least evoke silence are those least conflicted about such intrusions.) If silence is a void, it is a void that seems not of our own making, a reminder that our thought does not fill all space. Hesitation at the boundary of speech confirms our consciousness of speech's intrusion into the place of another, but speech, we know, is not merely some disembodied and neutral articulation of text. The presence of speech means that someone is speaking; speech means that our words go with us. Not only do our words venture into the space of another consciousness, but we too are the wanderers, the explorers, the invaders. With this in mind we may understand the biblical prohibition against taking God's name in vain as a prohibition against presuming to intrude upon the presence of the sacred. Only in circumstances where one consciously recognizes the separation between the human and the divine may one speak of divinity, such as in prayer or benediction, for these are occasions explicitly acknowledging that unequal, unfamiliar relationship.

Language therefore is the nontactile means by which we reach across the division between self and other. It is the conceptual means by which we also try to reach across conceptual or experiential divisions. Divided from one another and from the source of ourselves, which is the source of creation, we are continually challenged by what we do not grasp. Language is our fallible tool. Such intimacy carries risks, and consequently speaking and writing are both accompanied by apprehension. Not only accompanied, they are preceded even more intensely by apprehension. Nor are they as separate from one another as the distinctiveness might lead us to believe: they are related to one another like ego and alter ego, self and doppelgänger. Within what we take to be silence is sound we have forgotten to notice; prior and subsequent to silence is sound that defines silence, giving it meaning. But reverse "silence" and "sound" in that sentence and it remains true. The two phenomena share a common boundary. To speak of one of these necessarily involves remembering the border, even if one attempts to refrain from crossing or mapping it.

Silence propounds its own eloquence. Michelangelo, a poet as well as a painter and sculptor, faced the challenge of representing the orality of creation on the Sistine Chapel ceiling. His context, after all, was the explicit orality of the Jewish Bible's creation story and of John's Gospel allegory, "In the beginning was the Word, and the word was with God, and the word was God."

Instead of a creator miming Logos, Michelangelo represents a creative act more appropriate to the plastic arts, the silent animating gesture, the sweeping arm that swirls worlds into being, the near-touch when God stretches a hand toward the languid figure of the not yet vitalized Adam. It is as if the artist has found in a gesture a metaphor for the word and breath of God. It is a gesture more directly tactile than mime, but it is also the gesture expressing a creative power that works more subtly than any human being can on the medium of mere clay. Despite its physicality, the transformative act seems metaphysical.

One might look at a survey of great paintings—not just portraits, where one would expect this phenomenon, but narrative, dramatic, mythological, and emblematic works as well—and be struck by how many of them depict people with mouths closed, even when in putative conversation: Botticelli's *Calumny of Apelles,* a picture that even feels noisy; Raphael's *Disputation;* and Leonardo's almost boisterous *Last Supper.* Although clearly constructed on verbal exchanges, all of them depict discourses among individuals communicating through wordless yet eloquent gestures and expressions. The continent of painting seems peopled by thousands of human beings who do not part their lips. If a visitor from another planet were to scan these representations, could the function of that double willow leaf in the lower third of the face be deduced? Could it even be known that the dividing line parts?

Visual artists seem to have perceived by virtually intuited generic principles the tension between the eloquence (literally, the speaking out) of the mute but visually expressive and that of the verbal. Although art theory and poetic theory are not devoid of analyses of the conceptual relationships between the visual and verbal, the visual artists seem to have grasped outside of any theoretical discussion that figures in visual works of art must not only be silent perforce, they must appear silent. Their eloquence must be conceived wholly within the terms of unspoken yet nonetheless subtle (some would say more subtle) expression: because the communication takes place without words, it conveys the impression of expressing feelings on a level beyond verbal language.

The strength of the convention may be suggested by an incident from another art form in which figures communicate with voiceless expressiveness. Many ballets of the nineteenth century dramatic story-telling tradition require that some amount of apparent dialogue take place among the characters on stage. Choreographic tradition has developed a limited but nonetheless effective vocabulary of mime gestures to carry this communication wordlessly through movements of the hands and arms, facial expression, and body attitude. Mime can be done perfunctorily or well, but a dancer with a sense of artistry in mime can create a powerful impression. Although dance mime language may look old-fashioned and so stylized as to be ripe enough for parody, when performed with conviction and style it is succinct, often kinetically beautiful, and in the hands (literally) of a well-trained artist, occasionally eloquent. The convention absolutely depends on our belief that the people on stage express and communicate everything they need to say about themselves and to one another through gesture and movement. True, one might object that mime merely substitutes a code of gestures for a code of speaking or writing, that it is not true silence but merely a different way of speaking. It is still founded on the unstated implication that words are irrelevant appurtenances of some other mode of existence. To make mime plausible, that implication must be sustained. It can be if and only if the performers really believe this and have the training and discipline to communicate it on stage. Several years ago, a dance critic reviewing a major company's performance of the romantic ballet *Giselle* registered the disruptive effect on the stage illusion when one dancer at a critical moment of a mimed dispute clearly mouthed the retort, "No." Although no sound was heard, his seeming to speak brought into doubt, only for an instant but perhaps a fatal instant, the logic of the medium itself. The episode illustrates by contrast how silence can completely be a world sufficient to itself.

For this reason modern art can assault our sensibilities by means of a truly silent scream. Surely much of the shock of Munch's painting, *The Scream,* arises because it defies conventional visual language or rhetoric, because the screamer's mouth is actually open. Similarly, the horse in Picasso's *Guernica,* open-mouthed in terror, in pain, and in protest, is memorable not only because it is so powerfully depicted but also because we expect visually depicted terror to scream in the eyes, not the mouth. Of course, they are ambiguous declarations because they cannot communicate anything more specific than the scream itself, but beyond that is the ambiguity of the medium. The canvas condemns the cry to eternal silence, for the sound will never emerge from the depths of the work, yet each evokes an outcry whose source lies even deeper than sound.

We are drawn into texts' silences. Obsession with narratological lacunae is not purely postmodern. One recognizes it in the compelling power of the figure and stories of Rabbi Nachman of Bratslav, who wrote nothing and wanted his teachings, oral tales, and parables left to the muteness of unrecorded history.

24

Each story, cryptic and filled with interpretive holes, speaks of silence; lucid as they are in shape and language, they tell us nothing clearly. But the Bratslaver could have found his technique in the Talmud's way with the unexplained. Consider this example:

> The rabbis taught, four entered the garden: Ben Azzai, Ben Zoma, Akher, and Rabbi Akiba. R. Akiba said, "When you reach the stones of pure marble, do not say, 'Water, water,' for it is written, 'He that speaketh falsehoods shall not be established before My eyes'" [Ps. 101:7]. Ben Azzai looked about and died; Ben Zoma looked about and was stricken; Akher cut down shoots; R. Akiba emerged in peace. (Mishnah Ḥagigah 14b)

Not a single element in this oft-interpreted anecdote is self-explanatory, including "four" and "garden." The story, one may argue, initiates discussion. That indeed is important, for it shows that out of silence comes speech. Speech ventures into the text's voids, among which are voids of certain knowledge. Interpretive tradition gives us stories about what happened, but the language posits truth rather than revealing it.

To have the power of speech may never mean having power over language, even if we devote ourselves to "mastering" just one language. Still, words and power cannot easily be separated from one another, especially when choice of tongue or characteristics of speech are identifiable with class or caste. Furthermore, if we believe there is power in art, we cannot completely deny that artistic and linguistic mastery may in some circumstances provide a means of power over others, but only in some circumstances: if the shortcomings of cultural idealism had not been apparent earlier in history, then surely events during this century ought to make us embarrassed to quote too readily the aphorism that the pen is mightier than the sword. One needs to show some piety at least before the fates of writers such as Gertrud Kolmar, Bruno Schultz, Simon Dubnow, Mordechai Gebirtig, Yitzhak Katznelson, Miklos Rádnoti, Anne Frank, and even Walter Benjamin among Hitler's victims, or Osip Mandelshtam, Shloime Mikhoels, David Bergelson, Der Nister, Itzik Fefer, and Peretz Markish among Stalin's; nor dare one forget that in our own time Salman Rushdie still lives and writes under threat of a death sentence because of a work of fiction.

Nonetheless, literacy is a privilege, and facility with language can be a dangerous as well as agonizing gift. Under more conventional circumstances, the manipulative power of language can seem surprisingly strong, even brutal. Franz Kafka's "Letter to His Father" is a verbal assault by a writer who has felt overpowered by his physically self-confident but unintellectual father. The monologic character of the piece, which was composed as a letter and apparently neither sent nor intended to be published, imparts both its strength as a diatribe and its vulnerability as an ethical document. By controlling the narration and allowing his father to speak as a character in the work only in circumstances that the author manipulates, Kafka may satisfy his personal needs; however, he violates any moral obligation the artist may have (if not to people then at least to art) to be fair to the characters. But Hermann was not a man of letters, not eloquent with words, and it was Nadine Gordimer who extracted justice for him by contriving a "Letter from His Father" purporting to be Hermann Kafka's apologia.[14]

Why an apologia? Biography and history have judged Hermann through the criticism of Franz. To a literate and literary community, the son's protests against the older man's masculine crudity and insensitivity to art, as well as against his pragmatic mercantilism and superficiality of religious observance, seem enticingly plausible. Franz's verbal power effectively turned the tables on his father; indeed, one might say that it won for him a reversal of roles. Although the only offspring Franz passed on to the future were literary, through an act of artistic re-creation Franz Kafka authored, in a sense generated, his own father. His father became, in the eyes of the reading public, the man his son made him. This was the unpremeditated triumph of the young man who had been deeply disgusted by his father's determined effort to make a man of him. The father is rendered impotent by the son's almost unbroken recitation; the father's few ineffectual, vulgar words, put into his mouth by his son's prose, have reduced him and his life to blustering but impotent brutishness.

Gordimer's story redresses the father's silencing. In his narration he is able both to tell his side of the story, which he does with robust vigor, and to protest as well his son's self-pitying but otherwise pitiless literary exposure of private experiences large and small. "And that other business you *schlepped* up out of the past—the night I'm supposed to have shut you out on the *pavlatche*. Because of you the whole world knows the Czech word for the kind of balcony we had in Prague! Yes, the whole world knows that story, too. I am famous, too. You made me famous as the father who frightened his child once and for all; for life. Thank you very much. I want to tell you that I don't even remember that incident. I'm not saying it didn't happen, although you always had an imagination such as nobody ever had before or since, eh?"[15] Hermann Kafka attains a more complex personhood, in fact a more complex voice, more nuanced, more flexible rhetorically, more ironic, more Jewish, than his son allowed us to hear. Although not an imaginative man himself, Hermann Kafka knows that imagination and memory can shadow one another, and he is aware of how the telling detail commands attention. He also has the opportunity to counterpose his son's devotion to art against the challenges and opportunities of daily living that Franz seemed unable to meet and to raise a vain shield against the ice pick jabs of his own son's prose. "Your revenge, that you were too cowardly to take in life, you've taken here. We can't lie peacefully in our graves; dug up, unwrapped from our shrouds by your fame. To desecrate your parents' grave as well as their bed, aren't you ashamed?"[16]

In telling the other side Gordimer introduces at least an argument and at times even a debate in place of the monologue. Certainly in her closing paragraph, which hinges on a point of textual interpretation, she focuses the issue between father and son on the literal noncommunication between them. In that state of tacit hostility, the father's simple lack of sophistication seems less culpable than the intelligent and sensitive son's withholding of understanding or compassion. Hermann charges, "You once wrote 'Speech is possible only where one wants to lie.' You were too *ultra-sensitive* to speak to us, Franz. You kept silent, with the truth: those playing a game of cards, turning in bed on the other side of the wall—it was the sound of live people you didn't like." If the famous son was right, living with live people also means lying with live people.

Between human beings, this seems to be the choice, to keep silence with the truth or to lie with others. We understand, though, that the choice is deceptive and might as well be turned completely around, because silence can also be a lie, can be crueler—deadlier—than the lies we speak, and even faulty words can serve for a time as thumbtacks to stop elusive reality from sliding too quickly from us.

This is surely one of the most provocative paradoxes of the relationship between language and silence. What is most evanescent is the moment, and its slippery passage quickly eludes us unless we have language to hold its image and essence before us. Yet language seldom seems adequate, or our abilities to wield it seldom seem adequate, to the complex tonalities of the simplest experiences, with all the varieties of its "ineluctable modalities" (to recall Stephen

Dedalus's related efforts in *Ulysses*). Language appears better able to help us trace with mental fingers the more amenably stable (though less clearly visible) contours of the eternal. As Plato recognized, when the many varieties of a phenomenon or a concept that we have encountered in the empirical realm can be resolved into the common features of a universal and timeless ideal, then we can believe we have something to grasp. When the mutable world eludes our clutch, the immutable (though more distant) is at least more fixed and so available for our repeated sorties of exploration and mapping, as if we are testing staking our claims, whether to dominion, occupation, or residence.

But therein lies the next peril. Venturing to violate the territory of the timeless, we tread with profane feet onto holy ground and risk disrupting with our clumsy mortal language the equilibrium of eternal altars, bringing them down upon ourselves. For the Talmud cautions (Mishnah Ḥagigah 11b), with an uneasiness that seems as much psychological as theological, of the dangers that pursue those intruding upon metaphysics, prophecy, and eschatology: "Whoever speculates on what is above and what is below, what came before and what will come after, it would have been better for that person never to have been born."

2

A Sea of Ink

The Word in Jewish Religious Thought

IF, AS SOMEONE HAS SAID, Jews are like everyone else, only more so, Jewish experience embodies everyone else's. It may do that, however, in particular and intensified form. On some frequencies Jewish experience itself and Jewish analyses of experience resonate with the universal, although perhaps the pitches on which we hear harmony are the middle ones, just beyond the silences that are only apparent silences. In the profound depths below and in the peaks above the ordinarily audible vibrate tones singular to Jewish history and consciousness. Let us attend first to the more easily audible range.

Jewish tradition is keenly aware that anxiety accompanies all profound confrontations with language. While attempting to articulate the ineffable, we know nevertheless that speaking or writing will never express the totality. As an eleventh-century liturgical poem proclaims, "Were the sky made of parchment, each reed and grass a quill, were the seas filled with ink and everyone a scribe of skill," we would still be unable to recount God's glory.[1] In fact, spinning out the line of effort by continuing to speak seems only to confirm that it is impossible to say everything and that it is just as impossible to communicate the essence of truth. Edmond Jabès wrote, "I have spoken to you of the difficulty of being Jewish, which merges with the difficulty of writing, because Judaism and writing are one identical waiting, one identical hoping, one identical wearing out." ("Je vous ai parlé de la difficulté d'être Juif, qui se confond avec la difficulté d'écrire; car le judaisme et l'écriture ne sont qu'une même attente, un même espoir, une même usure.")[2]

That similar difficulties afflict non-Jewish writers may be exemplified through this passage by Gloria Anzaldúa, a self-described mestiza: "Writing produces anxiety. . . . Being a writer feels very much like being a Chicana, or being queer—a lot of squirming, coming up against all sorts of walls. Or its opposite: nothing defined or definite, a boundless, floating state of limbo where I kick my heels, brood, percolate, hibernate and wait for something to happen."[3] Although the experiential tones might seem different for a Jewish writer, the relationship between writing and cultural discomfort seems revealingly similar. To be a writer as well necessarily distances one. Judaism's distinctive element in this regard is longevity. We have consciously articulated for more centuries than any other group our awareness of anxiety, boundaries, and uprootedness.

Perhaps a contrast will dramatize the similarity between a Jewish sense of language and an imaginative writer's sense of language. Introducing the thought of Wittgenstein, Bertrand Russell asserted, "The essential business of language is to assert or deny facts."[4] Such words would seem alien even to a medieval mystic promulgating practical letter kabbalah (manipulating combinations of vowels and consonants to gain power over the objects of a world created by God through language). For reasons such as those Sander Gilman cited, to be a Jew, Chicana, or "queer"—the list need not stop here, nor are the terms mutually exclusive—is likely to mean that one is consciously aware and distanced from the current of uncritical living and intensely aware of the roles of language in expressing and bearing relationships. For the Jew, language is essential to the relationship between Creator and world. One can hear in Martin Buber's ideas of language a Jewish reply to such notions as Russell's, for Buber claimed, "Primary words do not signify things, but they intimate relations. Primary words do not describe something that might exist independently of them, but being spoken they bring about existence." Language precedes existence and is inseparable from its essence. "God's speech . . . penetrates what happens in the life of each one of us, and all that happens in the world around us, biographical and historical, and makes it for you and me into instruction, message, demand."[5] Through divine utterances an undifferentiated welter of experience is structured and given meanings, purposes, and priorities. Language makes mitzvot, the commandments that govern the Jew's relations with the sacral and the human spheres. Language, the Jew understands (as must any writer), resonates with implications, stretches and bends under its own pressures and weights of intimations and demands.

Jabès's string of substantives—waiting, hoping, wearing out—sighs with apparent defeat. It does not embrace (for example) fulfillment. He writes as if the practice of Judaism and the practice of writing were ongoing processes in which one never sees results. Perhaps that is deeply true. One still waits for the Messiah or (as Anzaldúa says) for something to happen, one continually hopes that the text will be complete (Jabès himself referred to his many books as simply parts of one book that he was in the process of writing through his entire career), yet one also knows that the book may be finished but will never be complete.

Further, the three terms do not necessarily describe a linear sequence through which one progresses in time, like the progressively deteriorating protagonists in Beckett's novels. The emotions overlap, so that amid the wearing out, the next cycle of waiting stirs. In the midst of these, hoping is the center. Without it, waiting is aimless; without the wearing down, hoping would be terminal. Hope is the core of energy that sustains both messianic conviction and any creative enterprise, for hope looks not merely to the future but to the possibility of attainment. In every realm of life—political, spiritual, emotional, expressive, erotic—hope the matchmaker encourages us to believe that desire and actuality may unite. For the Jew and for the artist, hope is our gamble with history.

This idea catches their common prophetic note and their mutual awareness of the antitheses bounding each enterprise. Neher, remarking on the dual biblical meanings of the Hebrew words *nehamah* (repentance / consolation) and *asaf* (abandonment / gathering in), argues, "Failure and hope are not separated moments in the work of God; one is implicit in the other, like opposite poles, so that failure and hope are expressed in the Bible by one word and occur at the same points of the story."[6] In regard to hoping, the artist and the prophet speak with similar voices, if only by speaking with a commitment to a tomorrow. There need be no sentimentality in that commitment, only the hazy dawn flush of a next moment where there could be an auditor. Our hope, surely, ought to be at bottom only that someone may happen to hear or come upon our words or works. Jonah, desperately fleeing the obligation to speak, resenting those to whom he must deliver his words, even felt that hope to be too burdensome.

Presuming beyond so modest a desire, however, by daring to hope that one's words will matter, risks disappointment. The prophet Elijah's dejection after what seemed to have been a momentous triumph, his defeat on Mount Carmel of the prophets of Baal, who could not bring forth fire from the heavens, reveals that he expected too much. Elijah believed that his faithful testimony and God's answering hand should have changed the world. On Mount Horeb he had to learn something else about God, that the holy is not "in" the wind, the earthquake, or the fire but that after the fire (*v'ahar ha-esh*) it can be heard in the *kol d'mamah dakah,* the narrow soundless voice, the "still small voice," the voice that speaks within the world's stillness (1 Kings 19:12). Others have also heard such a voice as an unarticulated but certain communication affirming that the Presence is with us, though unseen. Seldom has that voice given forth with such eloquence, such precision, as it does to Elijah.

Disagreeing with André Neher on a point of biblical interpretation feels presumptuous; however, he seems wrong to claim that in this episode Elijah discovers ultimately that God is also "the God of Silence and Withdrawal."[7] For the sequel to that barely heard contact is a more direct address from a more explicit voice, a differently pitched *kol,* presenting Elijah with a plan of action. Elijah's stroke of daring on Carmel was exactly that, as brief and brilliant in its immediate result as it was flamboyant in its rhetoricity. On Horeb an understanding of how to build for the future emerges from what Yiddish would call a *pintele,* the tiniest dot. That paradox suggests that God's withdrawal is only one part of the systolic and diastolic surges. It also suggests that the prophet, surely the greatest prophet, must also have moments of silence in which such a voice can be heard, not engulfed in the whirling sounds of the whirlwind or earthquake or fire. Elijah, who believed that he had demonstrated adequately to everyone through the test of the fire that none is like Adonai among the gods that are worshipped, is taught another and deeper way of knowing the divine presence by that same One, Adonai the triumphant God, who did, after all, also affirm Elijah. The lesson is not lost on the psalmist, who counsels, *"dom l'adonai v'hitholel lo,"* "Be still in God and await God" (37:7). In the tests of fire, we need the clear and strong voice; *v'ahar ha-esh kol d'mamah dakah.*

That is to speak of our need. We mortal beings always have cause to speak of it. What we believe we need and what we receive, however, are often at odds. There have been tests of fire answered in silence, and the sequel to the fire has also been silence at the core of being, at times when we listened intently and vainly for that *pintele* of a presence.

Consider, for instance, this paradoxical relationship between silence and language. Wiesel, who shares Picard's protest against modern civilization's noisiness, hears in our attachment to constant clamor an attempt to fill the spaces where we might be alone with our thoughts, to drown out the quiet voices of our restless consciences. However, Wiesel—whose discourse on this silence Neher has probed so perceptively—also hears on the other side an excruciating silence in the "chronotope" (the time-place, in Bakhtinian terminology) of the Holocaust.[8] That silence was formed by the disregard shown by nations and peoples during the catastrophe, by the suppressed and stilled voices of the victims, and by the subsequent silences that may be those of respect or of indifference or of protective complicity. Surrounding it all, Wiesel believes, is the more frightful deafening silence of God, who did not speak in that firestorm and whose still, small voice was not heard. In the murders of the Yiddish writers by Stalin in 1952, Wiesel found again the threat of silencing. "You must understand, the language of a people is its memory, and its memory is . . ."[9] The imprisoned poet's sentence in *The Testament* (a book whose every page is obsessed with silences) is terminated by a bullet he does not know to expect, denied even a chance to form a final statement or say what he has remembered of memory. Earlier, tortured through enforced muteness threatening to annihilate him, he has posited a way to understand why God created: "God Himself was afraid of silence."[10] Against these silences Wiesel counterposes the telling of true stories about the Holocaust, although not countenancing the making of fictions about it. Fictional works using the Holocaust from those who did not experience it inevitably profane and diminish (he believes) what they purport to represent. Although he accepts prayer, he praises it for its implicit defiant protest against the muteness marking the place of the object of prayer. We may inquire what silence does denote and ask of what value are words. Life and thought embedded in Jewish experience prove too complexly compounded of contrarieties to admit of a straightforward dichotomy between silence and language.

From a Jewish point of view (as exemplified by Buber's propositions cited above) Wittgenstein's efforts at stabilizing the relationship between language and empirical reality seem as quixotic as they are poignant. *"Ein Name steht für ein Ding, ein anderer für ein anderes Ding"* (One name stands for one thing, another for another thing), he wrote. So Francis Bacon near the beginning of the seventeenth century and the British Royal Society near the end had tried to pin word to object without allowing for ambiguity or uncertainty. Through brief, numbered statements (*Sätze*) suggestive of mathematical propositions, the philosopher attempted to construct a stable structure of meaning: *"Der Satz teilt uns eine Sachlage mit . . . als er ihr logisches Bild ist"* (the sentence communicates a situation to us insofar as it is its picture).[11] Wittgenstein, however, notwithstanding the stolid optimism of these pronouncements, seems to undo his own hypotheses as his line of reasoning takes him to the solipsistic subjectivity of experience itself: *"Die Welt und das Leben sind Eins. / Ich bin meine Welt."* (The world and life are one. / I am my world.)[12] The author's ontological context notwithstanding, the religiously aware Jewish reader is likely to hear as a countertext the core statement of Jewish faith, the Shema ("Hear, O Israel"), which concludes by affirming, "God is One." Acknowledging divine unity, one can accept language's simultaneous inexhaustibility and insufficiency. Finding one's world in oneself, on the other hand, may leave one with a proposition about language that seems at once tautological and frustrating, the final proposition of the *Tractatus:* *"Wovon man nicht sprechen kann, darüber muß man schweigen"* (Whatever one cannot speak of, of that one must be silent).[13]

For the Jew, silence before the ineffable retains the quality of the sacral rather than of failure. Franz Rosenzweig perceived that to be a fundamental consequence of Hebrew's sequestration from daily experience. (He was writing, of course, at a time in this century before the language had become the common tongue of a modern state.)[14] Maintaining both a holy language and a secular one means, according to Rosenzweig, that the Jew relinquishes "freedom and spontaneity" in expression: "He addresses God in a language different from the one he uses to speak to his brother. As a result he cannot speak to his brother at all. He communicates with him by a glance rather than in words, and nothing is more essentially Jewish in the deepest sense than a profound distrust of the power of the word and a fervent belief in the power of silence."[15] Silence is attainable only when the speaker directs common attention to the textual word of God, not to the speaker or the sermon text. Rosenzweig even excepts the auditor's mute communication of responsive gestures and expressions as merely a different mode of speaking. True silence, he emphasizes, rests in the audience's "unanimous attention" to the unfolded truth.

Still, as noted earlier, discussing silence in relation to Jewish religion and thought may at first seem paradoxical. That comment has nothing to do with stereotypes but with characteristic Jewish approaches to language, religion, and society that emphasize the speech preceding or accompanying the profound silence Rosenzweig perceived as the goal of religious understanding. Buber expressed speech's centrality in these terms: "The whole history of the world, the hidden, real world history, is a dialogue between God and his creature; a dialogue in which man is a true, legitimate partner, who is entitled and empowered to speak his own independent word out of his own being." Our glory, according to Buber, exists in being "mortal, brittle human beings who yet are able to face God and withstand his word."[16]

José Faur, drawing on the familiar antithesis between the Hellenic and Hebraic views of experience, points out, "The Greek truth is visual. . . . For the Hebrews the highest form of truth is perceived at the auditory level."[17] We have remarked before that in Hebrew the same word, *davar*, denotes "word" and "object." As Arthur Green tells us, "Humanity is defined and distinguished from other forms of life in our tradition by the term *medabber*; the human is a 'speaker'."[18] Contrasting the "Greco-Christian" hermeneutics of Western philosophy and literary criticism with the Jewish, Susan A. Handelman observes that the Greek term for word also means *name*, not *thing*. She claims, "It was precisely this original unity of word and thing, speech and thought, discourse and truth that the Greek Enlightenment disrupted."[19] Hebrew, Rosenzweig claimed, has "no word for 'reading' that does not mean 'learning' as well."[20] He rightly posited that engagement with words involves us with process and dialogue, and although these are necessary preliminaries to informed acceptance of truth, they are merely preliminaries.

Yet even the Jewish mystic must face and resolve, and might have to compromise on, the dilemma posed by knowing. "The secret of God is with the one who fears God," the Bible tells us (Psalm 25:14). That secret (*sod* in Hebrew), "the essence of divinity," according to the nineteenth-century Hasidic rabbi Kalonymus Kalman Epstein, one "cannot possibly communicate to others, to convey from the deepest recesses of the heart that which one has in heart and mind." Indeed, the more one comprehends of this mystery, the fuller becomes that inaccessible treasure trove. Suppose one wants to lead others to understand, however. Then an intermediary "of lesser spiritual rank" must bridge the gap between the more and less enlightened "who can understand that which he has been told and who can then communicate it to others."[21] The profoundly enlightened individual truly cannot open those chambers of secrecy, but obliged to return to the life of this lower world, one bears a double obligation as well as a divided soul.

As we have seen, spiritually infused meditative silence is often praised in Jewish texts, even as an end in itself. Nonetheless, we live in physical and social worlds resulting from divine action; in that world, we speak. Language is the medium through which we respond to experiences as profound and diverse as oppression and awe. The terms in which we respond are likely to owe much to biblical precedents of complaints, praise, protests, lamentations, psalmody, and prophecy, all of which afford a vast range of canonical and even formally shaped verbalizations.

Amid their outpourings of language, all religious forms of Jewish verbal expression—psalmody, liturgy, and theology—affirm that words are inadequate to God's praise. Abraham Joshua Heschel noted that Maimonides, rationalist though he was, affirmed that profundities such as God's unity are beyond language. In *Guide for the Perplexed* Maimonides wrote, "Words are altogether one of the main causes of error, because whatever language we employ, we find the restrictions it imposes on our expression extremely disturbing. We cannot even picture this concept by using inaccurate language." Heschel carries through the thought: "And all language is inaccurate." Experience and Scripture, Maimonides felt, were both on his side. "When our tongues desire to declare God's greatness by descriptive terms, all eloquence becomes impotence and imbecility." Even the Psalms, those great outpourings of poetic praise, affirm (he noted), "Silence is praise to Thee" (65:2) and instruct the righteous, "Commune with your own heart upon your bed and be still perpetually" (4:5). Heschel concluded, "Silence is preferable to speech. Words are not indispensible to cognition. They are only necessary when we wish to communicate our ideas to others or to prove to them that we have attained cognition."[22]

Rabbi Joseph Soloveitchik similarly expressed the delicate balance between language and silence in the process of revelation: "The message communicated from Adam to Eve certainly consists of words. However, words do not always have to be identified with sound. It is rather a soundless revelation accomplished in muteness and in the stillness of the covenantal community when God responds to the prayerful outcry of lonely man."[23] We think, feel, comprehend in words; we talk to ourselves in words, vocalized or not, and we may comprehend unseen truths through unspoken articulations of meanings. A thirteenth-century Jewish liturgical poet, David Hakohen, expressed the experience of being overwhelmed by divine majesty:

> I shall be silent, and by my silence shall thank the Eternal.
> Mutely, I proclaim that greatness is God's.
> I have become a byword for hoping in dumb silence.[24]

Having passed beyond rational understanding (*el aḥrei t'bunai*), the speaker proclaims that words are useless. Obviously, though, they remain inescapable even if unnecessary, for the poem is made of words. Furthermore, the poet also reminds us that God's vast magnificence should impel us to praise God even "as I pour out my supplicating speech" (*b'shafkhi siḥei taḥanunai*), perhaps in soundless words, mute and still confessions streaming forth out of this side of the covenantal community.

From the realm of essential truths we are essentially separated. We retain physical forms and remain things, not pure words or the pure ideas inside those words. Here we are, "stones, people, shards of glass in the sun, tin cans, cats and trees," in the words of the poet Aaron Zeitlin. He wrote that we all are *"ilustratsies tsu a tekst,"* illustrations for a text.

> Some other place we aren't needed;
> there the text alone is read—
> the pictures fall away like dead limbs.[25]

Our hands shuffle the pictures, manipulate the words that stand for things, doing our best with the grasp of reality vouchsafed us.

Jewish religious tradition draws from this realization the lesson that we must pour forth language in futile attempts to articulate the ineffable. Words, we realize, cannot describe or define the holy. Instead, they constitute both tribute and witness: the words of praise are our sacrificial gifts, and the celebrations of divine bounty and manifold attributes express our energetic commitment to appreciating the fullness of the divine. We may grasp that words are insufficient and that the fullest understanding should be expressed through awed appreciative silence. Being silent, however, seems even less adequate than manipulating our admittedly insufficient words. Therefore, we affirm in morning prayers that, "Were our mouths filled with song as the sea, our tongues with joyful praise as the multitude of its waves, our lips with adoration as the spacious firmament, . . . we would still be unable to thank and bless Thy name sufficiently." Given that one can praise inadequately or be silent, one praises inadequately but copiously. Consequently, the resort to silence may be even more startling when it appears in the context of Jewish texts, though it is validated (as we saw above) not only by mystics.

We must speak. Furthermore, we understand God also wanting (for how can one speak of God as needing?) to speak as the way to express the divine will. The Torah is filled with anthropomorphic allusions to God speaking, from the earliest moments of creation through the books of Moses and onward throughout the stories of the prophets. A passage of the Zohar, the central text of kabbalah, continuing that work's fascinated attempts to probe inside the mysteries of creation through the linguistic mysteries locked within the opening words of the Torah, turns to the logic of beginning with the second letter of the Hebrew alphabet (the *bet* of *b'reishit*, "in the beginning") and offers a midrash. "When the Holy One, praised be!, was about to make the world, all the letters of the aleph-bet were still embryonic, and for two thousand years the Holy One, praised be!, had contemplated them and played with them. When the Holy One was ready to create the world, all the letters presented themselves before God in reversed order. The letter *tav* advanced in front and pleaded, 'May it please Thee, O Sovereign of All, to place me first in the creation of the world, seeing that I am the final letter of *emet* [Truth].' " So the text proceeds through all the letters, arriving at last to grasp the logic for the disposition of the second and first letters.

It is the literarily dramatic concept that seems so remarkable here, as in pageantlike form each letter (still in the process of developing its essence) comes to plead its case orally, advancing its claims according to its importance in the spelling of some appropriate Hebrew word, to which God responds with an objection stemming from the letter's use in an unfavorable word. Before people exist, before the world is created, the letters are ready, and so is the language; as an earlier Talmudic-era text informs us, before creation a solitary God dwelt only "with God's own name."[26] In this context of divine orality we can understand more deeply Moses' reluctance to transmit God's message to the Israelites and Pharaoh when he protests (much as Isaiah later will) that he has *aral s'fatayim*, "uncircumcised lips" (Exod. 6:12). We can also grasp why his failure with words at Meribah (Num. 22:12) resulted in his being prohibited from entering the promised land (as is specified in Deut. 32:51–52): Told by God to speak to the rock to bring forth water for his parched followers, Moses instead spoke angrily to the people and smote the rock.

Not only does God speak, but as the preceding kabbalistic scenario implies, God's native language is the language in which the Torah was communicated to the world. Hebrew is therefore the *leshon ha-kodesh*, the holy tongue, for a reason more profound than the mere fact that it is the language of the Bible text. As secular Hebrew poetry began to flourish in medieval Andalusia while deriving greater formalistic complexity from the varieties of Arabic quantitative meters devised for the linguistic patterns of the Arabic language, traditionalists protested against the profanation of a language God created "before endowing the inhabitants of the world with intelligence or speech."[27]

Even if one does not pursue the idea that Hebrew is the language holy to God, it is indisputable that Hebrew is holy to Jews. In an early essay (1917) on the importance of Hebrew, Rosenzweig wrote that "The German—and this includes the German within the Jew—can and will read the Bible in German, read it as Luther, Herder, Mendelssohn, read it; the Jew can understand it only in Hebrew. Yet while [the Bible is] . . . property common to both German and Jew, in the matter of Jewish prayer it is otherwise. Of the language of the Jewish prayer we may state quite categorically that it is untranslatable." To the extent that the Jew's religious life is lived through Hebrew's historical continuum as a language, consciousness of one's exile is permanent. "So far as his language is concerned, the Jew feels always he is in a foreign land."[28]

Hebrew's spiritual significance extends for Jews even to the forms of the letters. Rabbi Lawrence Kushner, who has special interests in both mysticism and calligraphy, has expressed the underlying principle: "The OTIYOT [letters] exist independently of ink and paper or even words."[29] The sacral quality of the language has been reinforced through the precise rules for the proper shaping of the "square letters" of religious Hebrew established in the Mishnah and through the practices and attitudes discussed below. It is implied as well by Jewish traditions of biblical interpretation founded on manipulations of letters: *gematria* (substituting numerical values for letters to make equivalences between words), *t'murah* (transposing letters to turn a word into another), and *notarikon* (taking the letters of a word as an anagram for a phrase). These techniques treat words as temporary, mutable embodiments of even deeper truths resident within the letters and verbal structure of Hebrew itself. Rosenzweig posited that in adopting Hebrew characters for writing Jewish vernacular languages like Yiddish, we attempted to maintain some contact between the holy tongue, no longer spoken, and everyday speech. The substance of Jewish prayer and thought, therefore, does not stand separate from the language but rests within it.

Language is spoken as well as written. Among the greatest of Judaism's literary and religious texts—and the most widely known, loved, and influential of them—have been the words of the prophets, the poetry of the psalms and the Book of Lamentations, and the parables of the Hasidic rabbis. All of these signify a culture strongly given to expressing its most profound feelings and perceptions verbally in public. One is not surprised by the title of a recent work by a rabbi and scholar, Anson Laytner: *Arguing with God: A Jewish Tradition*. Indeed, although the Book of Job unquestionably enters world literature through the Jewish scriptures, rabbinic tradition casts doubt on Job himself being Jewish, precisely because he never demands justice even from the Eternal. David Wolpe points out that, confronted with persecution, the rabbis of the Talmud raised their voices against the silence of God, challenging the Eternal with evocative phrases that mock familiar biblical texts proclaiming God's supremacy. Amid Jerusalem's ruins the sages replaced the rhetorical question "Who is like you among the gods, glorious in holiness, awesome, doing wonders" with the challenge "Who is like you among the dumb? Who like you hears the humiliation of his children and remains silent?"[30]

An anecdote related in the Koran (Sura 18:64–80) amusingly underscores this association between Jews and the critical mind, although in our context it acquires a meaning different from the one in its source. The story (whose folkloric pattern will likely sound familiar) claims that Moses journeyed with a Muslim spiritual teacher, who agreed to the prophet's company only with the provision that Moses ask no questions about anything that might occur on their trip. Moses, however, in good Jewish fashion, cannot restrain himself: he must ask questions. Not only does he inquire but he also protests (unperspicaciously, according to the Koran) what he perceives as unjust.

The nature of the biblical relationships between God and human beings and between one person and another is complexly and intensely oral. Notwithstanding the Pentateuch's many enumerated exchanges of property and possessions, the detailing of positive and negative commandments along with the penalties for infringement, the accounts of obligatory gifts and sacrifices for worship, the essence of Torah is verbal. "I set before you this day blessing and curse," God warns (Deut. 30:19); we will experience the good and the bad in our lives as fulfillments of divinely articulated promises and admonitions. Those who reject the teachings are scorned through their words by God, who says that his commandment "is not in heaven, that you should say, 'Who shall go up to heaven for us and fetch it for us and let us hear it [*v'yashmieynu*] so that we can do it?'" (Deut. 30:12). Rather, the word (*ha-davar*) is intimately close by, "in your mouth and in your heart, that you may do it" (Deut. 30:14). "That you may 'do' the word [*la'asoto ha-davar*]" succinctly expresses the connection between holy language and righteous behavior.

Given the rabbinic teaching that there are no extraneous words in the To- rah, we must not pass inattentively over the phrase *b'fiḥa uvi-l'vavḥa* (in your mouth and in your heart). To feel or comprehend is not enough. We must also know the truth of what we are saying, whether it is what we routinely say, unthinkingly, by rote, or what merely receives our lip service and not the service of the heart or the deed. For this reason, Jewish benedictions are very specific about defining the category of the item for which one gives thanks: the blessing for meeting a religious scholar (and there is such a blessing) differs from the one for meeting a secular scholar (and there is also such a blessing), and the one for eating tree-grown foods differs from that for foods grown in the ground. One should be conscious of the nature of the source of one's gratitude, and one should be conscious of the connection between language and material reality.

"The study of God's word is greater than the rebuilding of the Temple," the Talmud tells us.[31] Such a statement, to be sure, does not come forth in theol- ogy's pure empyrean. The Talmudic assertion is sagely practical, insofar as God's word can be studied each day, whereas rebuilding the Temple depends on bringing the Messiah. It is also, one must admit, partisan within the Jewish milieu as much as politic in encouraging a circumspect relationship between Judaism and the public world. One could say that it expresses both a domestic and a foreign policy. Succinctly, this quintessential rabbinic text attests that rabbinic Judaism has superseded levitical rites and that Jews are to pursue mental and spiritual enlightenment in preference to temporal power. Granting all these interpretive caveats, one can nonetheless note that the Talmud's authority bestows its own honor on the spiritual value of studying written or spoken words. The religious culture that had been founded on the priestly sacrificial rites of an agrarian society became a religious culture centered on a text and its extensive system of satellite analyses and commentaries. That textual system became a code of living and a network for knowing God and God's word.

Exile from the Holy Name

The first difficulty in speaking about God, we have noted, is exactly that: How does one apply words to the inexpressible? Other difficulties follow. How can we grasp the concept that we are patterned after the divine without constraining that godhood into human form? How can we designate that which is the author of being, the sustainer of life, the giver of laws and precepts without reproducing a model of our own imperfect constructions? A significant achievement of the contemporary feminist critique of traditional God terms is to remind us that the nouns and pronouns by which we refer to God relate both to theology and to our own lives. The issues include not only how we refer to God but how we refer to God and who "we" think we are. Both Judaism and Christianity have been compelled to face issues raised by these critiques. The issues differ somewhat from religion to religion; within Judaism, for instance, no central organization can mandate linguistic practice even for its own member congregations. However, Jewish experience with gendered religious language can illuminate the central concerns that have arisen within Christian churches as well.

Within religious communities, linguistic revisions in prayer books and hymnals bespeak the changes behind the pulpit, behind the altar rail, in front of the Torah ark, and in the minds of congregants and celebrants. Exile has also included exile from cultural discourse, one main branch of which is theology, expressed through language about God and language of worship.

Simple revisions of traditional texts can raise complex rejoinders, as each suggested change redefines the issues involved. The tamest and therefore most easily and widely accepted textual revision within the liberal branches of Judaism has amended the roll call of our ancestral tradition. Specifically, the first blessing of the central Amidah prayer has been one addressing the God of our "*avot*" (literally, fathers), the patriarchs, Abraham, Isaac, and Jacob. Many progressive congregations now acknowledge in prayer that the deity is also the god of our "*imahot*," the matriarchs, Sarah, Rebecca, Leah, and Rachel; the "rock of Abraham" is as well the "helper of Sarah." Perhaps this alteration has proved widely acceptable, at least among social progressives, because it does not affect the essential nature of God but broadens our acknowledgment of the ways in which our religious tradition has been experienced and transmitted among people. This new wording begins to reclaim (as two female Jewish writers have entitled their works) "The Jew Who Wasn't There" and "The Woman Who Lost Her Name."[32] In addition, Jewish feminists have reemphasized the importance of the feminine Shekhinah in Jewish theology and directed our attention to some of the female ritual and prayer resources to be found in earlier Jewish cultures as well as in current traditional and nontraditional communities of Jewish women.[33]

Greater resistance confronts changes affecting how we think about the deity or the external manifestation of the divine and what words we use to characterize God. Balancing traditional paternal pronouns and metaphors for God with maternal ones, adding, for instance, blessings for a goddess-creator to the traditional ones for a god-creator, gives rise to an outcry such as Cynthia Ozick's against what she perceives as a longing for pagan goddess worship, "The answer stuns with its crudity . . . slanders and sullies monotheism." For Ozick, calling our divinity "goddess" or even "Queen of the Universe" (to parallel the traditional Hebrew *adonai melekh ha-olam*, usually translated "Lord, King of the Universe") evokes "a return to Astarte, Hera, Juno, Venus, and all their proliferating sisterhood." The female title conjures up a forbidden and horrific pantheon of strange gods from alien peoples and tongues for this observant Jew, who also describes herself as a liberal (not radical) feminist.[34]

On the other hand, rephrasing the traditional imagery so that God is characterized through female and male terms alike may also prompt the converse complaint that this is too traditional. For example, the Jewish feminist theologian Judith Plaskow, responding to such linguistic modifications, has objected that "Although changing pronouns and some imagery modifies and softens the traditional picture of God, it does not fundamentally alter the conception of a great potentate fighting for his/her people and ruling over the world. . . . [Authors of such revisions] are wrong in assuming that any attribute applied to 'God-He' is equally well applied to 'God-She'."[35] Plaskow, describing feminist theology as an effort "to rename and reconceptualize God," urges that we understand the divine as (among other qualities) "a power to be named through rhythm and movement as much as through words."[36] Words, she implies, are inadequate as well as obstructive.

Some Christian churches have similarly refined liturgies, hymnals, and biblical translations. The entire process is analogous to the more general critical and academic revision of the story of our cultural past. Jewish liturgical language raises particular problems because Hebrew, which is grammatically gendered, remains the standard language of prayer, ritual, and benediction for Jews worldwide. Changes often have been made in the English translations or paraphrases but not in the corresponding Hebrew, which is disjunctive for worshipers familiar enough with Hebrew to know what the words are and are not saying. Altering the Hebrew texts or substituting others is possible, and this certainly has been done within circles comfortable with such revisions.[37] This process seems essential, especially as progressive Judaism develops among native Hebrew speakers in the land of Israel.

However, these changes raise concern over the resulting discontinuity with the synchronic historical tradition of Jewish worship and the diachronic current community of Jewish worshipers. Jews feel our place in the universe to involve not only our individual relationship (diachronic as well as synchronic) with God but also those two other relationships—that is, with Jewish historicity and with Jewish contemporaneity. Most Jews, including feminists, who are connected at all with their religious (as distinct from solely ethnic or historical) tradition want to maintain some identifiable, familiar liturgical continuity with it; we are also likely to value sharing a religious language (broadly understood) with Jews around the world. Again, the situation is somewhat analogous to Christians wanting to broaden, not narrow, confessional relations among denominations.

Jews are caught in the tension between our evolved religious experience as one people (Jewish particularism, as some others term it) and our messianic mission to be a light to all peoples. Trying to resolve the perplexities, some have chosen (like the faithful Spanish *conversos,* who hid their Sabbath candles in jugs) to maintain the flame safely for their distinct guidance; some contrarily have joined their lights to countless others, adding to the universal glow an undifferentiable light. Speaking differently of and to God than we have in the past may be most troublesome when we find that the loss of traditional terms of reference threatens to obliterate our sense of our own conceptualizations. Adding distinctive words and visions to humankind's grasp of the eternal existing within or over nature and time must be among any people's most significant contributions. Franz Rosenzweig in *The Star of Redemption* argued that this made Judaism's survival essential especially amid the apparent triumph of Christianity in the temporal world. Jews long for the time when (as we say in the prayer known as the Aleinu) "God shall be One and God's Name shall be One." If we make the mistake of believing we can hasten that time by stilling our own distinctive voices or letting our own candle melt into a shapeless common torch, then we will end with a God produced from the lowest common denominators of all faiths rather than the richly complex originator and welcomer whom all of nature and humankind must hymn as they can.

We need to guard against inadvertent self-mockery, however, turning ourselves into the Tevye of *Fiddler on the Roof* bellowing "Tradition, tradition!" to defy change. Although for most of our history since late antiquity we have shared throughout our communities highly standardized rituals and texts, the turmoil caused by the rise of kabbalistic worship in the late Middle Ages and by Hasidism at the end of the eighteenth century attests that the introduction of major new texts and reinterpretations of old ones have been accompanied by terrific pains but that these innovations have contributed significantly to Judaism's survival and spiritual growth. Furthermore, as suggested above, some apparent innovations actually reinstate older practices and reintroduce ancient texts that also have legitimate claims to that tradition.

Reforming language in worship really means ending exiles that have been caused or reinforced by language. One exile is that of most men and women who have been separated from the feminine aspects of the divine in the world because those aspects have been suppressed in the verbal evocations of the deity, the "God-He." This is a lexical version of the exile of the Shekhinah. Another is the particular exile of women and men who have felt exiled from God because the names and concepts of divine masculinity have offered them a sense of the divine that was distant, alien, alienating. A current wave of Jewish theologians, particularly those rediscovering the midrashic and mystical currents, are demonstrating that conventional views of God are not only restricting but artificially constricted. We have lived with diminished images and terms giving us a mere fraction of what our heritage has articulated of understanding about sacredness. The return to tradition paradoxically may — though it certainly does not always—carry us from the shallow, narrow-channeled God-language of the traditional mainstream into a more vast sea.

If richness, even austere richness, dwells within the beating at the heart of life, we are unfair to it and ourselves to restrict our vocabulary and imagery for expressing and conceiving of it. Perhaps we did better in that regard when the Temple still stood and the high priest entered the Holy of Holies during the Yom Kippur service to speak that divine name that had been passed as a treasured secret inheritance through the generations since Moses. At that time it was possible to know that aside from the stories, laws and precepts, and figurative language accumulated around the concept of God, there was a moment of contact with the divine accessible only through the simplest and most primitive form of language, the speaking of God's name. It was a name at once verb and noun, abstract but particular, dissimilar from any other, a name not otherwise spoken and therefore free of the accumulated human aids and hinderances of gender and attributes. One could and did recite in petitioning for forgiveness the litany of divine attributes—"God merciful and compassionate, slow to anger"—but these were about God's relationship with us. They frankly attested to what we needed when we thought of divinity. Beyond those expressions, however, remained, more importantly, the name. Centuries of name substitutes and figurations of art have perhaps led us to imagine that God is merely the compilation of terms and images that come easily to mind and mouth.

We do well, not only for social but for theological reasons, to escape from the ensnaring routines of thought instilled by our verbal formulae. Plaskow's term for this effort is "reimaging the unimaginable." The desire for ritual is not base. Even those of us for whom "Lord God, King of the Universe" or "Our Father" has become an impossible formula (at least in English, regardless of what we speak in Hebrew) may need to adapt our own locutions to articulate and communicate what we feel needs to be said in moments of gratitude or of individual or communal need. At times each of us will need more strongly the historical connection, at other times, commonality with one community or another wants to be more clearly affirmed, and at still other times, what will matter most intensely for us is our relationship with the creative source of all life. These moments will call forth different sorts of prayers, blessings, and rituals, and we will need to have the words appropriate to each, in whichever language or languages we can find the connective bonds.

46

This may be another way to understand the Aleinu when it proclaims, "Then You shall be One and Your Name shall be One." Genesis tells us that we were created in God's image and also that God created male and female and called "them" Adam. According to the midrashic tradition, therefore, Adam was first created in God's image as both male and female conjoined as one. Division came subsequently.[38] When we can imagine God as one, we come closer to resolving the two separable images of male and female. In leading us to imagine God as one in the way that we human beings, now differentiably male and female, were once one being in God's image, language helps reunite us with the holy.

3

———

Letters in Love with Letters

Life is where nobody can live.
It's the Jewish quarter. ·
—*Marina Tsvetaeva*

BOTH LITERACY AND ORALITY have continued to occupy important places in Jewish scholarship and worship. The two activities of scholarship and worship are not readily separable in Judaism. In every religiously based facet of home and synagogue, the text of the Torah remains central. During periods of history when the ability to read the local vernacular tongue or the official language was reserved only for certain especially privileged classes in the general population, almost all Jewish boys could read some biblical Hebrew, and many could also read Aramaic. (Aramaic had an unusual role: an erstwhile late vernacular tongue of Jews, when it ceased to be commonly spoken it lived on as a scholarly language in the Talmud, Judaism's essential companion piece to the Bible.) Mishnah Avot 5:21, the Talmud's outline of a man's life, prescribes (albeit optimistically): Scripture at five, Mishnah at ten, religious obligations at thirteen, Talmud (i.e., Gemara) at fifteen. Although Jewish girls were not so privileged educationally, a substantial body of religious material written for women (even if mostly by men, usually rabbis) beginning in the Middle Ages attests to literacy among women probably more extensive than that within the general population. It is also clear that women sometimes had access to knowledge through, for instance, their brothers or educated older relatives.

Although exiled from their ancestral homeland and muted within the non-Jewish political and intellectual culture indigenous where they dwelt, Jews have sustained conversations in specifically Jewish secular and religious tongues through two thousand years of history in the *galut* (exile). This is especially remarkable because physical exile also meant that the Jew's traditional cultural language, Hebrew, was cast into a special form of silence. Although still spoken in benedictions and liturgy, Hebrew ceased as a conversational oral language, a tongue truly alive as an organic entity. A mid-nineteenth-century Jew quixotically determined to write in Hebrew necessarily did so using biblical vocabulary and grammar. Because that "fate" was imposed, Hebrew's situation was significantly different from that of (for instance) Church Slavonic or Sanskrit, which retained religious uses despite being superseded through normal processes of change. Along with the modern development of a Hebrew language went the development of a place in which to speak it; the resurgence, resuscitation, or reinvention of Hebrew coincided with the rise of political Zionism, both adjuncts to a modern reimagining of what being Jewish entailed. That was clear in the first writings of the originator of modern Hebrew, Eliezer Ben-Yehuda. In 1879, three years before Leon Pinsker's *Autoemancipation* and seventeen before Herzl's *Jewish State* (the two principal founding texts of modern political Zionism), Ben-Yehuda saw the return to the ancestral homeland and to the ancestral language as inseparable from one another and from the full emancipation of Jews. The voice and tongue of the people were not incidental to their autonomy but central to it.

Through the centuries of exile, language was essential to preserve Jewish identity and culture. What was studied and how it was studied significantly shaped Jewish thought and relationship with language itself. The most elementary grammar school (heder) tutelage in the Bible introduced a boy to the text itself but also to the rudiments of biblical scholarship in the form of grammatical and philological commentary. Any traditionally educated boy would begin learning Talmud before his teenage years. The idea that religious understanding emerged through verbal interaction would be conveyed at least implicitly. First, annotated Bibles and religious school teachers specified the sources of their lexical and interpretive insights; the names of great scholars of centuries past are part of the storehouse of a Jewish child's general knowledge, if that child has any Jewish education. As it was five hundred years ago, so today:

reading a copy of the Pentateuch printed with Rashi's twelfth-century commentary is not regarded as an abstruse scholarly enterprise but as an appropriate beginning for a student. For traditionally educated youths the "Chumash [Pentateuch] with Rashi" remains the benchmark of basic literacy in the biblical text. Consequently, centuries of Jews learned Hebrew biblical grammar and philology from one of the acknowledged great figures in Jewish learning.

The tradition has also developed a complex relationship between the written and oral word. What we think of as the Torah is traditionally designated as the written Torah, and its chief interpretive resource, the Talmud, is known as the oral Torah, notwithstanding that the former was also originally given orally and the latter has existed in writing for about fourteen centuries. Even within the written Torah a separate tradition exists (*qere/ketib*) designating oral substitutions for particular words, even though such substitutions may not be written into the scrolls used in synagogues or printed in place of those words in the transmitted text. A centuries-old tradition mandates the rules for hand lettering the Torah scrolls that may be read in the synagogue, but the scrolls that must be read literally cannot be read as written because they lack vowel markings, punctuation, and symbols for the traditional cantillation. In his detailed analysis of the semiotics of rabbinic texts, Faur observes, "The liturgical lesson of the Tora cannot be enunciated according to the written text (disregarding the vocal tradition of reading) and it is prohibited to write the text according to the vocal tradition (disregarding the scriptural tradition)."[1] The scribal tradition furthermore mandates meticulous rules for the physical appearance of the written text, including the formation and legibility of letters. Because letters were the building stones of creation, the significance of language begins with the physical markings that denote it and, according to Jewish tradition, precede and even transcend language.

Talmudic study concentrates even more intensely on the word as construct. The Talmud explicitly records scholarly discussions and disputes over fine interpretive points of biblical laws, carried out in dialogic fashion across the page of a text, with continual references to specifically named authorities dating from the first through sixth centuries C.E. whose opinions it quotes directly or paraphrases. The Talmud's discussions are knowingly oblivious to the real historical chronology of the authorities whose analyses are brought forth to challenge one another, who are allowed to support or refute one another not only across the page but across the divisions of its encyclopedic volumes and still more dramatically across the centuries in timeless dialogue. By contrast with such indifference to chronological sequence, Talmudic controversies evince a meticulous regard for the text's linguistic specificity: pages of speculative hypothetical analysis arise from the use of an ambiguous pronoun reference, one preposition versus another, singular versus plural, included versus omitted detail, even lexical and spelling variants.

Furthermore, the pedagogical method of studying Talmud emphasizes the verbal. Learning Talmud entails students in pairs reading and disputing aloud with one another, with the text and about the text, and with their teacher. Through the form of nonsyllogistic reasoning known as *pilpul*, the Talmudist draws deductions from ingeniously worked analogies. It is both mental discipline and a determined attempt to find how an old text that seems locked in place can be made to yield new meanings or provide guidance on material presumably not included in it. Fittingly, Edmond Jabès has written, "The country of the Jews is a holy text amid commentaries to which it gives rise" (La patrie des Juifs est un texte sacré au milieu des commentaires qu'il a suscités).[2] From the holy word to the promised land and then out again into the sacred text might be one way of summarizing Jewish history.

The gift given by a parsimonious "God of Israel," according to the Yiddish poet A. Leyeles, was "two handsful of letters" scattered like jewels across the world's roads. "They sparkled with speech, blazed with sayings" (zey hobn gefinklt mit reyd, mit mimros geflemlt) and set Jews on the road for thousands of years to seek and collect and interpret them. The legacy of that collecting proves to be, "Another manuscript, and another manuscript . . . letters in love with letters."[3] Because of that love, we are to understand that they seek one another and reproduce.

The poet's *farlibt*, "in love," is not pure hyperbole. It captures the genuinely passional relationship between the Jew and the word, one that is like other passional relationships in being not only intense but sometimes difficult, contentious, strained, and yet still loving—"Jewishly" loving (one may perhaps dare to say), unashamed to express that love emotionally and physically. Traditionally, when a Jewish child begins Hebrew school, a drop of honey has been placed on a book for the child to kiss, to associate reading with sweetness; from childhood to old age, the Jew who accidentally drops a prayer book will pick it up and kiss it, as one would kiss a child who had fallen. As David Wolpe notes in contrast, "Judaism has no sacred ritual objects. If a Jew drops any ritual object, a candlestick, a spice box, a wine cup, it is simply retrieved."[4] The people given the highest honors in synagogue worship are those called to recite the blessings before and after scriptural readings, and decorum requires that they touch a prayer book or prayer shawl to the scroll at the point of reading, before their blessings. Prayer books and scrolls too damaged to use are not just thrown away but specially stored until they may be buried in a Jewish cemetery, along with the rest of our cherished loved ones.

The text is both the place we love and the Jewish territory into which we are exiled or exile ourselves—in sometimes-painful love—by remaining Jews. Our country is the road that we travel along in quest of those glittering letters. Leyeles lived the paradox. Born in Russian-dominated Poland, he then moved to London and eventually "settled" in the United States, where he travelled extensively on behalf of Yiddish educational causes. Though his first language (his *mame-loshen,* or mother tongue) was Yiddish, his father taught Hebrew, and growing up he learned Russian and Polish also; later he would add German and English, all of them languages in which he wrote, though Yiddish became his exclusive poetic medium. His journey in an international tongue and several national ones was voluntary, at least within the definitions governing immigration offices. Only when one understands how such multilingualism signifies rootlessness can one sense in what way these migrations might be involuntary. If one belongs no place in particular, how can one stay anywhere in particular? Recognizing Leyeles's lack of a certain home, one may also recognize that his moves are only apparent emigrations. They might be better comprehended as migrations within the land called *Yiddishkeit,* a term meaning both Yiddishness and Jewishness.

Other conditions under which that quest frequently has been undertaken return to memory through the poignant commentary of the great scholar Isaac Abrabanel, who served as treasurer to Alfonso V of Portugal until the latter's death and subsequently as adviser and banker to Ferdinand and Isabella of Spain until the Spanish expulsion decree of 1492 turned his life into a succession of exiles. Writing of the ritual detailed in Deuteronomy 27 for claiming possession of the promised land, Abrabanel noted that other nations set up monuments celebrating their conquests and heroes; the Jews, however, were instructed in their moment of triumphant entrance into their promised homeland to "inscribe on stone the words of Torah."[5] The place of settlement was to become the place of the word, the place governed according to the holy words, the place in which the word of God would dwell. It was not to give us the word made flesh but rather the word made fruitful, and the word was to be experienced through milk and honey and each season's first growths of the land. Not the world's roadways but one land was to blaze forth in the word. Those roads have become the paths of diaspora, the extension of that land into the rest of the world, onto the surface of the world, trodden virtually unremarked by the exiles. In their exile and dispersion, often disregarded by the world at large, usually seemingly silent within those cultures, they maintained their conversation about God's ancient promises and the terms of a continuing covenant.

To be Jewish in the postbiblical world means to be exiled in different senses, which we can comprehend through lexical or linguistic means. First, we must understand that the Greek word *diaspora*, the most common term in non-Jewish contexts to refer to the scattering of the Jewish presence throughout the world, poorly connotes through its descriptively literal sense of "dispersion" the analogous but scarcely equivalent Hebrew word *galut*, denoting exile. Scattering is an experiential fact; to be in exile, by contrast, is to be in a particular state of mind. Actually, the phrase *state of mind* itself inadequately expresses the totality of experience, visceral as much as mental. One should also remember that exile has two components. One is exiled *from*, but one is also exiled *in*.

Nor need those components be equal in one's sensibilities. Franz Kafka, despite an attraction toward Zionism late in his short life, certainly never felt exiled from the Land of Israel per se, since he never had any such affection inculcated in him by his upbringing in a secularized and assimilationist familial environment. Unquestionably, though, he felt exiled in Prague and in the languages he knew. One could argue that Kafka as an individual, a pathological case, would have felt exiled anywhere, given that the exile began at home, but this seems to beg the question. Marthe Robert neatly summarized the question confronting him: "With what could Kafka, as a German-speaking Jew, an Austrian subject, and the inhabitant of a Czech city where the mere fact that he did not speak their language made the Czechs regard him as an enemy, have 'assimilated'? . . . His language was his only substitute for everything of which destiny had deprived him: a native soil, a fatherland, a present and a past."[6] However, Robert observes that even Kafka's language was a mark of exile, because he could not feel himself to be in any sense a native within the linguistic culture. The other languages with which he had contact were never his own spoken or written tongues, not Czech (disdained by Germanicized bourgeois Jews longing to identify with the esteemed German literary culture), not Yiddish (even more sharply spurned for social reasons), and not Hebrew (revered in principle as a religious language but as a modern language identified with a Zionist program threatening the acculturationist desires of most Prague Jews).

Robert records that Kafka eventually regretted his poor Czech, developed respect for Yiddish as a repository of Middle High German, even more notably experiencing a sentimental affection for its fusion of language and feelings, and learned to write and speak some modern Hebrew while considering emigration to Palestine. She cites his unease, however, even with the language that had been his from infancy. To that he referred disparagingly as, "the sort of German we have learned from the lips of our un-German mothers." The *mame-loshen* (his familial Yiddish inheritance) became his undoing, he implied. Jewish authors writing in German, Kafka asserted, "existed among three impossibilities, which I at random call linguistic impossibilities. It is simplest to call them that. But they might also be called something entirely different. These are: The impossibility of not writing, the impossibility of writing German, the impossibility of writing differently. One might also add a fourth possibility, the impossibility of writing (since the despair could not be assuaged by writing and was hostile to both life and writing)."[7] It seems notable that the first "impossibility" he rejects is "not writing," the "impossibility" of silence.

Even if one acknowledges the possibly distortive effect of Kafka's hypersensitivity, his insights transcend the purely autobiographical. At least the issue may be put in these terms. Every writer has wrestled with elusive, intractable words and sentences, no matter how fully native to the language the writer may be. When one is conscious of a particular source of estrangement, that source likely becomes the focus of one's difficulties. Whether that focal issue is actually the cause of some particular difficulty or whether it is simplest to call it that probably defies certain answer. Writers whose consciousness of that difference has been raised by the artistic struggle are likely to make that issue a major text or subtext of their careers. Grappling with an unwieldy syntax or hunting fruitlessly for a better word, one may feel that the solution to the problem would be found more readily by a writer for whom this is the "natural" language, a birthright inheritance. Falling mute would mean being swallowed up by one's circumstance.

This phenomenon of locating the tensions of one's creative struggles in a particular category of "otherness" appears even beyond the lexical level, as feminist criticism has certainly shown regarding the anxieties of women authors in using, rejecting, or subverting the literary genres, structures, and cultural language inherited from male authors or, to recall Kafka's own terms regarding the use of German, "appropriated," "stolen" from the native users. Virginia Woolf claimed to feel deprived of reading the Greek authors in the original, deprived of the university-developed intellectual training to which her stepbrothers exercised their claims by the mere facts of being male and coming from the same social class as she. We can probably agree that the kind of writer she became owes something to what was not instilled in her by education and training, and we can be thankful that she perhaps thereby avoided having her creative independence smothered. That she was the one who became a great writer may or may not be related to that impression of deprivation. That the impression itself affected many aspects of her writing and personal temperament seems certain.

So it is also when the ethnic, female, or gay writer contends with what might be called the normative literary culture. One may feel that the artist who protests of oppression, marginalization, or privation actually benefits artistically from those experiences, notwithstanding the personal pain and danger accompanying them. However, even if one takes advantage of the luxury of such an outlook, one cannot pretend that the artist's view of personal circumstances is irrelevant or remain oblivious to the writer's expressions of suffering, oppression, or exile. What can a black writer (for instance) make of centuries of European color coding of values, moods, morality, and status other than muse as Countee Cullen did on the sardonic humor of a deity who would "make a poet black and bid him sing" or poignantly ponder with Fats Waller the question raised in Andy Razaf's lyric, "What did I do to be so black and blue?" Audre Lorde said, "For those of us who write, it is necessary to scrutinize not only the truth of what we speak, but the truth of that language by which we speak it." Silence is intolerable for her: "In the cause of silence, each of us draws the face of her own fear."[8] Scrutiny of language is needed, however, because speech forms within a heavily determined linguistic milieu, a fact not lost on this black lesbian who would call one of her books *The Black Unicorn*, a title in which the adjective is not merely decorative or superficially categorical. It is essential, and if it suggests a paradox, in doing so it reminds us of the bond between the words we use and our inner sense of reality.

A Jew's relationship to the indigenous language and its culture still remains arguably unique, despite the suggestive homologies with other groups. At least it seems so for the Jew affected not only by ethnicity but also by the current of Jewish tradition. The relationship we have been examining exists between Judaism and the word, relying on a verbally specified covenantal relationship with God, on a textually based temporal scheme that encompasses not only the mythic and historical past but also the present (with its obligations of observance, charity, justice, righteousness) and the future (wherein redemption will be realized)—the Jew conscious of Judaism as well as Jewishness will live aware of a place in time and language shaped by the tales and text of Torah.

For the Jewish writer, who may say, as does even Cynthia Ozick (a precise English prose stylist), that when she writes in English, she is conscious of writing in Christendom, words are also filled with wrong or discomfiting implications. The English *charity,* from the Latin *caritas* (love) bears quite different implications from the Hebrew counterpart *tzedakah,* whose root means both justice and righteousness. The English word *redemption* carries Christian doctrinal freight unrelated to the Exodus-based historical meaning of the analogous Hebrew *geulah.*

In fact, to raise a relatively basic question, what does one call one's people and therefore oneself? This terminological issue concerning Jews has attracted less attention than the issue over denoting Americans of African origin, who have generally been labeled by people other than themselves. The issue is, however, far from simple for Jews, Israelites, Hebrews, those of the Jewish faith, children of Israel. Cassell's popular German-English dictionary (a 1906 edition, published—in London and New York—when Kafka was twenty-three and Jewish immigration to those two cities was extremely high) defines *Jude* as "Jew; usurer; miser" and *Jüdelei* as, "Jewish way of acting; usury; Jewish dialect; Yiddish."[9] If being exiled means that one has only the word as a home and inheritance, what language is it? What words are kosher? What words are bearable?

As an exile, in the indigenous language one might feel awkwardly conscious that one is not a native speaker; the accent one is aware of in one's own voice and cannot quite isolate or eradicate may dispose one to refrain from speaking or writing, exile one into the silence of the foreigner. For a people in exile, without territory, one's homeland is the homeland of one's language, in which all of one's people may lay claim to citizenship. This native homeland has meant the Hebrew of the Bible, Mishnah, and the prayer book, with Aramaic continuing to have commonwealth status. However, for most Jews over many centuries, this legacy has been principally hypothetical. For various large subgroupings within various chronotopes, another Jewish language has defined identity: Ladino, Judezmo, Judaeo-Arabic, Yiddish, and Hebrew again in its modern avatar. These have existed as Jewish tongues alongside every other language in which Jews have also lived, talked, sung, prayed, and written. The Sephardic Jews, driven from the Iberian peninsula at the end of the fifteenth century, have carried multiple cultural and linguistic citizenship for more than five hundred years, because they took into their second exile both the Hebrew language of their ancient home and the medieval Judeo-Spanish that became a vernacular of their speech and song throughout the Mediterranean and later the New World. While Jews of the *galut* may have been conversant with the local language, their principal medium of thought, communication, and expression remained throughout centuries (whether as a result of external or internal pressures) that of the Jewish linguistic territory.

That territory itself, though a place of exile, could double as sanctuary from an environment that, more often than not, has been not simply non-Jewish but more specifically anti-Jewish. What could or should one say amid such cultures? Some Jews surely have chosen voluntary exile in a Jewish lexicon of words, phrases, gestures, and cultural idioms. While the pagan cultures of Greeks and Romans on the one hand afforded a tempting and even seductive civilization and on the other hand effectively contained or suppressed Jewish national polity, the succeeding cultures dominating the Jewish environment have imposed more threatening constrictions on the spiritual citizenship of the individual Jew. Specifically, Christianity and Islam have both laid claims to being more than simply new or other religions vis-à-vis Judaism. They have professed to be corrective fulfillments of Judaism. Christianity, and less consistently Islam, have for that reason sought not just to dominate Jews and Judaism but to convert Jews either individually or en masse to fulfill the daughter religions' claims to the inheritance of their presumably dead mother. Since the late eighteenth century the civic religion of putatively secular (at least secularized) democracies has leveled its own claims as well to relieve Jews of ancient restrictions (from the endogenous as well as exogenous culture) in exchange for the voluntary diminution or abnegation of Jewish identity, the silencing of the Jewish voice insofar as it is Jewish (an idea explored at greater length in Chapter 8). Being exiled in the word therefore means being in a state of exile in one's surrounding culture and from one's surrounding culture; clinging to Jewish identity means living in the word, whether it be through ancestral language or convenantal teachings (*v'hayu ha-d'varim ha-eleh asher anokhi mitzavḥa ha-yom,* set these words which I command you this day).

Those teachings themselves became a place of exile in which one could dwell. Beyond the study of the Hebrew Bible, the specialized discourse of the Talmud that became the main area of study for male Jewish youths was, as one ancient commentator claimed, a "sea" in which to swim throughout one's days. The Talmud in turn was supplemented by a substantial body of commentary, and for the student who reached beyond, the enormous treasury of Jewish texts stretched through midrashic literature to the philosophical and spiritual commentaries of thinkers like Maimonides and onward into the mysteries of the kabbalah. Being literate in at least some of these texts was virtually synonymous with being a Jewish male; to be learned in them was a goal esteemed even by people who admired it only from a distance and who consequently enjoyed it vicariously by patronizing those engaged in the actual practice.

Although material success was probably no more widely disdained in Jewish circles than in the world at large, scholarly or intellectual attainments (or at worst the appearance thereof) were accorded particular honor even when they coexisted with poverty. To be poor because of the text but rich in the text was at least deemed honorable within Jewish circles. Occupied with close analysis and argumentation, the Jewish student or scholar—or, for that matter, the ordinary Jewish man or woman finding sustenance in the text of the psalms or the familiar home and synagogue liturgy of statutory prayers and benedictions— might well dwell in the word, exiled from prosperity but also from materialism.

For Jews who seized upon modernity, the Jewish cultural devotion to texts might be displaced rather than replaced. Perhaps the Mishnah and Gemara were superseded by Montaigne and Goethe or by Marx and Gorky, with attendant shifts in the fields of debate, but words remained central even when the nature of the library changed.[10] The Jewish Marxist Isaac Deutscher noted, "From the Jewish working class in Eastern Europe came the efflorescence of Yiddish literature." The making of literature was only a fraction of that intellectual involvement, however. He recalled one whose story was far from unique, a man who had grown up in poverty and remained illiterate until the age of seventeen. As an adult, he hungrily devoured "all that world literature and classical socialist literature had to offer. To this child of the most horrifying

Jewish poverty a crumb of knowledge was always far more precious than a chunk of bread." One can hardly resist bracketing an exclamation mark after the phrase "Jewish poverty," so redolent as it is of the understanding that this is not *mere* poverty but a misery manipulated to a great extent by social and political oppression. Even granted Deutscher's clear polemical interest throughout, countless similar narrations from other political vantage points amply corroborate his seemingly romanticized view of the hunger for literature shown by largely uneducated Jewish laborers in pre–World War II Warsaw. "I still see before me the masses of young and old, workers and artisans and paupers, who flocked in the evenings to listen to the readings of poetry and drama. They often came in their overalls to applaud Peretz Markish or Itzik Manger reciting poems, or Joseph Opatoshu or J. N. Weissenberg reading prose, or H. D. Nomburg reminiscing about Yiddish writers of the past." This was, as he stated, "a sharp break with the religious consciousness," but at the same time it suggested the shaping of "a new Jewish cultural consciousness."[11] We should note once again the particularity of its Jewishness. It is worth observing that when Leyeles, in the poem cited earlier, writes *manuskript,* he chooses a word more associated with secular than with religious writings. For him as a secular poet writing within a Jewish cultural context, all the pursuits of letters in that environment have become part of an ongoing Jewish search for the secrets and treasures of the dispersed and fragmented but still holy word.

The importance of both literacy and orality is sustained by the connections between education and worship and between worship and daily life. Much of that life's pattern is shaped by analyses laid forth in the Talmud, which we have noted is still studied regularly by ordinary Jews and which has shaped Jewish practices over the centuries. (Christians of comparable levels of intellect and devotion, by contrast, are not expected to make the writings of the Church fathers part of their weekly religious routine.) The traditionally observant Jewish man or woman prays at home upon rising in the morning and again at night before going to bed; men are expected to attend the morning, late afternoon, and early evening synagogue services that take place in between, as many Orthodox Jews continue to do. Throughout the day, events that might otherwise seem ordinary (eating a cookie, hearing distant thunder) become occasions for specific Hebrew benedictions. The Jewish home has, by definition, sacral components. These are not embodied in a specific spot designated for worship; rather, they are lived out in the temporal and social spheres. To inaugurate the Sabbath or a holy day in her home, for example, a Jewish woman lights candles before sundown—and she must be cognizant of when sundown occurs—and says the appropriate blessing. One of the most crucially defining elements of a traditional Jewish environment is observance of the commandments regarding food types and preparations, the laws of *kashrut* or "sanctity," requiring that observant Jews, women as well as men, irrespective of class, have some knowledge of what might be termed religious law and also be capable of reciting a variety of Hebrew prayers. For centuries that has been part of the normal daily life in traditional Jewish households.

To such examples one might add those embodied through other special holiday observances. The main feature of Rosh Hashanah is the sounding of the ram's horn, or shofar, an event accompanied by a blessing, not for the privilege of blowing the instrument but for fulfilling the commandment to hear its "voice" (*kol*); the most distinctive liturgical element of the Yom Kippur evening service is the chanting of Kol Nidre, a petition for divine remission of all our imprudently made vows—not what we have done or not done but what we have said must be given first attention.

Perhaps the most indicative ritual in regard to language is the Passover seder, which is celebrated in the home and structured by a lengthy written text, the Haggadah (literally, "the narration"), which must be read aloud. Written mostly in Hebrew, with passages in Aramaic and perhaps the local language as well, the ancient Haggadah might well be seen as the quintessential postmodernist text, comprising many verbal and musical genres, commentaries, even metacommentaries, inviting questions, further commentaries and discussions during the actual ceremony. As important as the required foods are, Passover has not really been celebrated unless one has explained the symbolic meaning of the three main food elements, literally, "spoken of the three words [items]." In fact, the Haggadah in telling us so specifically ascribes that view to Rabbi Gamaliel, a great scholar who lived about nineteen hundred years ago, thereby characteristically preserving as part of the text itself the record of its own authority. To hear the Haggadah each year is to be reminded of the names and texts of the sages whose words are woven into it, much like the patchwork quilt whose squares can be "read" by someone who still knows not only the names of the patterns but the genealogy of the scraps of material and the identities behind the piecers' initials. And what provides the crucial impetus for the unfolding of the whole narrative and commentary? Questions—specifically, the four questions read or chanted, usually in Hebrew, by the youngest person capable, inquiring why the customs of this night are different from the ordinary. Those questions, ritualistic as they are, pose a dialogue for the entire evening.

Living a Jewish life cannot be separated from active verbal engagement with the sacred acts or texts. That engagement occurs synchronously and diachronously, both at the given moment and across the historical expanse repeatedly evoked explicitly in those texts. The Talmudically based verbal formula for most Jewish benedictions connects them with God's commands to Jews, an unmistakable evocation of the verbalized revelation to Moses; the text blesses God "who has sanctified us through Your commandments and commanded us to . . ." In Sabbath or holiday blessings linking that particular observance with both the creation of the world and also the Jewish deliverance from Egyptian bondage, and particularly in the blessings and narrations for Passover, Chanukah, and Purim, the communal consciousness of the moment is infused with historical consciousness embedded in the story told as part of the observance and in fact as part of the benediction for observing the holiday itself.

If anything, the synagogue increases the emphasis on literacy and orality. Being present for worship services is traditionally an obligation for Jewish males. That obligation is both personal and communal because certain portions of the service may be performed only in the presence of a *minyan,* a minimum of ten adults (in Orthodoxy, ten adult males). All participants could be laypeople. Unlike a minister or priest, whose principal public function in the religious community might be officiating at worship services, the rabbi's functions have been principally legal, educational, and inspirational. In traditional settings it would be unusual for the rabbi to lead a complete service; worship would normally be led by congregants. Perhaps the leader is specially designated or even hired for that purpose, but it is usually a layperson nonetheless, and no parts of the liturgy mandate an ordained rabbi. Consequently, any member of the congregation (traditionally, any man over the age of thirteen) would understand a religious obligation to be able to read and say the textbook prayers which, until the nineteenth century, were always in Hebrew or Aramaic, and still are entirely or primarily so in most synagogues today. Therefore, transmitting enough knowledge to enable a Jewish male to conduct the prayers has been at least a theoretical goal of a boy's education and, more recently, a girl's as well. One could say that attending a service, especially in a small community or a traditional congregation, might well mean one would be expected to be a leader as well as an active participant and therefore to take a speaking role requiring the ability to read Hebrew (regardless of exactly what one might mean in this context by "read").

We also should consider the nature of prayer in Jewish worship. Because Judaism expects that Jews will pray at set times in groups as well as privately, the individual's prayer is public as well as private. However, although it is collective and stabilized by liturgy, the Jewish tradition of public worship preserves the autonomous, independent articulation of prayers by the individual worshipers. The biblical Hannah, mouthing her heartfelt personal petition in words that she and God alone could hear, has been praised in the Talmud as our proper model for sincere prayer. Consequently, in traditional Judaism public prayer is not easily subsumed into a disciplined unison recitation, even when the prayer book seems to imply it will be. One is more likely to find a congregation of individuals, each speaking the same text aloud within the same flexible stretch of time but with no desire or constraint to read simultaneously or to measure one's verbalization of the text in response to the group or even one's neighbor with whom one might well be sharing a prayer book.

During the Enlightenment and after the period of Jewish social and legal emancipation throughout Europe, "progressive" (or culturally assimilated) Jews expressed embarrassment (plentifully recorded in their letters, diaries, and speeches to Jewish gatherings) concerning the unseemly and ragged tumult characterizing Orthodox services, in which everyone in the congregation was reciting, chanting, or mumbling prayers (or for that matter talking with their neighbors), all at their own pace, in their own pitches and volumes, unconcerned by individual melodic idiosyncrasies, with the service leader virtually praying independently while signalling through a raised voice the rubrics of the ritual. Periods of apparent silence were generally not really silent times for focusing independent and private devotions but rather times when the worshipers were reading written prayers subvocally. After all, Orthodox Jews spent lengthy periods in synagogue worship every morning and evening of the week, not just once a week on the Sabbath; one could hardly expect the worship service to retain ceremoniousness when it was so thoroughly integrated with the patterns of daily life within that rather segregated Jewish environment.

The reformers' approach (aided by the shift toward holiday- and sabbath-only worship) was to insert a moment designated for silence but more importantly to encourage adapting to the "more decent" patterns of Christian services by means of truly unison reading of collective prayers or unison singing of them in Protestant fashion and by choral or expanded solo cantorial performances of parts of the service, eventually even to the addition of organ music. That is, reform changed the nature of orality in worship, rather than curtailing it. True, one consequence surely was that the worshipers were more silent more often in the service than before (since they had become sometime audience members rather than simply worshipers); nonetheless, that was not the same as increasing the importance of silent worship.

In the process of change we disregarded one great spiritual truth, incisively articulated by Franz Rosenzweig. "In eternity the spoken word fades away into the silence of perfect togetherness—for union occurs in silence only; the word unites, but those who are united fall silent." The purpose of liturgy, "the reflector which focuses the sunbeams of eternity," is to take us by means of words "to the point of learning how to share silence" by learning how to hear. What is needed, therefore, is not the dialogic seeming-silence in which the auditor is still actively engaged in conversing but the fully receptive silence through which one can perceive at least temporarily or partially the perfect unifying silence of the eternal.[12]

Ironically, liturgical reform in one instance eliminated from the Progressive or Reform order of service the most significant moment of silent worship in the tradition. At the heart of every Jewish service, public or private, is an extended passage of benedictions frequently referred to as the Amidah ("standing up") because it is recited while standing but generally known in early references simply as the Tefillah, "prayer," thus indicating its centrality as the quintessential prayer of the worship. In traditional Judaism even in our own time, that prayer is recited first by the worshipers silently; it is then repeated aloud, with appropriate insertions, by the service leader, thereby reasserting the public and collective nature of the service. Having two Tefillahs, one prayed in the voice of silence and the other voiced aloud, typifies the interplay between two ways of addressing and connecting with the sacral. Streamlining the worship entailed dropping the silent Amidah (as if to suggest that whatever is silent might as well be absent), thereby affirming the priority of the public and collective against the private and individual, speech against silence.

Reaction against the traditional style of worship, what one might call the unstylishness of the worship, can be understood within the terms of the Enlightenment's preference for the rational over the emotional. We find this at work as well in the contemporaneous contempt for Yiddish, which was described by the philosopher Moses Mendelssohn (who had been raised in it) as "corrupt and deformed, repulsive to those who are able to speak in a correct and orderly manner. . . . This jargon has contributed more than a little to the uncivilized bearing of the common man."[13] We have noted that reformers deemed Jewish services embarrassingly disorderly. Behavior during the liturgy did not show Jews as disciplined, self-restrained, and ready to subsume individual independence into the collective republican consensus.

Another frequently appearing adjective, if not directly pejorative at least indicative of estrangement, was *oriental*. That implied something other than a neutral modal designation of Jewish liturgical music; it meant not moderated by Western rationalism.[14] The term was one verbal element in the system of codes associating Jews not only with insular and unsound traditionalism but also with emotionalism as well as demonstrativeness. The latter trait was generally looked upon merely as a sign of bad breeding or inadequate socialization, both of which were capable of being remedied over time. Left unchecked, of course, demonstrativeness could be more than socially unpleasant; it could be politically destabilizing. Emotionalism, however, was always dangerous, because emotionalism undermined Western civilization's hard-won, ever-tentative rationalist triumphs. Jewish "oriental" emotion seemed volatile; more ominously in the eyes of some Jewish reformers and non-Jewish philo-Semites, it typified Jews in general as excitable, more passionate than rational, and consequently not fully integrated into modern Western culture. Emancipation's gains and assimilation's goals were threatened by this emotionalism, which seemed to give ammunition to anti-Semites. Measured against the self-restraint idealized by genteel society, Jews looked uninhibited (they even talked with their hands, for instance) and sounded boisterous. A German saying, used illustratively in the 1906 Cassell, carried the cautionary definition: "Es geht hier her wie in einer Judenschule" (What's going on here is like a Jew's school [*shul*, synagogue]). The dictionary gives this phrase as proverbial for "What an uproar, it is Bedlam broke loose."[15]

Nor can one take comfort in thinking of such attitudes as relegated to a quaint past or sunk in the swamp of Nazi racialism. In 1992 a magazine for California lawyers featuring a cover article on gay and lesbian attorneys evoked fulminations from one anonymous attorney against the story's manifestation of "the Jewish psyche—greed for money, inveterate vulgarity, complete disregard for non-Oriental norms of decency and an insatiable appetite for all the uglier aspects of sex," along with the claim "that the progressive deterioration of morality can be directly attributable to the growing predominance of Jews in our national life."[16] The letter writer's anti-Semitism was presumably stimulated by the surname of the article's author, who is also the magazine's executive editor. However, because "Jane Goldman" would not sound "oriental" to most people, that particular expression of hostility obviously has arisen from a much deeper complex of cultural contempt. Mad as it seems, such caustic language from a member of the bar clearly exposes the stakes that are involved in suppressing Jewish expressivity within safe norms determined by a different (and, one could say, repressed as well as repressive) culture. If Jews are "directly" responsible for "the progressive deterioration of morality," then civilization presumably can be saved by silencing them, especially (one gathers) if they have some authority with words as lawyers, publishers, and writers.

Whatever is spurned can also be welcomed. Sensing the broad cultural history involved, the contemporary American Jewish writer Gerald Stern, in his poem, "Behaving Like a Jew," claims the legacy and value of the passional as Jewish. One could say that he reclaims it from assimilation. Stern evokes Charles Lindbergh as his philosophical and ethnic antithesis. In the poem's context Lindbergh is a more complex cultural icon than usual. The deep background holds the latent image of the man himself and what his success first betokened. A young blond midwesterner, exuding the proverbial all-American appearance and candid manner, in his time of glory he was a world hero who conducted himself without undue self-aggrandizement. His achievement required daring as well as trust in the logic behind the physical forces of nature and our ability to construct machinery to overcome those physical forces.

In the nearer background (as Stern has remarked when commenting on this work at poetry readings) was the political consequence of Lindbergh's ethos, notably his later accolades for the technological achievements and charismatic leadership that he found when visiting Hitler's Germany in the 1930s. Lindbergh subsequently was prominent in the America First movement, actively opposing American intervention against Hitler even as technologically advanced German Panzer divisions overran Poland, with the 2.5 million doomed

Jews who lived there, and the Heinkels and Stukas of Göring's Luftwaffe, which Lindbergh had smilingly admired, pounded the cities of England and continental Europe. To Jews then and now, Lindbergh's praise of Nazi rule in Germany, politically naive and morally callous as it was, made the man himself merely a shell of a hero. Furthermore, it came to typify the ethical failings of a gentile transcendentalism that viewed a life as fundamentally insignificant except as a small transitory particle adding to the greater good. The notorious kidnapping and death of the Lindbergh's infant son (for which ironically a German immigrant was executed on still-controversial evidence) seemed to deepen in the flyer and his wife their inclination to acquiesce to death as a philosophical abstraction and biological inevitability.

In the foreground, referred to directly in the text of the poem, stand Lindbergh's published views about death, which Stern has said he remembered reading with annoyance in a magazine article. Before a dead opossum lying in the road, Stern, behaving like a Jew, refuses to be philosophically detached from the raw emotion of the loss. He specifically contrasts his feelings with the real-life foil, evoked here not only through his own name but also through allusion to the name of the airplane, "The Spirit of St. Louis," inevitably recalled along with its pilot as emblematic of his success.

> I am sick of the spirit of Lindbergh over everything,
> that joy in death, that philosophical
> understanding of carnage, that
> concentration on the species.

The poet's disgust at this "joy" and "understanding" may be precipitated by the nature of the animal's death; for although Stern has written poems lamenting other animals killed in the road, this one was not accidentally hit by a car. Rather, it was shot: The poet finds him (the personal pronoun is Stern's) lying "with the hole in his back." Although the poem posits no explicit connection, the need to mourn the dead opossum may evoke the Jewish need to mourn our human dead (especially after—but far from only after—the Holocaust), those killed with equal indifference, left to lie "like / an enormous baby" on some other road, with a bullet hole in the back. In this context of rejecting "joy in death" and "understanding of carnage," it may not be farfetched to sense a somber memorial lurking like a shadow in the word "concentration."

Stern's careful verb form in the line "I am going to be unappeased at the opossum's death" denotes a willful choice. To "praise the beauty and the balance / and lose myself in the immortal lifestream" would be unacceptable. He chooses instead "to touch his face, and stare into his eyes, / and pull him off the road." Wordlessly eloquent, the mourner makes himself into the burial society (the *ḥevra kaddisha* of Jewish tradition) that will attend piously to the corpse, in reverence for the wonderment of "his curved fingers / and his black whiskers and his little dancing feet." Whether or not we see the black-whiskered opossum as somehow analogous to Jews, the poem welcomes emotion. To look at the fact of death, to allow one's own human animal sorrow, to tend for the dead with one's own hands—these are not confined to Jews. However, in defiance of Lindbergh's aloofly Aryan embrace of death, Stern lays claim to the candid expression of emotion, to sensitivity, and to Jewishness.

Exalting each of these qualities, he undermines what he senses as the prevailing discourse from his standpoint as an outsider who opposes "the spirit of Lindbergh over everything" and who refuses to assimilate love for "the beauty and the balance." The phrase "over everything" offers another nucleus around which the poem's words cluster, for throughout the text the speaker's *I* opposes a pervasive spirit that has spread anonymously into a culture of destruction, broad, plural, impersonal:

> I am sick of the country, the bloodstained
> bumpers, the stiff hairs sticking out of the grilles,
> the slimy highways, the heavy birds
> refusing to move.[17]

Stern's speaker is "behaving like a Jew" not only in mourning but in resisting the non-Jewish cultural standard, subverting it with other premises about life and death. His solitary *I* affirms and denies simultaneously.

If that doubly defined response is another mark of exile, as if one were to acknowledge one's distance from the shared ceremonies even though one is present, it is not exclusively Jewish. Jews hold no monopoly on compassion, decency, or emotionalism. Instead, the poet affirms behavior that our cultural constructs conventionally associate with Jews and allows the concept of "Jew" to function metonymically for those values that also seem to be in exile.

Because the Jew is semiotically marked as an exile and an outsider, the terms can be reversed, and the exile can be a Jew even if not Jewish. Marina Tsvetaeva (who was not a Jew but was married to one) uses this metaphoric association in her "Poem of the End" ("Poema kontsa"), which she wrote as an émigré in Czechoslovakia in 1924 during a period of miserable poverty and professional disappointment. You might as well declare yourself forever a Jew, the Wandering Jew, the poem asserts, because any of the "chosen" remnant—that is, anyone unwilling to be absolutely vile—will be exiled from life and closed into a "ghetto." For anyone decent, life is a "pogrom." The idea that the Jew and the abused outcast are essentially interchangeable conceptually because their fortunes in life are interchangeable is further refined at the end of this passage when the figure of wretchedness specifically becomes the suffering artist. Tsvetaeva uses one of the Russian language's most contemptuous words for Jews, perhaps not merely a masochistic insult but a lexical strategy necessitated by the absence of a sufficiently contemptuous appellation for a poet: "In this most Christian world, / The poet's a Yid!"[18]

Albeit at a different rhetorical level, her declaration returns us to the passage from Edmond Jabès, quoted at the beginning of this chapter, on the fusion of the Jew's and the artist's outlook. The third of the French author's three terms, translated above as "wearing out," is *usure* in the original. Although it can refer to deterioration through use, that word's primary meaning is "usury." With his precise sense of language, Jabès selected a term that would evoke the stereotype of Jew as usurer and incorporates it with the implicit stereotype of the artist as a parasite, living off of other people's labors. Literally through the lexeme itself, we are drawn from the stereotype (*usury* will be the likely first reading of *usure*) into the less obvious level of meaning, the feeling of depletion.

The paradoxes of Jewish exile and of Jewish resistance to silence are thus realized through the artist. All exiled people take with them their stories and songs in addition to their cuisine. Jews took an entire library, including the native-language text of the book that is for much of the world's population The Book. Furthermore, when all else was barred or failed or was taken away, the text (understood in its broad sense as the entire body of writing) remained, the only homeland. That was territory to which even the poorest could lay claim. They could be citizens of that land, unlike the often-unlettered people among whom they dwelt. In fact, some of the poorest Jews were as nobles within it, traversing with affection and respect the domains of Torah and Talmud, midrash or mysticism, although admittedly contending like any would-be ruler with fractious and intractable elements that could be quieted temporarily but never totally brought under one's control. "The country of the Jews," Jabès claimed, "is at the cutting-edge of their universe [à la taille de leur univers] because it is a book."[19]

The Jew, in these ways so much like any artist, writer, or scholar, was nonetheless virtually excluded from the domain of European secular and even sacred culture, an exile from the civilization in which the same Jew lived. Jews, "the People of the Book" to Mohammed, studied books and even wrote books, notably books about The Book, but because of linguistic as well as broader cultural factors, they rarely had access as readers—and even more rarely as writers—to the contiguous non-Jewish society. Although this greatly simplifies a complex historical story (Jewish artists and intellectuals in Islamic Andalusia felt more integrally part of the indigenous culture, for example, as did Viennese Jews in the late nineteenth and early twentieth century, despite the evidence of anti-Semitism in both situations), it is in the main true, in ways that will be developed further in Chapter 6. The notion of Jewish and artistic similarity expresses the fact that Jews have occupied a cultural position leaving them with social and economic marginalization like the artist's, but without the artist's high-cultural centrality. If one seeks the Jewish Michelangelo or Mozart, for example, one cannot search before the twentieth century for artists or musicians but instead must look at Maimonides and Moses Mendelssohn, whose enormous achievements reside in their religious and philosophical writings, still studied inside Jewish intellectual circles if not outside. To the outside world, even when it seems obsessed by talking about Jews, the Jew is a silent presence, because the Jew's voice is not heard except as paraphrased or parodied by others.

Yet exiled in the word like the writer, the Jew carries on a discourse different from that of the world at large. The word *discourse* needs to be understood as pertaining to the broad means of communication and expression, including behavior, as Stern intends by "behaving like a Jew." Distinctive intonations or gestures (even the frequency of using these), emotionalism (or for that matter, analytic rationality instead), questioning, verbal or intellectual irony—these stereotypical Jewish behavioral characteristics all relate to Jewish rootedness in the word rather than the land. The Jewish response to being silenced in the halls of power and privilege has been a refusal to be silent outside of them. That has sometimes meant a speech of indirection, a vital skill for those who are politically or physically vulnerable. Raising questions, ironizing, undermining what appears to be said by the use of intonations and gestures can permit discreet apparent silence about the actual center of the discourse while allowing communication or eloquent expression about it. The Jew and the writer are both like the chess player, whose moves are totally visible to the opponent as well as everyone else but whose strategy succeeds by being obscured.

Thus results the paradoxical relationship of Jews to silence, and perhaps this is related after all to the biblical insight about creation. Only the word of God articulates an unequivocal, direct, unambiguous relationship between word and deed. The Jewish Sabbath morning service proclaims, in its conventional English translation, "Blessed be He who spoke and the world came into being." The Hebrew original is not only more powerful but more to the point: "*Barukh sheamar v'hayah haolam*," or, as one might translate more literally, "Praised be He who spoke and there was everything." How revealing that this should be the initial perception about what God is. God is not only the creator of all things, but God is specifically the perfect integration of will, word, and deed.

Having had this insight, we could not resist our own instinct (Jewish or human, who can say?) to rethink. Therefore, the creator who brought into being one person that was integrated and self-sufficient and, according to the Jewish mystical tradition, androgynous is understood to amend human development. God's second thought was that the single creature, though unified and singular, was also solitary and alone, an idea precipitating God to undertake a second creative process to bring forth Eve. Genesis 2 is deeply human, whatever else it might be. Even if one sees it as divinely dictated directly from God, one cannot deny its implication that God, author of all being, had not even finished creating before revising the text of the world, changing the cast of characters and, along with them, the plot, reconsidering the wisdom of the first version.

But in considering that idea, we are rushing ahead in the creative process. At one time the world was not yet, and there was silence. Or was there?

4

The Silence of Potentiality

Photographs of Lynn Seymour, the dramatically compelling dancer whose Juliet was recalled earlier, do not reveal her singular virtues as a performer. Neither do reviews, which dwell so often only on her emotive power. By contrast, even still photos of other great ballerinas from the 1960s to the early 1980s evoke some special qualities typifying their individual artistry: Margot Fonteyn's mercurial yet vulnerable passion, Alicia Alonso's optimistic self-confidence, Cynthia Gregory's regal brilliance, Carla Fracci's lyricism underpinned by tensile strength, Maya Plisetskaya's blazing dramatic intensity, Antoinette Sibley's sweet elegance untainted by coyness, Patricia McBride's Janus-like amalgam of the athletic and erotic. At the time, particularly within a dance culture strongly influenced by George Balanchine's penchant for the lean and linear look embodied by Tanaquil LeClerc, Allegra Kent, Mimi Paul, and Suzanne Farrell, Seymour's appearance in her photos even looked somehow unpromisingly "thicker" than those of many other treasured stars. Kenneth Macmillan's predeliction for choreographing entire ballets around Seymour seemed especially puzzling to ballet enthusiasts on this side of the Atlantic who had never seen her dance and knew of her only through such pictures, which now seem flawed mementos.

One needed to see her perform, perhaps ideally in a nonrepresentational work that had no overt story, to understand what made her a special artist. Having seen that, however, one would have understood much more than just the artistry of one individual. Here is one memory. Envision that the cast was already on the bare stage when the curtain went up. Seymour, the featured dancer, was downstage, at rest in first position, totally still.

Then she was in motion. She did not begin to move; she was simply suddenly moving. At one moment she might have been a photograph of a dancer illustrating a preparatory stance; there was not a flicker of process, of tension, of flex; not even the abdominal pulsations of deep precursory breathing could be seen. Inside, she must have been fully coiled, waiting for the cue more felt than heard that would fire her muscles at once, but the viewer was offered no sign other than the focused intensity of her gaze. In the next instant energy surged through her. It became her, or perhaps she became it.

Her attack of the opening phrase seemed then (not just now, nostalgically gold-haloed by the distance of twenty years or more) unimaginably and perfectly instantaneous. Because of its abruptness, it was stunningly forceful, unleashing a dynamic drive that felt unstoppably vital and was sustained in fact through Seymour's incandescent performance of the whole piece. Yet one could not say at what instant the movement commenced; it was simply there. The moment of apparent rest preceding it was as remarkable as the first movement, and as important, but only in retrospect; in itself, it too was simply there. Its sequel gave its meaning to the observers. Within a bar of the musical phrase, time enough for the viewer's unarticulated gasp to register in the mind, one could intuit the dimensions of Seymour's technical capability. That, however, was only the superficial revelation. We had seen in one small moment a miracle reminiscent of creation itself; we had witnessed the silence of potentiality.

Just before the creation unfolds, anything is possible, and everything. The great Hasidic mystic Yaakov Yitzhak, known as the Seer of Lublin, said about the prayer book's petition to God, "Renew our days as of old," that the phrase "of old" (which might be thought to refer to the prosperity of the Davidic kingdom or some other era of temporal glory) means "before creation," when nothing existed but the quickening power of the divine.[1] The prayer therefore is a prayer that we be renewed indeed, as if re-created. When we newly experience life, we can realize—we can make real to our own experience—the creative energy that filled the divine when creation was potential. At that point, the powerful energy was fullest.

On what did it act? According to pre-Hellenic Jewish thought, God shaped the world out of the "formlessness and emptiness" that was inchoate matter rather than out of a sheer vacancy. Later authorities (Saadia Gaon, for example, in the tenth century) would posit that creation was in fact out of nothingness. Later still, Jewish kabbalistic mystics imagined God creating the universe out of the substance of divine being itself, a being without form or matter and consequently appropriately represented by words. The innermost essence of that divine existence is acknowledged, the Zohar posits, by the first letter of the Torah, the *bet* in the first word, *b'reishit*. In Hebrew grammar a *bet* as a prefix denotes the preposition *in*. Consequently, "in the beginning" comes to mean, within that which is the origin of all, that is, within God.

David Slabotsky has written a parable illustrating what he calls the "Mind of Genesis," the precreative mind. Rabbi Yehuda, while studying the Talmud, becomes convinced that its details are drawing him further from the heart of the Torah. Attempting to focus his concentration, he withdraws to a room where he directs his attention on one letter, the not quite arbitrarily selected *alef*, first letter of the alphabet, hoping through it to achieve spiritual union with the holy name. The longer he contemplates, the more his mind encompasses, for the letter drawn on the wall cannot be separated from the wall, nor the wall from the room, the room from its house, and so on, until "he carried in his mind at one time the entire creation including the planets and the kingdom of heaven . . . and the universe proceeded without interruption from its source through the mind of Rabbi Yehuda." Responding to the inescapable question of how far one can admire devotion without doctrine or deeds, the fictive rabbi who has told the tale implies that such a person, such a mind, is beyond these sorts of concerns. "The sun may rise and set and the days are days and the nights are nights, but still in Rabbi Yehuda's mind the Lord has not as yet divided between them."[2] One might say that Rabbi Yehuda (whose name denotes "praise" and is the root of words like Jew and Judaism) in contemplating the letter has found a characteristically Jewish way to disregard Judaism in devotion to a vision of creation that seems constructed out of a biblically Jewish understanding. A rabbi who uses Jewish teachings and thereby Jewishly ignores Jewish tradition? This seems quintessentially, particularly Jewish, even in its transcendence of particularism. In Yehuda's condition, silence and stillness inevitably result from his full contemplation of the perfect coherence of all that is. Everything is ready and possible.

As soon as creation begins, the power of pent-up infinite possibility becomes vitiated. Infinite potential is turned into reality, and in so being changed it is channeled, limited. Although some would say it has been improved with (in Shakespeare's phrase) "a local habitation and a name," others would reply that it has been diminished into the merely material. Human beings are familiar with the experience because something similar happens to our idealizations: Embodied, they lose substance. The moment when the fullest experience of the divine would be possible is in that silence truly filled with potentiality, just before word is shaped into fact. However, calling this time "silence" means acquiescing to our convenient but limited perceptual categories. Surely within what we are inclined to imagine as silence actually exists a fully developed network of subaudible communication, like the architect's blueprints. André Neher has termed this " 'energetic' silence."[3] An important ontological implication of the creation story was developed (Faur has shown) by the nineteenth-century rabbi Elie Benamozegh. Benamozegh pointed out that we might think it odd that the work of creation (*ma'asei b'reishit,* as the benediction says) is celebrated on the Sabbath, the day of rest after its completion. Benamozegh observes, "Interruption actually demonstrates His power more than continuous activity, since there is no greater power than to put an end and a limit to an infinite power."[4] So a midrash claims, God is called *El shaddai* (God of power) because God is the One who said "*dai!,*" "enough!"

In risking a metaphysical oxymoron by speaking of such silence, we may succeed in denoting a unique event of creativity, but that unique event in turn speaks to us of a deep truth always with us, though unnoticed, unheard. Let one overheard story afford us a parable. After a heart operation, a man called his surgeon to ask about a persistent thudding sound in his chest. What he was hearing, he was told, was his own heart's sound. Because the heart was slightly displaced in the chest cavity after the surgery, its resonance had changed and was newly audible. But that was temporary. The physician said that the recovering patient would notice the sound of his heart for a few days, and then, "You'll never hear it again."

Silence must be illusory. It surrounds us without being noticed (much as Neher claims that it "forms the landscape of the Bible"), and when it is noticed, it is only apparent.[5] To answer the question "What do you hear?" with "Nothing" must tell us more about our own attentiveness than about the external phenomena to which we think we are listening. Helen Keller, deaf and blind, used to inquire of visitors what they had seen or heard in their walk to her house. Perhaps it was embarrassment that led so many of them to reply that they had seen and heard nothing, or maybe they were confused about how they could communicate whatever they had noticed. However, we might as well believe instead that they reported the truth. Keller, eager for reports from what Thoreau would have identified as one of the strangest of the strange countries, the place where objects can be seen and even heard as well as touched, remained incredulous and disappointed in us. She could not have understood the numbing effect of sensory attentiveness, from which sleep is the one vain resort in life. We are overwhelmed at last by the unceasing cadenzas of "all the pianos in the woods" (Emily Dickinson's phrase). We need what we take to be silence, although in believing we have found it, we are inevitably mistaken. Fittingly, a composer perceived this.

John Cage wrote of the difference between silence as a form of punctuation within the traditional musical grammar and supposed silence as an apparent phenomenon in human life. Musical silence is usually heard as the instant of pause between the rounding out of one phrase, section, aria, or movement and the succeeding one, or it is perceived as a deliberate withholding of sound for a specified and notated length of time significantly designated as a rest. As Cage explained, "Formerly, silence was the time lapse between sounds, useful toward a victory of ends, among them that of tasteful arrangement, where by separating two sounds or two groups of sounds their differences or relationships might receive emphasis; or that of expressivity, where silences in a musical discourse might provide pause or punctuation; or again, that of architecture, where the introduction or interruption of silence might give definition either to a predetermined structure or to an organically developing one." Cage offered a different conception of silence, arising from his experience in an anechoic chamber.

Regardless of its particular polemical relevance to his personal aesthetic position, this reflection can be extracted nonetheless for its value as part of the discourse on the teachings of silence. Here Cage is not only theorizing but also drawing on his own discovery of sound in a scientifically silent room:

Where none of these or other goals is present, silence becomes something else—not silence at all, but sounds, the ambient sounds. The nature of these is unpredictable and changing. These sounds (which are called silence only because they do not form part of a musical intention) may be depended on to exist. The world teems with them, and is, in fact, at no point free of them. He who has entered an anechoic chamber, a room made as silent as technologically possible, has heard there two sounds, one high, one low—the high the listener's nervous system in operation, the low his blood in circulation. There are, demonstrably, sounds to be heard and forever, given ears to hear.[6]

Cage's observation implies that silence—what we might speak of as absolute silence, by analogy to absolute zero—is not a natural fact but a concept defined by human beings.

The phenomena that he experienced suggest that we are generally not tuned to two monologues constantly carried on within us, synchronously but not synchronized, harmoniously (one hopes) but not harmonized, on the highest and lowest levels of our being. Unless we make the effort deliberately to be still, we will not hear the discourse of the heart or that of our finest nerves. The heart patient's experience implies that even in our stillest moments, we will not perceive those ever-present articulations unless some extraordinary intervention brings them to our notice, perhaps against our will and our pleasure. Imagine being attuned to the essential rhythm of one's own heart, to hear it working, to be personally familiar with the voice of that indispensable organ and know it as it lives inside, more intimate to us than any fetus because more permanently part of us. Imagine one day being conscious that one can no longer hear it, and will never again hear it, all the normal days of one's life. Would we want to grieve over that loss of communication with one of the most cherished companions of our natural life? Would we greet the silence instead with relief, knowing that we truly could not tolerate forever being aware of the incessant—one fraudulently hopes—rhythmic pulse, that we could not possibly have the stamina to sustain our attention to it?

That is surely a key to our mental survival, albeit maintained at a great cost. We survive, that is, by allowing the constant realities to fall beneath our threshold of awareness. We manage to be oblivious to the familiar. Only when the familiar becomes estranged from us, or we from it, does it make itself heard again, in which case it is like new. Arthur Green, drawing on Hasidic mystics, has suggested an analogous truth about our apparent separation from the God who is all: "We mortals are both blessed and condemned to live in a world of separateness, one in which each ego-consciousness sees itself as individual. Our maturity and our sanity are themselves largely created by the success of this ongoing process of individuation. . . . The greatest gift God gives us . . . is the illusion of our separate identity."[7]

Hearing the seemingly new or seemingly different, turning our face to it with attention, is at least risky and demanding, whether the experience proves gratifying or not. And what we will have to report once we have explored in the regions beyond our known borders is likely to be as ambiguous as the conflicting reports brought back from the land of Canaan by Moses' scouts, with some daring spirits extolling the rich life to be found there but most cautioning against the giants threatening to humiliate and destroy us. Of course, Caleb and Joshua dwell within each of us, as do their ten antagonistic, persuasive kinsmen. The challenge of the new is not meager.

The metaphysical, theological, and even social implications of the knowledge demonstrated by Cage's experience are the materials of centuries of mysticism. For, as we observed in the second chapter, within the mystical experience the quietest voices of silence seem to be most distinctly perceived. A passage of the Zohar describes a process of syllabic manipulation whereby "the whole creation was in suspense until the name of Abraham was created, and as soon as the name of Abraham was completed the Sacred Name was completed along with it, as it says further [viz., Gen. 2:4], 'in the day that the Lord God effected the creation of earth and heaven.' "[8] Even the silence before creation is filled with discourse. What we imagine as silence may be only the quiet intensity of a conversation too fundamental for us to hear or a concentration too complex for words or movement. Arranging letters to form words before speaking them is one way of imagining the divine preparing for the process of creating. The Torah, according to rabbinic tradition, preceded creation in exactly the way that a blueprint precedes the structure it details.

According to a fourteenth-century Spanish Jewish kabbalist, the high priest's role in the Temple's Holy of Holies during the Yom Kippur service was to reconstruct the unity of creation simultaneously with our personal union with the divine through the properly ritualized enunciation of the divine name. The vowel symbols in the name, claimed Abraham ben Isaac of Granada, embodied the "illuminations" or spiritual influences of divinity extended into our natural sphere. By pronouncing the tetragrammaton with full vowel values in a ritualistic way and meditating intensely on the spiritual energy contained in each consonant and vowel, the high priest held together the forces of the universe and as supplicant on our behalf made contact with the creator and sustainer of all.[9]

The biblical creation story implies that in the seeming silence inhabited only by God accompanied by the divine name, all is potential, all possible. Because nothing is yet done, nothing yet spoken and consequently nothing beyond recall, both power and liberty exist as potential. For us, realizing such pure potential is impossible. God's power and liberty are absolute. However, the creative artist can experience momentary connections with that autonomy, for the artist maintains some measure of control over the articulations and silences in the text, its onward propulsion and its cessations, its explicitness and its reserve.

The artist also comprehends, perhaps too fully, how precious and tenuous the flow of human creativity is. God, we are told in the Jewish tradition, spent the eons before the creation of this world by making and unmaking others (some say at least twenty-six) until generating one that seemed "very good."[10] We might go through fewer drafts. Is this because we are satisfied with lower standards? Or rather, perhaps our creative energy gives out before our vain quest for perfection is satisfied, since we seem not to be content with the divine measure of sufficiency, "very good," and demand "excellent" (that is, a grade of *A* rather than *B*) instead. Whichever answer one prefers, certainly every creative artist works against, in defiance of, and in fear of the failure of inspiration or powers. Consequently, the artist's display of autonomy over the material may be suffused by desperation; the bravura reminders of the artist's control over the unfolding of the text may be indeed death defying.

A musical example, from the final movement of Beethoven's String Quartet op. 18, no. 6, may illustrate this. Around the time of this composition, 1799, Beethoven began to experience the hearing problems that would eventually culminate in his profound deafness. Some listeners have found in this movement's strikingly pensive adagio opening—which Beethoven himself labeled "*La Malinconia,*" melancholy— a premonitory response to his loss of hearing. Absence of any correlative commentary from the composer constitutes one variety of silent ambiguity. Although the biographical interpretation strikes others as too literally allegorical and even sentimental, formalistically the movement does suggest restless shifts of mood. Consisting of the slower introspective section (to be played, the composer wrote in the score, with "*più gran delicatezza,*" the greatest delicacy) and a sprightly allegretto section more characteristic of this quartet as a whole, the movement is punctuated by rallentandos and even by a brief moment of silence, following which the music takes a sudden turn of melody and tempo. For example, the *Malinconia* motif that begins the movement is discontinued with a sudden diminution of volume (from *ff* to *pp*), after which standard critical editions instruct, *"attacca subito il allegretto,"* i.e., immediately begin the allegretto. So sudden a shift to new melodic material in a strikingly different mood and tempo seems daring and may even startle the listener. The allegretto section itself winds down with an unexpectedly quiet cadence later in the movement, followed by a recapitulation of the first motif lasting for less than ten measures; the allegretto then recommences, but this restatement is terminated unexpectedly in the fifth measure, followed by a full measure of silence. That ensuing bar of rest (at this point less a rest than a void) after that allegretto passage leaves the listener uncertain as to the direction or development of the piece. The next return of the adagio (*Malinconia*) may seem logical in its way even following an unusual number of measures, but its curt termination after merely one bar and a half by the first violin's sudden reassertion of the allegretto feels totally unsettling.

Each transition is like a pivot. During the musical shift we truly do not know what will enter next, what Beethoven will spring upon us in melody, mood, or tempo or how the composition will end. We may interpret this as expressing in musical form the deeper splits, the powerful conflicts, within Beethoven himself as an individual and as an artist. In this movement, that is, we too can hear the auditory cracks, the troubled wide shifts of mood from gaiety to brooding, the pulling against form that would eventually take Beethoven to more daring compositional inventiveness but that we hear manifested in this work by his melancholic disturbances of the quartet's prevailing mood. However, we may want to think of this in other terms as displaying the composer's autonomy as a dominant creator playfully reveling in his power over the audience and in his defiant mastery of musical structure. According to such an interpretation, the work's apparent fits and starts and disturbing interjection of silence, if they are thought premonitory of anything at all, presage larger and more significant fissures between this text and its musical context, indicative of the artist's autonomous hand. Beethoven seems to be demonstrating his rights over the language of the composition.

Even as he does so, however, the way in which he demonstrates this, by focusing the issue on beginnings and endings (the significance of which is emphasized by the shifts in mood attendant upon each), locates the particular source of Beethoven's creative tension as anxiety about endings and beginnings: about concluding and thereby falling into silence, about being able to begin again after that silence. Like Michelangelo's *schiave* or *prigioniere* sculptures, twisting incomplete figures partially emergent from their marble, Beethoven's composition embodies the struggle, the defeat, and the triumph of the artist contesting with the medium. Even the apparently unfinished form or imperfect form may be the right form.

Creating does not mean imposing form, even if to do so entails allowing areas of formlessness or making the topic of the work its challenge to conventional form. A. R. Ammons, in his poem "Coon Song," deliberately stops the poem's narrative line at its most dramatic moment, when the dogs have cornered the raccoon, to challenge the reader's almost prurient interest in having emotions exercised and curiosity satisfied by knowing the actual fate of a presumed real raccoon. A writer's difficulty (in fact, even a widely read person's difficulty) in reacting unproblematically and directly to an immediate experience is demonstrated when the speaker at the beginning of the second stanza recalls that Dostoevsky would explore whether the animal could choose to be somewhere else. When one lives amid texts and makes texts, how can one escape their presence even in an emergency? Such frank admission that one comprehends life through art prepares one for discerning the raccoon's simple bold judgment, "reality can go to hell." That defiant rejection of brute fact or mundane probability in turn suggests "that my / problem," could be solved by denying it.[11]

The pronoun *my* seems to refer to the raccoon. It is, however, grammatically ambiguous and can just as appropriately refer to the writer, whose "problem" is the literary problem of finding what is to be said about this event, whether real or imagined, and how to say it. Turning, so to speak, from the action of the poem to the reader looking over the poet's shoulder, Ammons's narrator lays claim to the work of art as the artist's property, consisting of the poet's personal shaping of language, rather than the reader's property, consisting of a sensational anecdote. He directly refuses to entertain at our beck and call. Tauntingly, the narrator holds us at bay by simply counting, first to five, then to ten, as we wait for the story to be continued. Along the way to the poem's ending (which is no conclusion), we are chided by being given summaries of possible endings, much as Milton's Raphael, gently mocking Adam's flawed but familiar rationale for a heliocentric universe in Book 8 of *Paradise Lost*, offers him compellingly plausible metaphoric descriptions of both heliocentric and geocentric models, as if to say that Adam can live his life—or for that matter, make poetry—with either. The raccoon's death is not so much avoided or confronted as it is averted by being turned into a literary issue: "the coon will end in disorder." The truth, both poets suggest, is that the work of creation is not random and the details we are shown are sufficient unto themselves. "Omissions are not accidents," Marianne Moore wrote regarding her *Complete Poems* (which did not exactly comprise her "complete" poems but only those that she wanted included in the final reckoning).

The biblical mythos suggests that to create was not only to bring into being but to end the formlessness that had been before and to separate all that would exist thereafter into discreet entities, linked by having a common source and by dependence on a mutually governing process or power. Bringing humankind into social relationships meant to continue the process of *havdalah,* differentiation, such as we enact at the conclusion of Shabbat in separating the Sabbath from ordinary time. Along with that process, or so the biblical story seems to suggest, came the separations that segregated self from other, and continue to do so. "If we say 'I,'" claimed Edmond Jabès, "we already say *difference.*"[12] We become not merely neutrally differentiated from God and one another but may allow ourselves to become alienated from the source that gives coherence to all. Differentiation becomes alienation which becomes opposition, from the loss of Eden to the present day, and the consequences are the destruction of life's apparent certainties (beginning with the acceptance of temptation), the destruction of cultures (beginning with Eden), and the destruction of people (beginning with Adam, primordial creature of earth). As (among others) Milton understood, "eternal providence" or biblical truth may be asserted, but the justification of what it asserts is demonstrated through life's experiences. The Christian may say that the Bible shows that we sin because Adam and Eve were disobedient; the Jew may say instead that Adam and Eve's disobedience shows that we all sin. Thus allegorizing the Bible's creation story is one way of remembering how its familiar narrative line expresses patterns of human experience.

Breaking the silence of unity entails differentiating items, whether physically by giving them independent form or conceptually by articulating them. Naming is not precisely the same as bringing them into being, but neither is it superficial to their existence. God's conjunction of the two acts (in speaking and dividing) really starts both time and space by beginning to distinguish separateness; the human being contributes to the process by naming. In becoming partners in the work of creation, we also become complicitous in the process of separating. When divine and human actualities—what they do, what they say—break the silence of potentiality, the building blocks of language and reality come forth: nouns and verbs, words for objects and actions. "God said, Let light be, and light was." Fittingly, the penultimate devotion (known as the Aleinu) in every public Jewish worship service concludes with a petition for that messianic time in which "Your Name shall be one." Within its immediate context, the prayer expresses the wish that we may be united in unity of devotion rather than divided by differences of religions. Understood more spiritually, it identifies the time of our redemption with the time of God's redemption from division.

In a modern midrash on the mystical meaning of the tetragrammaton, Arthur Green notes that it includes letters that are merely aspirated or are equivocal of pronunciation, capable of being read as either vowels or consonants. The third letter (the only one that may be naturally vocalized) distinguishes the human consciousness of God as distinct from the natural reality of God. Green claims, "with the addition of the *Vav,* that One enters in a wholly different way into the human mind; the all-pervasive presence is now *spoken* within us, and that can happen only to us creatures of speech. *God becomes word as we become human.*"[13] In becoming word, God loses and gains, or rather, in turning God into the articulated, we gain and lose something in our grasp of the divine essence. We may increase our ability to communicate and express our experience of it; we may diminish our ability to experience it. This seems inevitable for the human being, *medabber,* "speaker." Only by consciously working against speech into an informed silence can the mystic strive to escape language's confines; such mysticism is not mere muteness but stillness, not just silence but "silence." It is such a silence as can be used by one who knows how far language can take us and how far short it falls of the goal.

Herein lies the source of Isaiah's agony, which comes upon him at his first great moment of revelation. The prophet realizes that he, a profane person, has envisioned the sacred, seen God, even heard the seraphim call "Holy, holy, holy is the God of Hosts" one to another; yet he feels compelled to profess, "Woe to me, for I am a man of unclean lips and I dwell among people of unclean lips" (Isa. 6:5). Those lips must be touched by the purifying coal before replying to the holy voice by requesting a prophetic role as messenger of the sacred, "Here I am; send me" (Isa. 6:8). The Hebrew for "unclean" in this passage is *t'mey,* a three-letter word spelled *tet-mem-aleph;* not far from it in pronunciation is the word *tameyah* (*tav-mem-hay*), "amazed, surprised." Isaiah's impure language registers the distance between what he is and what he would be. In the presence of holiness, he is more conscious of his own unworthiness than of wonderment.

He specifically associates that unworthiness with unfit speech. At that personally and historically critical moment, with Assyria threatening the kingdom, Isaiah's anxiety seems to recall King David's traditional legacy of teaching in Psalm 34, "I will bless God at all times, praise always upon my lips. . . . Who is the man that desires life, loves days to behold good? Keep your tongue from evil and your lips from speaking deceitfully." Only the sanctified mouth can risk speaking sacred truths amid people of unclean lips. Isaiah needs to feel that divine intervention absolves him from this penalty of mortality. The corrupted tools of expression and communication he has shared with all others must suffice.

Henry Roth, specifically citing Isaiah and the purifying coal in *Call It Sleep,* his great novel of American Jewish immigrant life, allows his main character, a young boy named David, to strive for similar purification of his words and thoughts. After hearing the passage read and expounded in heder (religious school), David becomes obsessed with the mysterious purification, effected paradoxically with a coal, an object he associates with physical dirt, a child's fears of the dark, and his unwilling initiation into sexuality's mystery. In flight later from his parents, David receives an electrical shock that takes the place of God's "angel-coal." Stunned, as he lies in the street he hears a Babel-like welter of language, languages, and dialects cascading around him; when he rises again into private consciousness in the concluding paragraph, the language of his thoughts has acquired a new stylistic sophistication. David thinks in the elegance of a literary American English removed from past insecurities but also uprooted from its personal past, its ethnic and linguistic soil. The final paragraph begins with "He might as well call it sleep" and Roth subtly rephrases that in his penultimate sentence to "One might as well call it sleep." By that slight alteration the narrative point of view becomes objectified; the ostensibly autobiographical is transformed into the universal, a process that can liberate a voice from its own subjectivity or (as seems to have happened to Roth, whose next novel appeared sixty years later) render it dumb in the befuddlement of tonelessness.[14]

Isaiah's revelation does not lead him into glossolalia or silence. His orders are couched in terms specifying the verbal character of his task: "And God said, 'Go and say to this people, you hear and hear but do not understand.'" Like all of them, Isaiah dwells in language, and it is common language. To speak to them in uncommon ways of things uncommon, he must believe he has been touched with a gift. (Some would find that touch painful, although Isaiah says nothing of pain.) He must believe that he is the vehicle for what must be said, as his first lines proclaim, "Hear, heaven, and give ear, earth, for God has spoken."

Being human brings us into speech. With speech we enter social relationships, and with speech we articulate what lies unseen within us. Through language we make and are made. The possibility of communicating and expressing affords us the opportunities for splendor and the hope of being memorialized. That is not all, for God has set before us the choice between blessings and curses. With the possibilities of speech we also hear how language fails us and how we fail it and one another. We live amid words said and unsaid, monuments and ruins, gems and shards.

5

Limen / Mezuzah

> "But Rabbi," the students asked, "if everything
> has a sacred meaning, what does the telegraph
> teach us?"
> "It teaches that every word is counted and
> charged for."
>
> —*A Hasidic story*

LIMEN AND MEZUZAH: both words signify boundary markers, doorways between where we are at one within ourselves and where we negotiate between ourselves and external experiential realities, between being at home and being at large in the world. Yet these two words denote sharply differing ways of defining consciousness.

The word *limen,* from the Latin for threshold, is itself part of a network of etymologically related words (*limit* and *limb* are included) denoting margins or boundaries. It sits unobtrusively in more familiar words like *subliminal* and even *sublime.* This nexus suggests some conceptual boundaries that writers test and negotiate in dividing speech from silence, inching toward the limits of the subliminal and stretching for the borders of the sublime. Somewhere out there these profundities are thought to reside, regardless of whether these are thought to "lie too deep for tears" (Wordsworth), to be something "without name—it is a word unsaid, / It is not in any dictionary, utterance, symbol" (Whitman, "Song of Myself," sec. 50), or whether they can be attained only when "the afflatus surging and surging" allows the poet or bard to "speak the pass-word primeval" so that "My voice goes after what my eye cannot reach, / With the twirl of my tongue I encompass worlds and volumes of worlds" (also Whitman, "Song of Myself," secs. 24 and 25).

Limen itself has an etymology: it comes from the Greek *leimon*, "meadow." To step over the threshold is to go out into the open, free space of the natural world, the world not segmented or controlled by human constructs. Perhaps that open field feels exhilaratingly unlimited or perhaps frighteningly unmarked.

The Hebrew *mezuzah*, which means "doorpost," also designates metonymously the small case affixed to the doorposts of Jewish homes and rooms. The case is usually mounted diagonally, angled with the top pointing toward the house, as if implying that one ascends by entering and descends by exiting to the outer world. The case encloses a parchment scroll bearing two biblical passages (Deut. 6:4–9 and 11:13–21), written in Hebrew by a specially trained scribe. The texts are generally not visible. One does not take the scroll out of the case to read it, and one does not recite the texts as one goes in or out; it is safe to say that many people who have observed the commandment to install it do not really know exactly what the text says. The mezuzah seems metonymous of the Bible itself and even of religious tradition: it stands for that which people put up to guard the portals of their lives but which they might not know through intimate contact.

Case and parchment do not constitute an amulet; rather, they fulfill the twice-articulated commandment contained within the texts on the scroll, to inscribe the teachings of the Torah "on the doorposts of your house and on your gates." In other words, they designate that space as the home of a Jew who remembers the commandments, and the cases are themselves visible reminders of the covenantal obligations.

The mezuzah is interestingly situated on three boundaries. Physically, it marks the boundary between the domestic enclosure and the outside. Culturally, it marks the boundary between the specifically Jewish space and the world at large, shared in common with everyone. As a result, one can say that the mezuzah marks the boundary between the ways specifically appropriate to the Jew and the ways that lie outside Jewish tradition, whether compatible with that tradition or not. Semiotically, the mezuzah is positioned astride the division between text and symbol. It bears a text, and that text can be known, but the scroll bearing the text is not read once it is installed, and in fact it may not even be visible; however, the container itself, no matter how ornamental, is irrelevant without the scroll, and the scroll, although accurately lettered, has no purpose until it is placed in the container. Furthermore, the unseen text encased within the mezuzah declares the obligation that the affixing fulfills. The mezuzah seems an appropriate image for texts concerned with the boundary between what can or should be said and what can or should only be acknowledged.

The mezuzah's power as a defining symbol is acknowledged in Chaim Potok's *The Gift of Asher Lev*. In this novel the noted artist, Lev, who has defied his Orthodox upbringing by committing himself to making painted images, discovers that his recently deceased uncle, an influential and respected Hasid known for his piety, has amassed in his study an impressive collection of modern art, to the scandal of the other members of his immediate family. The transgression is indicated through the absence of the mezuzah that had once marked the entry to that room, an absence that Lev at once recognizes as enormously significant: "A riddle. What can be put into a room that will so profane it that the mezuzah should be removed from its doorpost?"[1] Secular art, regarded as frivolous if not actually prohibited by his sect's tradition, is consigned to territory unmarked by the sacral. It lies outside the boundaries protected through "the words I command you."

Setting a limit, even for oneself, indeed for oneself, marks one's control over compulsion; it allows one to recognize one's autonomy from the merely animal, material, and mechanical. "El shaddai," the midrash explained, is called that because God's power is revealed through the capability to finish the process of creating and say *dai,* "Enough!" Judaism, a religion of commandments (traditionally 613 of them) as well as of faith, deems boundary markers essential. We place them on the doorposts of our houses and on our gates; on and around our bodies through the covenant of circumcision, the binding of tefillin (phylacteries), wrapping of tallit (prayer shawl), and immersion in the *mikveh* (ritual bath); as well as in our voices and thoughts through the actions and texts of benedictions, welcoming of holidays, and *havdalah,* the separation between particular and universal, designated and unmarked, the ways for Jews and those for "the nations."

The liminal boundary does not have the cultural implications borne by the mezuzah. Instead, it holds a different psychological meaning. Mezuzah marks the boundary between Jewish and non-Jewish (and other symbols can work appropriately for other sorts of cultural differentiation). Some feelings of capability or vulnerability as we prepare to step across the threshold are particular to our self-definitions. We know or aspire to believe that we speak or appear *as* something. The terms following the preposition will lengthen and change as one recognizes affective categories: an American, a white lesbian mother, an unemployed blue-collar worker, a Jew in the twentieth century. Limen marks our common human border between familiar (at home) and unfamiliar (out there) or between the place where something special occurs and the undifferentiated exterior. So, both architecturally and emotionally, the theater needs its transitional lobby and, on a different emotional level, the U.S. Holocaust Museum must have its Hall of Remembrance modulating between the gripping inner environment and the outer spectacle of Washington's monumental Mall. To be more precise: the buildings may not need these, but we do.

Notwithstanding the Western- and Bible-originated orientation of our discussion, it seems worth noting that moving between silence and speech is problematic in other cultures as well. Furthermore, cultural predispositions have literary, social, and personal repercussions. Masao Miyoshi, in a study of the modern Japanese novel, has remarked that in Japanese society, "reticence, not eloquence, is rewarded. Similarly, in art it is not articulation but the subtle art of silence that is valued."[2] Miyoshi's literary analogy is haiku; one could also think of the laconic eloquence of the Japanese garden, especially in contrast to the exuberance of, for example, the English cottage garden, which might actually be even smaller and just as quiet aurally but will seem bursting with energy by contrast with the Japanese design penchant for visual stillness, harmonious spaces directed toward contemplation of one focal element, be it a rock or a pattern or a tree. The "passion for silence," as Miyoshi calls it, can be found in narrative techniques also, such as the inclination to set a scene "by suggestion and evocation rather than description."

This artistic predilection, the author argues, is related to a "Japanese hostility toward personality" that becomes inseparable from the literary language system. Among the salient recurrent features that Miyoshi notes are "its tendency to omit the subject, especially the first-person pronominal subject, in its sentences; . . . its writing medium whose ideograms resist being spoken aloud"; and a language "severely ritualistic and ceremonial, particularly in its dedication to silence." Such a literary culture "discourages formation of tangible individuals and a distinctly personal experience."[3] One might envision within the mind a Japanese-style gate or sliding door functioning ideologically somewhat like a mezuzah, erecting for the Japanese speaker or writer a separation between Japanese and un-Japanese language acts.

Not only does this guarding of silence and the accompanying resistance to asserting personality carry consequences for the literary work, but it also has consequences for the personality and life of the artist. Miyoshi notes that the three most prominent Japanese novelists in the latter half of this century (Kawabata, Dazai, and Mishima) all ended their lives by suicide. "Silence not only invites and seduces all would-be speakers and writers, but it is in fact a powerful compulsion throughout the whole society. To bring forth a written word to break this silence is thus often tantamount to the writer's sacrifice of himself, via defeat and exhaustion."[4] Therefore, the risks are only partly artistic. "Japanese is iron-tight once the speaker violates the rites of community and the sanctity of silence. He must learn to hum along very measuredly as he performs the ceremonial dance, or his speech will become a shriek, or a futile stammer. . . . Silence powerfully invites the Japanese. But for the writer, accepting the invitation is always fatal."[5] In Miyoshi's view, Kawabata and Mishima, the two best-known Japanese writers in the West, took different paths, both inevitably destructive. The former "learned this language of silence to perfection—at the expense of his personality"; Mishima turned instead to what the novelist himself called "a language of the body" that forsook artistry and art in favor of an anachronistic militarism. One might venture to see in this also a form of nihilism. Texts last; the body does not. If Mishima ended in inscribing the body (so to speak), the final inscription was made by the sword of hara-kiri that eviscerated him, and he became thereafter, stunningly, the text that induced its own burning. He reached that silence striven for by Ihab Hassan's exemplars, through annihilation of the word made incarnate in himself, a grizzly inversion of the creative act.

Still, aesthetic silences may call to us, not sirenlike but like the voice out of the bush, offering a way to shape experience and hold at bay the welter of worldly confusion. The possibility emerges fervidly in the diaries of Etty Hillesum, a young Dutch Jewish woman who became a victim of the Nazis. An entry from May 1942, while she was still free and could believe she would have a future, reveals how Japanese formalistic principles retained their aesthetic virtue for her, not only as stylistic pleasure but as a means for articulating truth. Her insight arises not from haiku or gardens but from graphics.

Looked at Japanese prints with Glassner this afternoon. That's how I want to write. With that much space round a few words. They should simply emphasize the silence. Just like that print with the sprig of blossom in the lower corner. A few delicate brush strokes—but with what attention to the smallest detail—and all around it space, not empty but inspired. The few great things in life that matter can be said in a few words. If I should ever write—but what?—I would like to brush in a few words against a wordless background. To describe the silence and the stillness and to inspire them. What matters is the right relationship between words and wordlessness, the wordlessness in which much more happens than in all the words one can string together. And the wordless background of each short story—or whatever it may be—must have a distinct hue and a distinct content, just like those Japanese prints. It is not some vague and incomprehensible silence, for silence too must have contours and form. All that words should do is to lend the silence form and contours.[6]

"Silence too must have contours and form." Hillesum, striving for a voice as a writer that she never had life enough to develop except through her remarkable journal and letters, honors but does not sacralize silence, "not empty but inspired." Language does more than emit the vocalizations that make silence meaningful; it is the way to express the "few great things in life that matter." That which is unsaid, the silence of space around the text, should make an environment commanding attention for significant pronouncements. Slightly earlier she had hungered for "every word born of an inner necessity. . . . I still need to write things down. I should like, as it were, to caress the paper with just the right word. . . . Sometimes I have a fleeting urge to express this or that in elegant words, but I kill the urge straightaway, finding all that now much too contrived."[7] Those forms and contours, tracings of the liminal line, respect the importance of what lies on each side of the boundary. In tandem, silence and the sparse brush strokes of words would make an artistic environment engaged with the eternal and "the few great things in life that matter." Etty Hillesum's life illustrates the principle and its undermining by life. In the spring of 1942, in German-occupied Holland, Jews had already been segregated into ghettos and were forced to wear the yellow star; in the Pacific, Japanese conquests had sunk Dutch naval vessels and sent Dutch colonial women, men, and children to miserable internment camps. Meanwhile, a young Dutch Jewish woman was trying to fathom art's stylistic secrets by reading Rilke and studying Japanese prints. Within two months she would be working for the Jewish Agency. Shortly after, she voluntarily joined the first Jewish deportees to Westerbork and thence to Auschwitz. Her letters and journals record her spiritual journey;

the artistic adventure was never able to find fruition, and she could not apply to her exquisite balancing of word and silence the lessons of language she recorded and pondered in one of her letters from Westerbork concentration camp: "When I think of the faces of that squad of armed, green-uniformed guards—my God, those faces! . . . I sank to my knees with the words that preside over human life: And God made man after His likeness. That passage spent a difficult morning with me. . . . 'God Almighty, what are You doing to us?' The words just escape me."[8] Experience answered that question in its way. The theological and literary have been left for others to try to coax out of silence.

Still, silence awaits us all, a term of our natural condition. One of life's many paradoxes is that mortals cannot avoid being consumed by the very process of living. God alone, the Rock of Ages, does not erode through time's passage. Such is surely one of the teachings of the biblical story of the burning bush at Horeb: The sacral presence is denoted because the bush burned and was *not* burnt up, unlike natural bushes and real people.

However, as was true also of Jacob's vision of the ladder, revelation of the divine presence is merely a prelude to the divine message. A voice accompanies the vision, turning the miraculous from the merely phenomenal into the inspirational. In the wilderness it comes to one through the sounds emitting from the sizzling thornbush in which he hears his own name, "Moshe, Moshe"— Moses, Moses. A midrash explains that he approached without fear because the voice was that of his father, Amram. This remarkable notion acknowledges the liminal function of language in mediating between the familiar and strange, like the "explanation kind" that Emily Dickinson says we use with children to facilitate comprehension, for "Truth must dazzle gradually / Or every man be blind." The blind poet Milton, envisioning God in the third book of *Paradise Lost*, pictured effulgent but impenetrable light; out of that light poured forth speech by which God was knowable. If those words diminish the divine essence, only diminution can close the gap between our comprehension and divine knowledge. The fullness of light dazzles, and we are all blinded by it.

Although the liminal experience may be turned into a welcoming one, the mezuzah-like sacral boundaries are more guarded, even when the doorway seems to stand open. Moses asks God what name he shall give to the people when they demand to know which god he is speaking about, and the reply is a linguistic puzzle. "*Ehyeh asher ehyeh*" can mean "I am that [which] I am," "I will be that [which] I will be," "Is-Was-Will Be" (this last is Arthur Green's construction); countless permutations are possible. But what does this mean, what does it imply? Should we understand it in the terms of the favorite motto of Queen Elizabeth I, *semper eadem,* always the same? Rabbinic tradition recorded in the Talmud and midrash approves that idea, understanding God's message as "I shall be with you then as now." But this does not exhaust all the possibilities. Might not the phrase rather imply "I am all that is and will be; I am both existence and potentiality"? Might we succinctly paraphrase the phrase as "eternity"? Does its importance lie in the fact that it is so clearly not a proper name and not associated with a place but rather is formed of common verbs (a nexus of noun and verb, Green notes), suggesting both universality and the fusion of stasis and action?

Even as we receive an apparent disclosure about the divine nature, we find that it puzzles at least as much as it illumines us. That is not even the end of the puzzlement; for although God then almost comically advances a virtual nickname—"but you may tell them 'Ehyeh'"—neither the longer nor the shorter version ever comes into use. For philologists the issue is linguistic, inasmuch as some have read the divine pronouncement as equivalent to the tetragrammaton (the letters *aleph-hey-yud-hey* standing for the more familiar *yud-hey-vav-hey*). For the theologian, however, the questions are epistemological: What does this tell us and why have we been told it?

We may find ourselves conflictedly shifting from one viewpoint to another, wondering whether we have been given more names for God and therefore more ways of comprehending the divine or whether the cloud has parted for a brief instant and in hearing the name we have received the one moment of real revelation; but if the latter, what exactly has been revealed? Is it not in truth a sleight of voice? For after all, the purpose of the entire episode has not been self-revelatory on God's part but rather motivational for Moses. The issue at hand is not for Moses to know God but for Moses to know that the force at the center of existence is moving him to public consciousness and his people to liberation. *Ehyeh asher ehyeh* could as well be paraphrased as "whatever you want." God tells Moses, "Call me whatever you want. I am whatever you want, whatever you will be or want to be; and as for you, Moses, when you speak *my* name to them, you will actually say, '*Ehyeh,*' which means that you will say, 'I am.' Acknowledging me, you will declare your own existence."

This suggests that the boundary marker of the sacred can be crossed without transgression when the sacred becomes personal. The human being, said to be made in God's image, after God's likeness, cannot see how that is so; language forms the bridge by letting awareness of existence connect us with the source of existence.

Joseph Gikatilla, a kabbalist of the late thirteenth and early fourteenth centuries, expounded on the mysterious multiplicity of the holy names of God, as well as on their efficacy. Approaching the topic in a cautionary way, Gikatilla himself acknowledged what might be thought of as the unseen mezuzah identifying the entryway to specially defined territory within Judaism. Because he is about to expound on the merits of studying God's holy names, he feels that not only must he affirm the biblical injunction against taking the name in vain, but he must also mark a clear protective boundary around that possibility with the aid of Talmudic expositions. Cautioning against intruding on holiness by failing to respect the teaching of guarding the protected names of God, Gikatilla repeats the Mishnah (Sanhedrin 10:1), "Whoever pronounces God's name as written will have no share in the world-to-come," i.e., no resurrection or eternal spiritual reward. This, he observes, explains the wording of the prohibition in Exodus 20:7, "You shall not speak the name of the Lord your God in vain." Because the biblical text says "not speak" (*lo tissa lashav'*, not bring to your lips), the commandment obviously goes beyond merely swearing a false oath, which could have been more narrowly proscribed. Gikatilla cites the cautionary tale of a revered rabbi who violated the proscription only to study and understand God's ways through the holy name and was punished by heaven for his presumption. Especially to be guarded against is the Faustian temptation of using the holy names for their great legendary powers of practical kabbalah, for material or pragmatic results. Though awesome power was said to be available through pronouncing the most mysterious of the holy names, "like the seventy-two letter name, the forty-two letter name, the twelve-letter name and many other holy names," the enormous personal jeopardy attendant upon doing so was equalled by the shameful effrontery of such presumption, to be risked if at all only in the past in circumstances of momentous significance. Furthermore, he observes (intruding a practical note), no one in our time has the knowledge to pronounce the name properly and turn it to use, even if doing so could ever be permitted because of public needs.

Nevertheless, Gikatilla encourages reverential study of the known names as a spiritual aid to understanding God's greatness more fully. The religiously legitimate use of the names lies in our studying them to help us appreciate the power of the one who is named. The kabbalist is therefore in an interesting border position as someone who warns us to respect the sacred names by neither speaking nor using them while simultaneously urging us to study and comprehend their meanings. The potency and significance of the names, which require that they be shielded from us, also attract us and merit our engagement with them. The ceremonial observance of their sanctity and due preservation of silence around them (to recall terms of Miyoshi's discussion) are the ritual requirements of our access to the names. However, the names are not ends in themselves. Rather, they are critical terms that turn us back to the central cultural text with new sources of illumination for understanding it. Furthermore, these do not merely reveal some hidden odd treasure boxes secreted in out-of-the-way corners. Instead, as we shall see, they will illuminate the internal structure of the whole edifice.

Gikatilla explains that the unpronounced tetragrammaton "is like the trunk of the tree," of which *ehyeh* (the name God reveals to Moses in Exodus 3:14) is the main root. The other names for God "are all like branches and leaves that spread from the body of the tree, and each of the branches bears its own fruit." Furthermore, "there are many appelatives derived from each name," which is to say qualities ascribed to God in the Torah, all deriving from these particular names. In a bolder intellectual move, the kabbalist advances the broader significance of this insight. "All of these appelatives have appelatives of their own, and they make up all the words of the Torah. You end up by realizing that the entire Torah is woven together out of appelatives, and the appelatives out of the names," all of which are derived from the tetragrammaton (traditionally translated as "Lord"), thus explaining the verse (Psalm 19:8), "The Torah of the Lord is perfect."[9]

The words of the Torah lead us into the mysterious knowledge of the divine at the core of existence. Yet as we penetrate ever more closely toward that inner reality, what do we find? Names. And within the names are letters. Behind the letters are sounds. Somewhere, a silence, perhaps, and that silence is God, who dwells not quite alone but rather in oneness with the divine name. In God the silence and the name are one.

No wonder that although creation moves us out of silence, our speech is fraught with multiple anxieties. One of the earliest and most famous medieval Spanish Jewish poems is Dunash ben Labrat's wine song, a precursor of many with that motif. Beginning with a nine-line invitation to disdain sleep in favor of a seductively described wine banquet, the poem suddenly shifts narrator (from "he" to "I") as well as attitude for a four-line pietistic protest that one cannot rejoice while Zion is oppressed. However this was understood in its own time, the change rouses interpretive controversy in ours over whether it is politically defensive (directed against the resistance we noted earlier to secular and Arabic-influenced Hebrew verse), whether it is drolly cynical, honestly pious, mimetically ambivalent.[10]

One could invoke the metaphor of the mezuzah to understand this division in the poem. At the peripetaeia, the poem's first-person narrator rejects his companion's carpe diem inducements, "*g'artihu: dom, dom*" (I rebuke him, "Silence, silence"). One voice is to be suppressed while the next comes forth. The secular, having forsaken the study of "*torat eyl elyon*" (the teaching of God the most high), allowed itself to engage fully in the rhetorical as well as physical pleasures of sensual secularity. Its lyricism now yields place to a more austere voice imparting the sacred message of Torah through a denunciation reminiscent of Jeremiah. We noted earlier that the Jewish sabbath concludes in a ceremony called *havdalah*, "separation." The religious tradition commands that we remember and acknowledge that division between the profane and the sacred. Even speaking unrestrainedly of earthly joys may call forth the answering voice demanding we remember who we are. Although this text is specifically Jewish, the situation is not. James Weldon Johnson and R. Rosamond Johnson's "Lift Every Voice and Sing" attests to the like fear in its last stanza. Addressed to "God of our weary years, God of our silent tears," it asks for divine aid "Lest our hearts, drunk with the wine of the world, we forget Thee." On the doorways of homes and hearts, the mezuzah recalls the boundaries.

Naming, that most basic transaction of verbal currency, discomfits. There may still be some who cling to an earlier gentility that held that one's name should appear in the press only on three occasions: announcements of births, marriages, and deaths. The authority of the name has lingered in folklore through the story of Rumpelstiltskin, whose own dominance lay precisely in keeping his name hidden. Once that name is revealed, he is immediately diminished and rendered harmless; his only strength consists in a hidden identity. Rumpelstiltskin embodies the secret, which can exercise force over others only so long as it remains secret. The artistic counterbalance to this is Wagner's *Lohengrin*, in which the eponymous hero's power to effect good depends on his betrothed, Elsa, not asking him his name to prove her complete faith in his goodness. The significance of naming can be felt in the history of name changes of countries and of people. Many of what we think of as "Jewish" names were imposed by non-Jewish European government officials in the eighteenth and nineteenth centuries; these surnames in turn were later changed or corrupted through misunderstanding by English-speaking American immigration officials or altered by their bearers to camouflage their Jewishness; completing the eccentric circuit, in Germany in the 1930s the Nazi government bizarrely dictated that "Aryans" could not give their children "Jewish" names (such as those from the Hebrew Bible) or Jews "Aryan" names, and any Jews already bearing atypical given names were designated with the middle name of Sarah for women and Israel for men. The next twist was wrought after the war by the poet who renamed herself Sarah (Kirsch) in defiance of her family's Nazi past.

We are dismayed by the slippery ground and slender resources of our own creative processes. The nineteenth-century Russian poet Fedor Tyutchev asserted in a poem entitled "Silentium," as only one well acquainted with language can presume to assert, "A thought spoken is a lie." Truthful language, Tyutchev writes, comes from nonverbal origins inside and outside oneself. The silence of the inner being, he claims, preserves the imagination's beauty, which is vulnerable to "the noise without," and therefore one should "listen to their singing, and be silent." Nature's voice, expressed in the night breeze, speaks "a language intelligible to the heart" and deeply expressive to it, even raising "frenzied sounds in the heart."[11] Words draw us out of experience itself into formulation. Transforming our own living into bits of language makes us a puzzling "beast," Adrienne Rich has suggested.[12] In speaking of experience, we hold it away from us. We lose oneness with it, and it becomes "something out there." The implications are many, including political: Nadine Gordimer's novella *Something Out There* exposes the obliviousness of people who want to believe that *there* is where violence is, not knowing that it is next to them and in a different sense within them.

This belief that language alienates us from feeling is a Romantic analogue to more traditionally sacral expressions of praise for nature or for divinity. Much earlier, however, a poet of very different temperament had registered the terrible, ambiguous conflicts at the boundaries of religious silence and speech. In his treatise "The Reason of Church Government," John Milton recalled that the prophet Jeremiah's futile silence gave way to divine compulsion, because God's "word was in my heart as a burning fire shut up in my bones." The English writer himself knew "those sharp but saving words which would be a terror and a torment in him to keep back." In the merely literary world (Milton noted), one's language forms amid "waste from the pen of some vulgar amorist, or the trencher fury of a rhyming parasite," and even worse, the scholar is compelled to "club quotations with men whose learning and belief lies in marginal stuffings." No wonder the honorable theologian would "prefer a blameless silence before the sacred act of speaking, bought and begun with servitude and forswearing."

Only the urgency of the prophetic moment compels Milton himself to abandon "a calm and pleasing solitariness fed with cheerful and confident thoughts, to embark in a troubled sea of noises and hoarse disputes, put from beholding the bright countenance of truth in the quiet and still air of delightful studies." Sharp but saving words: in like spirit he observes that, "although divine inspiration must certainly have been sweet to those ancient prophets, yet the irksomeness of that truth which they brought was so unpleasant to them that everywhere they call it a burden." Regardless of the sacred origins of expression, the fallen world corrupts speech and menaces the honest speaker. But the honorable person still must answer the challenge Milton feels directed against himself: "Where canst thou show any word or deed of thine which might have hastened her [the Church's] peace"?[13]

In "calm and pleasing solitariness" one might enjoy spiritual peace without tension or equivocation, although there may be a complementary refinement in what is meant by language. Psalm 19, a traditional Sabbath text since the time of the First Temple, affirms: "The heavens declare the glory of God, the firmament proclaims God's handiwork. Day proclaims it to day, and night to night reveals knowledge. Without speaking, without speech, their voice is not heard; yet they link together through the whole earth, and their words to the end of the world." This translation attempts to reflect the variety of words for language and speech contained in this passage, to show that despite the poet's consciousness that this language of cosmic polyphony between day and day, night and night, is metaphorical, the metaphor of language nevertheless prevails.

Yet how can we presume to create when the universe is already filled with such eloquent communication and profound understanding beyond our hearing? Our creations can only be imperfect testimonies. We offer them up because the songs of the heavens demonstrate that no less is required of us (though we know we are at best capable of much less), and so we attempt through them to placate our conscious senses and inferior comprehension. Even this can only be temporarily satisfying. The psalmist promises that in the time of revelation, "all the trees shall sing before the Lord" (Ps. 96:13). Though we (like Longfellow) might only be able to conjure "murmuring pines," our songs are no less valuable. That is because we sing them, and songs are the best we can offer. We may recall also how lucky we are when we are able to sing.

Gloria Anzaldúa, conscious of the creative dilemmas involved in her living as "a new mestiza" in the "borderland" of complex Mexican and Anglo cultures, finds more appropriate the terminology of another liminal experience, childbirth. "Something is trying to come out. She fights the words, pushes them down, down, a woman with morning sickness in the middle of the night. How much easier it would be to carry a baby for nine months and then expel it permanently. These continuous multiple pregnancies are going to kill her. She is the battlefield for the pitched fight between the inner image and the words trying to recreate it."[14] Hillesum summoned the same metaphor, affirming that "I want every word I write to be born, truly born."[15] Many kabbalists seemed to imagine the birth trope as they explained the process of the world's creation through rhythms of contracting, fragmenting, and expanding (*tsimtsum* and *hitpashtut*). When God decided to manifest the divine perfection through physical form, the great mystic Isaac Luria wrote, "then He contracted himself within the middle point in Himself, at the very center. . . . There was now available an area in which there could be the emanations, the beings created, formed and made."[16]

Unlike God, we experience the creative process as painful. Anzaldúa's images of morning sickness and battlefield evoke its violence and turmoil. Some Jewish eschatology envisions the world eventually experiencing "the birth pains of the Messiah," when suffering, wars, and moral chaos prepare for the Messiah to come forth. Perhaps Yeats's "rough beast slouching toward Bethlehem to be born" recalls that idea, which also found its way into Christian messianism. This image of a tumultuous time prior to redemption is virtually a counterimage of the world's creation.

Without stretching allegory too far we can at least imagine that the Torah gives us insight into how and why suffering and creativity are joined in human experience. Perhaps this is what we are being told when Eve is made to know that she will give birth painfully (Gen. 3:16). The Jewish tradition has always held that this was not punishment for original sin but explanation of cause and effect. Eve and Adam preferred knowledge to life and so separated the two.[17] Because for human beings knowing and living are now in conflict with one another, bringing forth requires struggle, suffering, travail. As with childbirth, so with the birth of ideas and forms. Kate Chopin divides the two roles in *The Awakening* between the archtypal "mother-woman" Adèle Ratignolle, suffering through excruciating labor pains because she is devoted to bearing children, and the would-be artist Edna Pontellier, who is more completely destroyed by trying to give birth to herself. As Anzaldúa writes, "How much easier it would be. . . . These continuous multiple pregnancies are going to kill her."

The danger of supererogation (violating the sacred), the danger of insufficiency (which may be simply another form of violating the sacred) are but two dangers of speech. Some truths are dangerous to tell; sometimes the simplest truths are dangerous to tell. Here is an incident narrated by Irena Klepfisz, a recollection from her aunt. "During the war the Polish woman [who was hiding her from the Nazis] sends her to buy a notebook for school. She is given the wrong change and points it out. The shopkeeper eyes her sharply: 'Very accurate. Just like a Jew. Perhaps you are a little Jewess?' "[18] To speak may mean being exposed.

Or it may mean exposing. Maya Angelou, raped as an eight-year-old child by an adult friend of the family, was persuaded to reveal his name. At the trial, she lied by suppressing a previous unreported episode when he had not penetrated her, and within hours of sentencing, the man was murdered. Believing that she had caused his death by lying, the young girl sequestered herself into virtual muteness from which she would not fully emerge for years. Abetted by her Grandmother Baxter's solution of banning any mention of the episode or the man's name, the girl forsakes speaking for listening. Without knowing the literary work, she imagines herself a lethal agent like Rappacini's daughter in Melville's story: "Just my breath, carrying my words out, might poison people. . . . I simply stood still—in the midst of the riot of sound. After a minute or two, silence would rush into the room from its hiding place because I had eaten up all the sounds."[19] Angelou describes that experience, now well known, in a powerful section of *I Know Why the Caged Bird Sings*. What was not known earlier is the refinement of her memory that emerged much more recently in an interview between Angelou and a longtime friend, the scholar Dolly A. McPherson.[20] The knowledgeable interviewer's probings elicited the fact that during those seemingly silent years Angelou did speak, not only to her brother but also her uncle and her revered Grandmother Henderson, those few people in her family with whom she felt absolutely safe, and Angelou suggests that there may have been periods of more general speech. Her experience does not tell us about catatonia but about permission of the will, not whether one is capable of speaking but whether one allows oneself to do so.

Angelou grew more than comfortable with language as she became exposed to its music and its special qualities through the tutelage of a gracious black woman who loved it. Asked to carry the woman's groceries home, the girl hears but does not respond to a gentle inducement to conversation about her silence. Instead, "I hung back in the separate unasked and unanswerable questions." Mrs. Flowers's own use of language begins to draw the child from her estrangement: "She pronounced my name so nicely. Or more correctly, she spoke each word with such clarity that I was certain a foreigner who didn't understand English could have understood her." Language, the woman's lesson continues, separates us "from the lower animals," but "It takes the human voice to infuse them with the shades of deeper meaning." Lending the child books, Mrs. Flowers insists that "I must read them aloud. She suggested that I try to make a sentence sound in as many different ways as possible."[21] One can both respect the power of words and find playful delight in them if language seems more than the agency of harm. The style of communicating attests to language's preciousness; it also allows language to reach between the speaker and the person alienated from speech.

Similarly, one can enjoy language's mysterious associations with objects or experience when borders around language do not seem threatening. Bella Akhmadulina, a modern Russian poet, evokes the potential within language for the liminal, creative power to evoke "reality." Language dips into "the din of silence" to draw forth what it can.[22] Language masquerades as reality—or equals it. Verbal image and empirical reality become interchangeable. Writing a poem centering on a flower, she senses herself beelike, and then: a real bee lands on the poem she is writing (or so the speaker claims). Flowers and words become one another; earth's layer of vegetation is the thickness of "a dictionary." Akhmadulina's metaphors never completely take over to impose art's primacy. Instead, the narrator continually calls our attention to her crossing and recrossing of the boundaries. Characteristically, one of her most complex poems tantalizes us with the odd double vision of garden-horserider beginning with the title's wordplay phrase "*Sad / Vsadnik*" (translated by F. D. Reeve as "The Garden / The Guardsman"). Regardless of other "characters" mentioned in her poems, in each work there seem to be at least three: the speaker, the supposed experience, and the poet's language, each wary of the other. Her phrase *ne predast slovam,* not betraying into language, acknowledges the risk of transgression. Somehow, poetry seems to have a will of its own. It might have a mind to turn those secrets into language, at which point the poet becomes watcher, guardian, the one who experiences more than controls the experience. Word and experience turn into mentally interchangeable counterparts of one another. "I went out to the garden," a poem called "The Garden" (*Sad,* in Russian) begins. Such evocative power dwells in the title-word that by the end of this poetic homage to the garden's life we discover that the garden has been entered through the word and is the word. She has not moved, merely written. In place of liminal anxiety, Akhmadulina offers liminal awareness. She is not a tightrope walker so much as an acrobat vaulting from one side to the other, and the line she spans is not invisible but deliberately drawn for us to appreciate the feat. That she traverses this boundary in curiosity rather than anxiety seems un-Jewish. To her, writing "garden" conjures a garden seemingly unproblematically, as if the poet shared God's easy correlation between word and object. The Israeli poet Amir Gilboa, treading similar territory, encounters dialogically the disjunction between language and reality. Words turn from simple denotations into a kind of Rorschach test.

> If they show me a tree and I say tree they say tree.
> But if they show me blood and I say blood they say paint.[23]

However one challenges the boundaries, either transgression itself or the threat of transgression is essential to the risk of venturing language. Some words seem riskier than others, as do some recognitions: "If they *show* me blood and I say blood . . ." Very accurate. Just like a Jew? Does the poet command the language? Precise to the letter of the text and law—like Shylock? But of course it was Portia who noticed that the letter of the loan agreement between Shylock and Antonio said nothing about blood and knew how to apply the letter of the law to confiscate Shylock's wealth and forcibly convert him. Who does command the language? I say blood, they say paint.

We go over the lintel, past the doorpost, into the garden, into language, a contested field. Words abound. Are they ours? Can we claim them? May we? We pass from liminal anxiety into agoraphobia, from reluctance to emerge from inner silence (even muteness) to inchoate openness. We step through the gateway and are exiled in language.

6

_____

Compulsion for the Word

ARE ANY OF Philip Roth's characters acquainted with silence? Are Isaac Bashevis Singer's? They seem made of words. Indeed, they and the books in which they live seem to have no silences within, nothing unreachable or protected. One wonders, however, whether such impressions warrant closer scrutiny. To consider an analogous case: At first impression one suspects that an oxymoronic imp suggested Ihab Hassan's pairing of Henry Miller, that man of unceasing garrulity and self-revelation, with the verbally parsimonious Samuel Beckett to represent the complementary poles of "the literature of silence." But the joke is on the skeptic, for, as Hassan points out, Miller claimed, "The word is always the reminder of a more perfect state, of a union or unity which is ineffable and undescribable."[1] Miller "speaks endlessly" because silence is, for him, prelapsarian, and he can only hope to get close to it by exhausting either language itself or his compulsion to use it.

What Hassan terms Miller's "Orphic" compulsion arises from a yearning to approximate that original and inexpressible simplicity, much as the attempt to get closer to the real value of pi necessitates an increasingly large string of numbers defining ever-smaller increments. Whitman similarly generated his enormous catalogues of American experiences in "Song of Myself" to express the ideas that he himself gave the truest poetic voice to America and that "the United States are [*sic*] the greatest poem." The greatest oneness can only be represented to our material consciousness by the richest multiplicity. Or, to switch the field of reference to theology, one might interpret Miller's verbal outpouring as a parody of the sacred acts by which creation unfolds. As Arthur Green expresses the connection between creation and variety, "The undefined One puts on the coat of many colors. In this, the One is seeking, as it were, to enter into a world of infinite variety so that its oneness might be attested to the ultimate degree. *Only in that garbing does the Divine sufficiently hide itself that it might be revealed.*"[2]

Other writers, as prolific and oral in their compositional styles, may surprise us by the extent of their silences. Consider an example from the literary background in which Singer and Roth grew up. The great Yiddish writer Sholem Aleichem's Tevye is famous for his garrulity; however, when observed closely, his rapid verbal footwork describes elaborate patterns around his experiences, drawing attention away from the feelings, which must be inferred through what he does not disclose and through what he discloses only indirectly. As confessional as Tevye seems to be, he is also evasive in the way of a nonintellectual about his own inner life, comprising the difficult balancing of beliefs and experiences.

Discussing Sholem Aleichem, the translator and critic Hillel Halkin remarks that, "His characters chute on torrents of words and seek to drag others into the current with them." That phenomenon is not motivated simply by the love of language, however. Halkin notes the difference between the traditional Jewish use of words in Talmudic discourse, for instance, and that of Sholem Aleichem's characters, to whom language constitutes, "a club, a cloud, a twitch, a labyrinth, a smokescreen, a magic wand, a madly waved paper fan, a perpetual motion machine, a breastwork against chaos, the very voice of chaos itself." Indeed, this critic observes, "Nothing frightens them so much as silence—most of all, their own."

Such compulsiveness is more than a stylistic trait of the author. It relates, Halkin observes, to the importance of verbal energy as a substitute for material wealth and power. As he claims, "No one understood better than Sholem Aleichem that this astonishing verbosity, this virtuoso command of and abuse of language, was at once the greatest strength and the ultimate pathology of East European Jewish life." (One suspects that this analysis might apply as well to contemporary displays of verbal flamboyance, such as rap music, which developed from the culture of a different sort of ghetto and emitting loudly from enormous semiportable stereos, the insistent and rapid-fire language not contained within the discrete and individual headsets of the appropriately termed "personal portables" but projected—some would say inflicted—onto the surrounding society.) Halkin continues, "Reviled, ghettoized, impoverished, powerless, [Sholem Aleichem's] Jews have only one weapon: the power of speech."[3]

Although language is a political tool for those fictive Jews, they are not using it for explicitly political aims. The stories, published between the 1880s and 1916, take note of both casual and organized anti-Semitism on the part of mobs and governments, but one would need to scrutinize the characters' comments with a police informant's eye to discern hints of the developing political and social movements that were then attracting extensive Jewish participation, among them Marxism, Zionism, and socialism (manifested in the Jewish Bund). Rather, the verbosity of Sholem Aleichem's characters constructs a rich linguistic environment, at once playful and subversive, aggressive and palliative, a verbal world of their own devising set inside and set against the world of factual reality against which they had no practical defenses.

The fear of silence, "most of all, their own" (as Halkin phrased it), was neither idle nor frivolous. A silent Jew was, in spirit or mind, a dead Jew. This is no mere figure of speech. In one of the most painful of all of Sholem Aleichem's stories, Tevye's daughter Shprintze, seduced and abandoned, withdraws into the deep silence that culminates in her suicide by drowning. "Don't imagine, though, that she ever said a word to me about it. Do you think she complained? Do you think she cried even once? . . . She just flickered out like a candle, without a word of protest, keeping it all to herself except for a sigh now and then—but such a sigh, I tell you, as could break a heart of iron"—and, one might add, does.[4]

That, however, is not where the story ends. Tevye, who has told it, carries on with his incessant repartee, his questions, aphorisms, and even characteristic but frequently off-center quotations from religious texts. This speech is not callousness but the need to survive, because surviving is one's obligation to the fact of being in this world. Sholem Aleichem's artistry also demonstrates that the grief and determination required to survive are borne on Tevye's resourceful verbosity; through it, they make themselves known. What is the stunning question to which Tevye distractedly wends his way? Why do drowned people die with their eyes open? We are compelled to recognize that such a question is not merely an inquiry, it is the exposure of a wound and with that exposure a covert indictment of life's injustices.

Yet there is more, and it is more subtly wrought. Acknowledging that God's judgments are beyond human reach, Tevye quotes and succinctly paraphrases a Hebrew prayer book phrase (Halkin notes) from the morning ritual that Tevye, poorly educated but observant Jew that we know him to be, would say each day: "As long as the soul is in me, I shall thank Thee, O God and God of my forebears." Given his circumstance, this would seem poignant enough. An even bolder irony than that which Halkin indicates is evoked by this quotation, however. Tevye's text is part of a blessing (*"Elohai, n'shamah"*) concluding with the formula acknowledging the promise of resurrection, "Praised are You, God, who restores souls to the dead." Does Tevye's quotation suggest purely an affirmation of faith in divine compassion, uttered through stoic endurance even when faced by that human tragedy encompassed in his pathetically curious question about the drowned? Or does it not at least imply a challenge to the one who expects so to be blessed, no matter what? Having raised these questions, the critic of Sholem Aleichem would also need to consider whether the irony is Tevye's or the author's.

Tevye's compulsive monologue is, to be sure, not merely symptomatic of his immediate situation; such garrulousness always typifies him. He seems to embody the concept of the human being as *medabber*, "one who speaks." Through his chatter Tevye's humanness becomes manifest. He is as unguarded in what comes out of his mouth as Joyce's Jewish protagonist, Leopold Bloom, is about what goes through his head. According to Benjamin Harshav's summation, "Tevye's *kaleidoscopic* visions result from the Yiddish folk ethos in which all things are linked with all things in one, transhistoric destiny, prefigured in the Holy Scriptures."[5] His prolixity keeps silence at bay.

One of Freud's great insights, of course, was to perceive the unheard or disguised volubility within verbal silences. Peter Gay expressed that idea well: "The psychoanalyst becomes the detective of absences: of subjects dropped, overtures rejected, silences prolonged. 'He who has eyes to see and ears to hear,' Freud wrote with supreme self-confidence in his account of 'Dora,' 'grows convinced that mortals can conceal no secrets. He whose lips are silent, chatters with his fingertips; betrayal oozes through every pore.' "[6]

Other authors seem to find silence almost obsessive, whether as a motif or theme. In Georg Trakl's poetry, silence is a recurrent motif. Poem after poem returns to the words *Stille, Schweigen,* and *sprachlos,* which together control the mood of "Nachtlied." Whether it is suggestive of loneliness or isolation or of pastoral quiet and blissful solitude, silence dominates Trakl's environment but with increasing interruptions from the screams and clamor that disrupt it and eventually take over toward the end of his life. For Samuel Beckett, Elie Wiesel, or Ingeborg Bachmann, silence is less a mood than an issue to contend with or confront. To be sure, the themes differ for each. Beckett's silence stands for the metaphysical void, Wiesel's the moral abdication of human beings and God, Bachmann's the frustrating inadequacies of language. Still, each finds the concept of silence definitional for treating these concerns that become central to their work.

This concept that we achieve knowing through the word and through silence resonate through Jewish thought, as evidenced by André Neher's magisterial theological study of the theme in the Hebrew Bible, *The Exile of the Word: From the Silence of the Bible to the Silence of Auschwitz,* and by Jerome Rothenberg's conceptually devised and mystical anthology of Jewish religious and literary texts, *Exiled in the Word.* The concept seems compelling because it contains our skepticism along with faith. While acknowledging our capacity for verbal engagement with others, Rabbi Joseph Soloveitchik challenges, "What really can this dialogue reveal of the numinous in-depth personality? Nothing! Yes, words are spoken, but these words reflect not the unique and intimate, but the universal and public in man. . . . Distress and bliss, joy and frustrations are incommunicable within the framework of the natural dialogue consisting of common words." As Soloveitchik also comprehends, common silence is no refuge. "Who knows what kind of loneliness is more agonizing: the one which befalls man when he casts his glance at the mute cosmos, at its dark spaces and monotonous drama, or the one that besets man exchanging glances with his fellow man in silence?"[7]

It is typical of contemporary thought in general, like Jewish thought in particular (though for different reasons), to concentrate on the negativity or at least the tension of involvement with "the word." Yet at the doorway to Jewish consciousness of the world stands another conceptualization of the word: *vayomer elohim y'hi or* (So God said, Let there be light). A rabbinic commentary on the text of Genesis (in Hebrew, *B'reishit*) inquires why the first letter of the

Bible (the letter *bet*) is the second, rather than the first letter, of the alphabet (in Hebrew, the *alef-bet*). This commentary characteristically proceeds to answer its own question. A *bet*, it observes, is closed on three sides, open only on the side facing inward toward the text that follows it. We can know what follows that initial articulation, not what existed before, above, or below it.[8] Hebrew's first letter, *alef*, is a silent letter; *alef*, implied in the silence preceding the point at which understanding begins to unfold, in the time before we begin positing whatever might be spoken about creation, is the letter of unity and therefore the initial letter of God (*Adonai, Elohim*) and of God's "I" (*ani, anokhi*).

Speaking brings about creation, as if the word itself (actually, in some Jewish traditional teachings, the Hebrew letters themselves) constructed the physical universe, not just conceptually but physically. Before words or letters was silence, and at the heart of the silence was the creative source whose truest names, we subsequently learn, are a grammatical puzzle (*"ehyeh-asher-ehyeh,"* which might be read as, "I am / will be what I am / will be") or the name hidden within the tetragrammaton, a name whose correct pronunciation was to be known only to the High Priest and pronounced only in the Holy of Holies in one moment of one service a year amid a tumult from the assembly that would mask its hearing from any except the one who was intended to hear and recognize it, the deity identified with that name that must be protected from desecration and not written unless in a sacred text, if written not to be erased or destroyed, never "taken in vain," the deity to whom orthodox Jews most frequently refer except in actual prayer by the periphrasis *ha-shem*, "the name." The Mishnah records among the offenders who will not know eternal bliss "one who pronounces the name of God as written."[9]

Readers of the Jewish Bible may come to know God as the one who speaks and the one who commands speech. In a preliterate society it is understandable that divine communication be represented as oral, yet Judaism seems to stress this concept even urgently: "And God *spoke* to Moses, *saying*, '*Speak* to the Israelites and *tell* them.'" The fourfold emphasis on verbs for speaking is no translator's indulgence but a fact of the original text. Jewish tradition emphasizes the oral nature of the relationship between the Creator and the creation and between creatures. Orality is present, we have noted, as the universe comes into shape: *"vayomer elohim"* (and God said). This may represent one way of explaining that even the physical world begins to make sense when we can articulate some understanding of its order and process, when it exists for us as something more than a physical reality at which to gaze. By predicating a statement about it, we acknowledge its existence independent of us; we accept that it is something to be spoken about or spoken to, precisely because we recognize a difference between ourselves and it. The original material of the universe took shape through the divine words that defined it by naming it; the naming separated it from everything else, from the original nature of matter, *tohu v'bohu*. The word *bohu*, usually translated as "void," may instead be glossed as "chaotic," so that the divine word does not so much bring matter into being within an expanse that is without form and void as it does bring order to what had been formlessness and confusion.[10]

If even the inanimate universe moves in response to the divine word, it is no wonder that God's relationship with us is expressed through verbal summonses and instructions, from the naturalness of the instructions given to Adam about his proper rights and limits to the urgency of the voices that called Abraham and Moses by name, recalling them to their right identities. Temptation to sin is also verbal; it is induced from the outside, not instinctive. Eve, for example, is not merely stimulated by her senses but led verbally to disobedience.

Many later examples of sin will follow that pattern, whereby the misdeed is articulated, even though the verbalization itself may not constitute the sin. Sometimes the sin seems compounded by what is said—such as Cain's response as to his brother's whereabouts, "I know not; am I my brother's guardian?" wherein the fact of his being his brother's destroyer is matter of callous irony. His retort actually seems another sin. Even a good deed may seem marred by silence. Such may be the case when Noah unprotestingly accepts the world's doom. Although some authorities find him perfect through his righteous obedience, others view him (though "righteous in his generation," as the biblical text precisely specifies) as an imperfect model of righteousness for all time when set beside the more active models of Abraham and Moses, who argued with God for the sake of flawed humanity. Concern over the moral implications of Noah's apparent silence is reflected in the midrashic tradition that posited Noah repeatedly but unavailedly imploring his neighbors to repent. Jewish sages were obviously troubled to reconcile a text specifying Noah's righteousness with his apparent failure to plead or warn, his failure to speak on behalf of others, either by appealing to the authority in charge or by cautioning the wrongdoer. The Talmud makes clear that anyone witnessing a person about to commit a crime must verbally warn that such a deed is prohibited and must specify the punishment mandated by law for it, admonitions without which corporal or capital punishment may not be given. Seeing and knowing oblige one to speak.

Neither speaking nor remaining silent, however, can be taken lightly. From a Jewish perspective, King Lear is culpably foolish in demanding that his daughters "tell" him, by means of what they "say" in a public ceremony, the answer to that most elusive puzzle, "Which of you shall we say doth love us most?"[11] Because the matter is reduced to a show of words—indeed, in Soloveitchik's terms, not "the unique and intimate, but the universal and public" expressed by "common language"—the honest Cordelia has nothing to show and is cast off with nothing. Making himself a captive to words, Lear becomes tragic but fails morally, rather like the biblical character Jephtha, whose imprudent vow led to his daughter being sacrificed (Judg. 11). Jewish tradition, clearly appalled by Jephtha's rashness, uses his story to define what constitutes an inadmissible vow and what steps are taken to rescind one; further, midrashic literature does its best to answer the heart's desire by sending the daughter into exile rather than death, with greater wisdom than Nahum Tate displayed by saving Cordelia in his Restoration revision of Shakespeare's play.

Answering Lear's failure, however, is Cordelia's. Hers is the fault of someone too virtuous to engage the world's folly for the sake even of love (if not of herself). Addressing herself, she responds to her father's challenge with the words, "What shall Cordelia speak? Love, and be silent" (1.1.62). "Love, and be silent" sequesters love within the inner space of the one who feels it. Language brings it forth. Her words, however, are not spoken to the one who needs to hear them. They are for herself (and of course for the audience as privileged but helpless auditors). True, what comes forth in public from the lips of others may be sham; yet what if the sham pleases like love? And what if love-filled muteness offers only what Cordelia can say, "nothing"?

"O reason not the need" (2.4.264), Lear protests to his two vicious other daughters as they reduce their proud royal father to penury. So might he say to Cordelia, whose truth and love do not reach forth to his need by saying what he needs to hear. To him, Goneril's and Regan's lies feel like truth because they are the lies he needs beyond reason. "I cannot heave / My heart into my mouth," Cordelia nobly informs her father (1.1.91–92). Paradoxically, the expression of emotional truth would feel to her like an emotional falsehood and her metaphors almost persuade us that she has nature on her side. But to what purpose have we a voice if not to speak what is in our heart and mind? The play reminds us that words are no substitute for deeds, and Cordelia's deeds (though they fail of their aims) will prove to be those of love. The play also demonstrates the power of words and silences over feelings and behavior.

Respect for the power of the spoken to define the self, shape or deform reality, claim or abuse divine respect seems to motivate the remarkable rabbinic concern shown in the Talmud to avoid compelling witnesses in cases of law to swear oaths, except as a final resort.[12] Adin Steinsalz notes, "Although there is a positive commandment in the Torah (Deut. 6:13) to take oaths under certain circumstances, it was said that a person taking an oath must be worthy, and that there must be no suspicion of falsehood, either intentional or unintentional, in an oath. For that reason the Sages almost completely abolished oaths from court procedure and substituted other regulations."[13] Even in seemingly petty disputes that we might refer to small claims court, Talmudic law goes to considerable lengths to settle the conflict through judgment or compromise while avoiding compelling either party to take an oath. Rabbinic procedures imply that reaching an incorrect or unjust decision is less worrisome than inducing someone into swearing a false oath and thereby profaning God's name.

This may help us understand why the ritual for Yom Kippur, the Day of Atonement, begins with Kol Nidre. The most famous element of the service (largely because of its haunting, insistent traditional melody), this is not a prayer but a legal formula renouncing "all vows" and other sorts of promises and pledges that one has been unable to fulfill or that never should have been made. Kol Nidre must be recited just before Yom Kippur itself actually commences because one cannot accomplish the work of atonement unless one acknowledges the possibility of such transgressions against the eternal judge of all truth and all deeds. We are compelled to remember that what is spoken does not simply evaporate into thin air.

The next level of anxiety about speech arises from the way that speech leads us into strange paths. Because we go with our words, imagination and understanding are at risk by what we hear and say. This may be truer of articulated speech than of thought, although obviously the separation cannot be neat. "Evil into the mind of God or man / May come and go, so unapproved,"[14] Milton's Adam reassures Eve after a troubling dream. Bringing that evil forth from the inner mind into the resounding air allows the evil to become palpable, to be spoken of. That which can be spoken of can be done; that which can be spoken of already has a place in the universe. Moreover, to speak even speculatively means stepping into minds and experiences one cannot know.

The Mishnah, that most pragmatic and rational of Jewish texts, therefore counsels, "The subject of forbidden incestuous marriages may not be expounded in the presence of three, nor the work of creation in the presence of two, nor the work of the chariot in the presence of one, unless he is a sage who has innate understanding."[15] These warnings surely are intended to prevent enticing the minds of others into distracting speculations. Why not explain the laws regarding incestuous marriages "in the presence of three"? How would three differ from two or one? As the group widens, so does the likelihood of addressing someone whose mind and extended familial relationships one cannot know. There is greater danger of stirring turmoil in the imagination or in the family that cannot be quelled or pacified. By extension of the same principle, the rabbis caution that in speaking to one whose relative has died by hanging, one never uses a phrase like "Hang this up." The magic within the words lie in their power of implication and evocation.

Another sort of power resides in the capacity of speech or silence alike to wound. "A conversation begins / with a lie," Adrienne Rich postulates in a poem called "Cartographies of Silence."[16] The poem beginning with a lie can be destroyed, whereas a conversation persists perniciously. Silence, she observes, is also ruinous and (as she elsewhere writes) personally destructive, leaving the person smothered by it, "drowning" amid all that is unspoken.[17] Because we are creatures of words, there is meaning even in our withholding of them. Poets may know this more directly than theologians; all of us, however, have felt that truth.

Is this not the familiar process as experience gives rise to language?

silence — word — cry — silence

Anxiety over the power of the word may occasion the separate and subversive anxiety over the power of one's own words. The artist characteristically will query, "What can I say?" The deeper artistic question is "What can words, what can my medium, what can my artistic language say?" Rich's poems insist on the value and the difficulty of speaking a common language with one another even when we speak the same language, and Ingeborg Bachmann raises as an issue our possibly problematic relationship with our own language. For Bachmann that issue was focused by her being an Austrian writing in German after the Second World War (and furthermore by her eventually residing in Italy).

> I with the German language
> this cloud around me
> that I keep as a house
> push through all languages.[18]

Though the problem begins as an issue of this language within this life, for Bachmann the difficulties reveal themselves eventually as inherent in language itself. The author of a significant early essay on Wittgenstein's linguistic theory, she remarked on the philosopher's "despairing attempt to chart the limits of linguistic expression" in the *Tractatus*.[19] Her poetry directly admits, even esteems, the struggle with words. In a work called "Wahrlich" ("Truly"), addressed to her Russian colleague Anna Akhmatova, she writes,

> Whoever has never coaxed out a word,
> And this I say to you,
> whoever knows to help oneself barehanded
> and with words—
>
> such can't be helped.
> Not in the short run
> and not in the long.
>
> To make one single sentence solid,
> sustained amid the ding-dong of words.
>
> Nobody writes that sentence
> who doesn't underwrite it.[20]

The play on *unterschreiben*, "to underwrite," affirms that commitment is necessary: One must be ready to put one's name to that work, to record that one has earned it but also to own up to it. Grabbing what comes to hand, chiming in with the familiar bim-bam of verbiage will never produce a real sentence. (The word *haltbar*, translated above as "solid," can also mean "durable" as well as "defensible"—as Mark Anderson translates it, "tenable"—all relevant to Bachmann's meaning.)

Scrupulousness about words would lead Bachmann eventually to what virtually all her readers interpret as her valedictory to poetry, a poem called "Keine Delikatessen," "No Delicacies."[21] The pun works in both languages. Like the seventeenth-century Anglican poet George Herbert in his two "Jordan" poems, rejecting verbal elegance and metaphysical conceits in favor of plainly spoken religious truths, Bachmann asks rhetorically if she should "equip" (*ausstaffieren*) a metaphor with an almond blossom or "crucify" (*kreuzigen*) syntax with a lighting effect. Quoting herself, she acknowledges that others "know to help themselves with words." In the context, the preposition *mit* equivocally implies "help themselves *to* words" or "help themselves *with*," a significant ambiguity given Bachmann's own struggle. Her "*Einsehn*" ("insight") occurs through words significant for "the lowest class," words she lists as,

> Hunger
> shame
> tears
> and
> darkness.

Rather than leading her into the language of proletarian literature, even (for instance) the sardonic hard edge of Brecht, however, Bachmann's awareness seems to make writing poetry even less possible. Perhaps through those words she has come close enough to the Wittgensteinian ideal of one word standing for one thing, and the result for her is what she saw in the *Tractatus*, "a tension into which [the author] eventually disappears."[22] So she concludes "Keine Delikatessen" (not absolutely her last poem but usually regarded as if it were), "My part, it should get lost."

To these stylistic, compositional, and conceptual worries common to all literary artists, the Jewish artist is likely to add, "What indeed is my language?" This question may be as fundamental as uncertainty over one's literary tongue: Hebrew, Yiddish, another vernacular language (especially earlier and elsewhere, Greek, Latin, or Arabic)? Language may also extend beyond the purely lexical. To find one's language also means to locate or make one's vocabulary and grammar of operative concepts and values. The Jewish writer who writes from within Jewishness or Judaism, Levinas has argued, "writes" Hebrew even when writing in, for example, French, and similarly "writes"

Greek while engaged with philosophical issues that are among Greek culture's legacy.[23]

For an artist particularly, finding one's language means finding one's voice. The poetry of Paul Celan, who lived through the Holocaust, reflects in its own ways an austere reduction of language, as if every word were hewn out of silence itself. Readers coming to Celan's work aware of his experiences may see in his poems (the first collection of which appeared in 1948) an aesthetic of artistry striven for in a time of deprivation and hardship, as if every word were heavy and lifted into place with difficulty, like the debris and rocks that the poet spent his years of captivity clearing as a forced laborer. The short-breathed lines and curt stanzas of the ensuing poem, given in its entirety, characterize Celan's work. The style seems strikingly different from that of (for instance) Nelly Sachs, another Jewish poet who wrote in German about the ḥurban. Sachs, however, was personally safe during the war. Her full-voiced lamentations from abroad, rhetorically antithetical to the tight-lipped parsimoniousness with words or emotions found in the texts of those like Levi, Wiesel, and Celan, who were there, attest to a stylistic difference arising from this crucial difference in personal experience.

Still, it should be acknowledged that Celan, more committed to making poetry his métier than Levi was, shows that we cannot take verbal leanness simply as the legacy of the concentration camp. Although autobiographical experiences resonate continually throughout Celan's poetry, we must recognize that his art was formed in a wide intellectual and aesthetic context. As noted by one of his translators, Katherine Washburn, "The range of associations, even in *Last Poems*, . . . includes Whitman, the Gospels, the Tenth Duino Elegy, the Kabbalistic theory of left-side Emanations, Christopher Marlowe, Jacobin argot, the events of 1968 in Paris."[24] Celan's poetry was informed by extensive reading and experiences not dependent on his experiences during his years in the grip of the Nazis. He created it with broader understanding of the aesthetic issues in his own era.

The reader familiar with the music of the earlier twentieth century may think of the analogies with the works of the Viennese composer Anton Webern, whose tightly wrought, tiny, austerely orchestrated pieces unfold amid silence that seems not to indicate pauses but rather seems to be the medium out of which the composer wrests brief moments of precisely nuanced tones and timbres. Within his famous *Five Pieces* for orchestra (Op. 10, composed in

1913), whose five sections take a total of approximately two minutes to play, or his only symphony (Op. 21, 1928), which can be performed in under ten minutes, each note (like Celan's sparse words) registers as a separately perceived articulation. Unlike his teacher, Arnold Schoenberg, Webern suppressed the expressionistic.[25] Phrases are not sustained or developed; instead, they seem discontinuous and nervous remarks ventured amid sonic emptiness.

To look at a page of an orchestral score by Webern or a page of poetry by Celan is to be struck by the amount of white space. As Donald Jay Grout wrote of Webern's compositions, "Textures are stripped to bare essentials; rhythmic patterns are complex, . . . and the sound, with all its fine gradation of dynamics, seldom rises above the level of a *forte*."[26] His so-called symphony is remarkably lightly scored; indeed, it can be considered a nonet for clarinet, bass clarinet, harp, two horns, two violins, viola, and cello, each of which has long passages of rests even in this short work. The dynamic markings are especially relevant for our discussion. Notwithstanding the occasional forte, far more prevalent are the pianissimos (*p*, *pp*, even *ppp*); many passages call for the instrumentalists to use mutes. Returning then to Celan's poetry with this aesthetic background in mind, without denying the relevance of his wartime experiences to the formation of Celan's art, the analogy with Webern may suggest that what Washburn termed his "silence of the unutterable" included the silences that some may hear surrounding all utterance.

There is certainly more here than aesthetic precision in selecting or devising the mot juste. There is certainly care for and care about words. However, this poetry implies a struggle for words, a struggle with words, an uneasy relationship with language that needs to be articulated and positioned with immaculate precision because it is otherwise in danger of slipping off center.

Celan's is a style well suited to mark the enigmatic shape of experience, for his texts seem only to notate rather than unfold. The opening line, for example, although more natural in German than an English translation may suggest, bears even in the original a sense of the periphrastic, as if adequate expression is beyond reach of ordinary language and must be notated by what is at best an approximation.

> What is needed regarding stars
> showers down,

> your hands' leaf-green shadow
> collects it,
>
> happily I champ through
> that bit of coin
> Fate.[27]

Both vocabulary and meter suggest the effort. Consider, for instance, that in the original language, of the poem's twenty-one words, nine are monosyllables; of the remaining twelve, only the two compound adjectives have more than two syllables. Utterance itself seems both precious and hard earned. That impression is augmented by the rhythmic structure. The opening line is metrically analogous (allowing for the difference between quantitative and accentual verse) to the first hemistych of the epic dactylic hexameter, but any implication of such reach is curtailed by the clipped second line. One could also perceive each of the first two stanzas as comprising a fractured elegiac line. Appropriate to the motifs of shedding and gathering, the short and rhythmically identical second and fourth lines (which begin and end with stressed syllables and strongly alliterate with one another) seem to pull the poetic action inward, as if in preparation for the verb *zerbeiß*, not merely eating but violently biting off. By a sleight of ear, the apparent lengthening of the third stanza with a third line has the opposite effect. The third stanza is syllabically no longer than the previous two; its first two lines are each shorter than the first lines of the preceding stanzas, and the final line, a single word of two syllables, terminates the poem with a finality that probably would seem heavily weighted even if one did not know that *Schicksal* means "fate." Thematically, the poem may suggest the inmate's ravenous gnawing at whatever scraps and kernels of food can be scrounged, which in this instance means devouring fate, right from the hands. Such a topical reading aside, Celan's poetry is that of life lived on the margins of survival and art wrought on the edge of communication.

His is exilic art, but such an exile is only partly geographical, and that may not be its salient form. From the vantage point of the general culture, Jewish postbiblical experience may seem marginal, but we know that the marginal may in fact be liminal. Edmond Jabès, for one, claimed, "Being Jewish means exiling yourself in the word and, at the same time, weeping for your exile."[28] What is the nature of that exile?

The biblical account of what happened "in the beginning" of human consciousness conceives that we are all exiles from Eden, our original home. Although that story appears near the start of a Jewish text, the loss of Eden has never been seen as a particularly Jewish experience. The prominent theme of exile within Jewish writing has arisen because of our exiles from a specifically Jewish location. Judaism has not claimed that Adam was Jewish, and the promised Jewish national homeland has always been Canaan, Zion, or Eretz Yisrael (the land of Israel), its center Jerusalem, not paradise or the Garden of Eden.

Nonetheless, Jewish tradition explores the meaning of the Eden story for our individual spiritual relationship with the source of all creation. Jewish mystical and especially kabbalistic thought has understood that story of exile as explaining our improvident exile of ourselves (as mortal beings, not specifically as Jews) from the physical manifestation of God, the longed-for feminine Shekhinah. The Zohar, for instance, develops that concept through a grammatical ambiguity in the Hebrew text *vaygaresh et-ha-adam* (Gen. 3:24), normally translated, "And he [God] drove out the man." The mystical interpretation advances the following revision: "We naturally suppose that 'he' is the subject and 'man' the object. The truth is, however, that 'man' is the subject and the object is the accusative particle *et,* so that we render 'and [he] the man drove out *et.*' Hence it is written, 'And God sent him forth from the Garden of Eden,' for the reason that he [man] had divorced [i.e., driven out] *et.*" According to that linguistically grounded interpretation, the word *et,* which normally precedes and therefore simply designates a grammatical object, is taken to be the object itself (like the English pronoun *it*), and *et* is thereby understood to mean the divine presence in the world, our erstwhile companion the Shekhinah.[29] In this metaphoric way human beings have all exiled the divine from themselves, so that loss of Eden means we have had to turn to words to substitute for direct experience.

The story of the Tower of Babel (Gen. 11) is more than a legend explaining the origins of language; it is also an allegory of the difficulty attendant upon being left with language as the medium through which we must apprehend reality and share experiences when we dwell as aliens from one another. The Tower of Babel leads to the confusion of languages, the de-creative act, a perfect mockery of the clarity of divine locution in which word equals fact and becomes fact, with no ambiguity. Divine speech comprehends and is comprehended by matter, whereas human speech after the Tower of Babel fails to communicate correctly to the human auditor. The demonstration of how distant humans are from God follows as their speech fails to connect with action and matter, fails to bring something into being. Those seventy languages produce noise, a clatter or cacophony, neither the language of prayer nor the piety of silence. Only when the Messiah comes will the problem of language be solved. Rosenzweig quoted Zephaniah 3:9, the pledge that the messianic age will both reunify and refine language: "Yea, at that time I will change the speech of the peoples to a pure speech, that all of them may call upon the name of the Lord and serve God with one accord."[30] André Neher in turn recalled Rosenzweig's insights to remind us of "the silence of Jewish Messianism," consisting of the fact that because the Messiah has not yet arrived, "the Messiah's word has not yet been spoken."[31]

So the Babel story is a parable of communication within our current human condition. Because we are not one—you and I, I and thou—we must speak. In so doing, we erect our individual structures of meaning, reference, experience; all of us speak our own tongues. As Rosenzweig expressed it, "Everyone must translate and everyone does translate. . . . Everyone has his own language if there were really such a thing as a monologue, . . . if all speech were not really dialogue to begin with, and hence translation."[32] Language's performative element complicates the dialogue: conscious of I, you, and it (the ostensible subject or the text in itself), I value the singularity of the sound of my voice, rendering more difficult the task of the "translator." Silence seems less valuable and less attainable, even that spiritual silence in which we are all joined as listeners attempting to understand. We glimpse that state of spiritual perfection in rare moments of artistic appreciation when an audience, as if joined together by the performance, seems to lose its sense of individuation to become one; in rare moments also a religious experience may attain a religious end. One such moment: "It happened during a Shabbat meal. Our holy teacher, the Tzaddik of Worke, was presiding. Lost in thought, he looked at us and at the twilight looming behind us, and said nothing; and we, at his table, listened and said nothing. For a while we could hear only the buzzing of flies on the walls; then we didn't even hear that. . . . Finally we heard only the silence that emanated from the Rebbe united with our own; solemn and grave, but passionate and vibrant, it called for beauty and friendship. We had rarely experienced such communion."[33] Returning to language returns us to time, process, and separateness.

A midrashic commentary on, "Therefore was its name called Babel" (Gen. 11:9), suggests that the Babel story holds the kernel of all our miscommunications and befuddlements. "A disciple of Rabbi Yokhanan was sitting before him and could not grasp his teaching, 'What is the cause of this?' the teacher demanded. 'It is because I am exiled from my home,' replied the pupil. 'Whence do you come?' inquired he. 'From Borsif,' he answered. 'That is not its name,' he rejoined, 'but Balsif,' in accordance with the text, 'Because there the Lord did confound (*bilbel*) the language (*safat*) of all the earth.' "[34] Metacritically, the midrash illustrates the result of that confounding, when the pupil from Borsif, near Babylon, seems to have linguistic difficulty understanding his teacher, and the teacher alleges that even the name of that town is simultaneously the testimony and the result of the primal linguistic confusion. On a deeper level, the profound connections of thought, language, and place seem to be registered in the pupil's laconic, oblique reply to the teacher's first question, which contains a nuance not developed in the midrash. The answer given to "Why don't you understand?" proves not to be the specific "I don't understand that word or pronunciation," a reply that would suggest a lexical or dialectal problem. Instead, he responds with the epistemologically far-reaching "Because I am exiled from my home," as if exile itself caused thorough disorientation or failure of comprehension. One becomes exiled from words and into words, so that the foreign vocabulary or even intonations and rhythms comprise the medium through which one remains conscious of being exiled in the word.

Here again Peter Gay's citation of Freud's comments on stylistics seems apposite. " 'A clear and unambiguous manner of writing,' [Freud] said in *The Psychopathology of Everyday Life*, 'teaches us that here the author is at one with himself,' while, in contrast, 'where we find a strained and tortuous expression,' we recognize the presence of an 'inadequately settled and complicated idea or the stifled voice of the author's self-criticism.' "[35] Freud describes the psychological equivalents of being at home in language ("at one" with oneself) and being exiled in it, "inadequately settled" or "stifled." Freud's formulation was restated in more political terms by George Orwell in his post–World War II essay "Politics and the English Language," in which he similarly argued that tortuous style reveals self-deception, confusion, or duplicity. Freud's positive assertion is intellectually and even morally problematic, of course; although clarity and unambiguity in one's statements might be psychologically healthy because it expresses the absence of inner conflicts, that absence might betoken only that one is ignorant or has made oneself oblivious of the errors or deleterious consequences of one's statements. Are the pronouncements of tyrants not usually clear and unambiguous? Notwithstanding this caveat, Freud correctly recognizes how deeply language relates, as source and effect, to the formation of our entire inner being.

We can apply this to a specific example. Primo Levi's poem "Cantare" is dated 3 January 1946, one year after his liberation from the Buna-Monowitz labor camp, a satellite facility of Auschwitz. The poem begins provocatively with elision marks and the conjunction *ma* (but), as if to start by jolting us into the latter part of a recollection whose earlier portions hold tales neither to be spoken of directly nor to be silenced. More as context than as past, those experiences rise from the poem's language, like moaning intrusions from another frequency, continuing to be heard in the midst of the songs to which the poem only alludes. In this poem Levi does not describe life in the *Lager,* but he evokes it just beyond the denotative margins of the text.

> . . . Ma quando poi cominciammo a cantare
> Le buone nostre canzoni insensate,
> Allore avvenne che tutte le cose
> Furono ancora com'erano state.
>
> Un giorno non fu che un giorno:
> Sette fanno una settimana.
> Cosa cattiva ci parve uccidere;
> Morire, una cosa lontana.
>
> E i mesi passano piuttosto rapidi,
> Ma davanti ne abbiamo tanti!
> Fummo di nuovo soltanto giovani:
> Non martiri, non infami, non santi.
>
> Questo ed altro ci veniva in mente
> Mentre continuavamo a cantare;
> Ma erano cose come le nuvole,
> E difficili da spiegare.

But when we started singing
Those good foolish songs of ours,
Then everything was again
As it always had been.

A day was no more than a day,
Seven make up a week.
To kill seemed like something wicked;
To die, something remote.

The months go by at a rapid pace,
But so many still lie ahead!
Once again we were just young fellows:
Not martyrs, not scoundrels, not saints.

This and that came to our minds
While we sang on;
But they were like the clouds,
And hard to explain.[36]

These songs link the present through the memory to a normal past, comfortingly mundane. Similarly mundane was the time when one could be merely a youth, safe from the present, in which one acquires a designation, marked out, marked as a "marked man" or a distinguished personage, whether martyr, scoundrel, or saint. Perhaps such a past is no longer neutrally "mere youthfulness" but must be marked or defined even negatively, as "not martyrdom," "not notoriety," "not sainthood." Levi's formulation indicates both the experiential suffering and the conceptual burden of taking on the roles that others ascribed to those who were in the camps or that survivors felt by themselves, even when the burden is the relatively positive one bestowed by hagiography. Memories ride on the music, the recollection of which dominates the poem's aesthetic: the strophic form, rhyme, and musicality of the language, all of which are atypical in Levi's work. The songs, insensate, are not important for what they may denote; however, they must be sung.

Notwithstanding Keats's claim that unheard melodies are sweeter than those that are heard, Levi eschews the romantic immersion into a recollection of personal significance; he does not call attention to any particular melody rich with a specific memory or associations. Instead, he gives us the collective experience of people whose suffering is collective in its origin and in its experience. This is not a reminiscence about "my youth" or of the days "when we were young together" but the recollection of a time when it was still possible to be merely young. Regardless of what is sung, group singing affirms some shared experiential reality. Indeed, at the point at which the memories promise to become most personal, Levi the poet obscures them in clouds: they were, he claims, *come le nuvole,* hard to explain, and consequently not to be spoken of. The personal recollection, the private experience, remains private, a mark of Levi's characteristic reticence in writing of his inner life except in regard to camp-related circumstances. In addition, Levi espouses the idea that the merely personal is—at least in the face of the common situation—insubstantial and therefore far less worthy of serious record than the collective consciousness of the gap separating now from then.

Shared memory seems to carry not only mutual experience but the promise of life beyond the individual, beyond in both numbers and spiritual transcendence that is valuable when it can be communicated. For example, in *Survival in Auschwitz* the narrator is not satisfied merely to recall for himself verses from the Canto of Ulysses in Dante's *Commedia;* it is necessary that he transmit them as a legacy of civilization to a young, uneducated fellow inmate.[37] Levi's poetic record of the life of memory and hope in the camps expresses most often a temporally and socially composite experience whose typical grammar is plural. Another of his poems, "Alzarsi," ("Get Up") substantiates this.

> Sognavamo nelle notti feroci
> Sogni densi e violenti
> Sognati con anima e corpo:
> Tornare; mangiare; raccontare. . . .
> Ora abbiamo ritrovato la casa,
> Il nostro ventre è sazio,
> Abbiamo finto di raccontare.
>
> In the brutal nights we'd dream
> Dense violent dreams
> Dreamed with soul and body:

To return; to eat; to tell the story. . . .
Now we have found our homes again,
Our bellies are full,
We've finished telling the story.[38]

In this survivor's representation of the group's consciousness, and not to
him alone, narrating is as important as returning and eating; it has become the
third essential term in a tripartite reconstituting of life. The infinitive forms of
the verbs in the poem's fourth line imply an ongoing process of returning
(perhaps to all of the dimensions of one's life), eating, and telling. Such open-
endedness (which is not necessarily optimistic but at least suggestive of a continuing future) is terminated by the past-tense closure of these actions in the
beginning of the second stanza. To return means to find the house again; to eat
means filling the stomach. And what of *raccontare*, to tell? To say it and have
done with saying it—*finito*—posits that the telling can be finished.

But is it ever? Perhaps imagining that it can be is only wishful thinking.
Contrast the rushing turbulence of the first three lines, "dense and violent" not
solely in imagery but even more strikingly in phonic and metric structure, with
the laconic but prosodically rigid austerity of the fourth line; there, the three
unadorned and stolidly assonantal verbs, segregated from each other by their
semicolons, convey the predictable sterility of a grammatical paradigm. The
wished-for future life seems almost primitive when glimpsed through this
forthright articulation of three needs, this outline of a simple life paratactic in
its structure of behavior, uncomplicated by hierarchizing, unpresumptuous
about positing connections.[39] There are none. Prioritizing occurs only through
the clear logic of a simple sequence: to go back, to eat, to recount. Because
those verbs are disconnected from one another by Levi's use of the semicolon,
they complement the disconnectedness of the actions to which they refer. We
recognize that the first two are clearly self-referential: returning is something
that one does oneself, regardless of whether one returns to anyone or anything
in particular, just as eating does not necessarily involve anyone else's presence.
Perhaps less obviously, telling may be just as self-referential. Levi noted in his
prose works the prisoners' fears that they would not be believed back in the
normal world, even if they were to survive.

The vast possibility implied through the verb *raccontare*, unconstrained by a
grammatical direct object (as if one might tell anything and everything) or an

indirect object (as if it were immaterial to whom one told) seems to be snapped like the poet's heart by a jagged and alien Polish imperative. " 'Wstawać': / E si spezzava in petto il cuore" (" 'Get up!' / And the heart cracked in the breast"). Although it does not prescribe any precise activity, the Polish word (untranslated in the poem except through the title) bespeaks an experiential specificity that carries its environment with it. The word becomes the verbal echo of the camp.[40] Precisely because it is not Levi's normal Italian *alʒarsi*, the word contextualizes far more than it denotes. It proclaims, not only by what it says but by saying it in Polish, the inescapable fact of being caught in the system of the camp. Quietly and matter-of-factly spoken in the camp, this word ended the tempestuous dreams and (seemingly) the hopes for the future that those dreams expressed. Now that those hopes have been realized, the word itself foreshadows at the poem's end the end of dreams, the end of life.[41]

> È tempo. Presto udremo ancora
> Il comando straniero:
> "Wstawać."

> It's time. Soon we'll hear again
> The strange command:
> "Wstawać."

Such is the power, whether insidious or tenacious, of language. This foreign directive will suggest either the last reveille or the persistence of memory. The last stanza indicates that everything that one wanted to do, hoped to do, or dreamed of doing has been done and that all is finished, allowing the camp word to represent the final awakening into death; a *comando straniero,* an alien command, it is like a voice from the other side, the *sitra aḥra* (as the world beyond the grave is known in Jewish lore). The suggestion seems appropriate, given the command's historical association in the camps with brutalization and death. Such a reading certainly accords with the mythology of Levi's depression. Still, given the early date of this poem (precisely given as 11 January 1946), one may prefer the interpretation that the survivor understands that this word will bear the memory that cannot be long repressed after those desires of liberation (to go back, to eat, to recount) have been satisfied. Once the simple goals are attained and there is nothing more to which one looks forward, the Buna-Monowitz concentration camp remains the past place whose memories are inescapable. Not only do words carry memory as vehicles for explaining or narrating experience, but they also carry memory because one could say that they are a form of experience. Memories arise from verbal evocations, which therefore seem horrid parodies of the way that songs sung in the camp linked uprooted and nameless people with their normal past. The tale may be recounted, but the bad magic of this word refuses to be quieted.

Levi himself ascribed the tonal dryness characteristic of both his prose and poetry to his individual character and craving for justice. Artistic control rather than the venting of anger characterizes his writings, but not because he was an aesthete. Indeed, the reverse was true. He wrote, "My personal temperament is not inclined to hatred. I regard it as bestial. . . . I prefer justice. Precisely for this reason, when describing the tragic world of Auschwitz, I have deliberately assumed the calm, sober language of the witness, neither the lamenting tones of the victim nor the irate voice of someone seeking revenge. . . . Only in this way does a witness in matters of justice perform his task, which is that of preparing the ground for the judge. The judges are my readers."[42] Slipping behind the author's public language, we notice that this measured pitch of voice is one he had to take on. His lean narrative style results from the labor of self-restraint, and his poem is the product of the labor of reclaiming speech from that special silence in which it is possible to sing what one remembers but not possible to speak of what one has undergone.

We live in language, because reality slips from us. For all of us, but especially those who grapple with the unseen and intangible realities, Freud's words still should seem vital: "Psychology we can describe only with the aid of analogies. That is nothing unusual; the same is true elsewhere. But we must keep changing these analogies; none of them bears up long enough."[43] We should not be concerned, therefore, that the verbal paradigms for theories, ideologies, and theologies change. Rather, we should worry when they hang about unchanged for too long. We live in language but must not forget that we are never fully at home in it. We live exiled in language.

Censors and terror squads alike work by silencing people; in less horrid but more pervasive ways we censor, silence, and repress ourselves and one another. Our lives record the damages of what is said and unsaid. Sometimes the repression occurs on the grand scale of national politics. During the congressional political repression of dissent in the United States during the early 1950s, the challenge to witnesses before the Senate Select Committee and the

House Un-American Affairs Committee was to "name names," to designate people with leftist sympathies by naming them as having been present at meetings or associating with those who had. To be a "named person" under repressive South African legislation meant not only that one was banned from public gatherings but also that one could not be quoted in print, a remarkable instance of the use of one's name as a way to silence one.

But such political usage carries into public an understanding we grasp familiarly in ordinary circumstances. Consider that a child's name spoken with a rising inflection serves as a warning about behavior; with a falling inflection, it is likely to condemn what has just been said or done; and to the child usually addressed by a nickname or endearment, the full formal name constitutes a verbal stick. To withhold speech, to give someone the silent treatment, can mean administering a soundless beating the pain of which is felt only inside, although it is real pain. This is a form of violence that one could truly say pains both parties, however, because the repressive silence of the silent, as much as the suppressed speech of the muted, weighs down with a painful burden that gets heavier as the silence continues, as the unspoken builds. Adrienne Rich has written of the tension between one's "swirling wants" and the lover's "frozen lips." But the one whose lips are frozen is also recoiling from suffering and therefore withdrawing into silence's security.[44] The adolescent boy in one of Nadine Gordimer's short stories recognized that something had gone wrong in his family when personal communications changed. "My mother and father were almost silent at meals. The private language we used to speak together—cat-language—we didn't use any more. . . . We have a different kind of voice for each of the three cats I have here, and we used to pretend the cats were making remarks about us. . . . But the cats stopped speaking; they became just cats. I couldn't be the only one to use their voices. A child can't use even a cat voice to ask: what's the matter? You can't ask grown-ups that."[45]

Within relationships, language is the miner's canary. Like the playful ventriloquism in this story, the special terms of endearment lovers choose for each other will be among the earliest casualties of the bad air. This is not confined to the home. In those wars that we term "civil" and amid the hatreds of racial, religious, and ethnic hostilities, those whom one might have called neighbor, sister, brother, or countryman are instead decked with the labels of hostility, contempt, and fear. Conversation turns into Caliban's snarl, "You taught me language, and my profit on't / Is, I know how to curse."[46] In a corrosive environment, pronouns will record the split as *we* divides into *us* and *them*. Neighbors become "those people," until intensifying hatred leads to the dropping of "people" and its replacement with something nonhuman, something dehumanizing. Long before that, we are no longer on speaking terms.

We live and die amid the spoken and unspoken, resulting in the power of Kol Nidre and the even more imposing power of the principle that the prayers of atonement from Rosh Hashanah through Yom Kippur atone only for one's relationship with God. Atonement of one's relationship with another person depends on making amends or asking forgiveness. Not once but repeatedly during that time, we name specifically and confess collectively litanies of sins. We articulate even sins that we do not think we have committed because by bringing them forth through speech we may be struck with recognition. Although we may agree with Fyodor Tyutchev's claim that an idea spoken is a lie, we surely know that the idea not spoken also lies.

The silences of tales untold carry their own pain. At the end of one of Grace Paley's short stories, appropriately entitled "Listening," the friend of the main character (who is a writer) turns to her with an accusatory question: "Listen, Faith, why don't you tell my story? You've told everybody's story but mine." The narrator's tales of heterosexual relationships—as the friend, Cassie, summarizes this, "women and men, women and men, fucking, fucking"—ignore the particular natural reality of her lesbian friend. Invisible, Cassie feels dismissed. "Where is *my* life?" Her complaint makes clear that she is not demanding merely that Faith write about lesbian relationships. Rather, she wants something more important: to know that her sort of life is seen, remembered, acknowledged as one of the ways in which people live. Despite Faith's personal cordiality, which Cassie grants, if Faith's fiction overlooks her, Cassie knows that Faith has pushed her friend's affectional life beyond the margins of her own awareness. Faith grasps the core issue: "It must feel for you like a great absence of yourself."[47] Her attempt at an apology is rebuffed, however, by Cassie's indication that their friendship will now be joined by vigilance.

Paley's story illustrates a connection between the personal and political. The marginalized or excluded person feels impelled to insist on the recognition that comes partly through acknowledgment of one's stories. Such connections have been insisted on increasingly in our own time in academic syllabi and curricula, in pulpits, prayer books, and hymnals, by those seeking to end their involuntary exile from the word.

7

Exiles from Their Words

"For humanity he speaks?"
—*Cynthia Ozick*

"As one of the dumb, voiceless ones I speak. One of the millions of immigrants beating, beating out their hearts at your gates for a breath of understanding."[1] In these words of Anzia Yezierska—words declaring their collective rather individualistic significance—we can hear a voice from Jewish history speaking out of a Jewish experience. The author's family was among the huge numbers of Eastern European Jewish immigrants from shtetls and urban ghettos who came to the United States early in the twentieth century. That remarkable period of migration did not constitute only a Jewish experience, however; the author's phrasing recognizes it as broadly composite. Yezierska's transgressive act—although one of the "dumb, voiceless," she speaks—impels her to shun both the ethnic specificity of her experience and the drive for purely personal success. Taking on her prophetic role leads her to address not the particular concerns of Jews or Jewish immigrants or, in this instance, even those of women; instead, she speaks to the millions of newcomers to the United States who may have felt that their talents were being left fallow even as their hopes withered. Her seeming humility in sharing alleged voicelessness "as one . . . of the millions" actually gives her the privilege to speak on behalf of them.

But the writer who "speaks" as "one of the millions" has put aside her quest for a personal voice, the distinctive style and personal story characterizing the art most highly valued by the individualistic culture of the modern and western world. Finding a voice, she endangers her artistry by risking the loss of her particular voice. Tucked between "ones" and "speak," her "I" seems to lose the focus of identity as it attempts to place itself at the fulcrum, balancing those voiceless millions on the one side and her own speech on the other. If the burden is the prophet's, so too is the risk. However, the lips of the prophet of the divine are purified by the touch of holy fire to speak of truths eternal emitting from a source that is one. The prophet of peoples at a moment in history speaks with time-bound words of the pressing needs of a changing multitude. Although the needs of the people are no less real, even urgent, the individual trying to articulate a common theme in a clear voice will likely grope for the key lost amid the silent dissonance of so many yearnings, including her own, overwhelmed by (as Adrienne Rich phrased it in a different context) "My swirling wants. Your frozen lips."[2] Yezierska had her literary and prophetic moment and in it she claimed a reshaped identity and a transformed role.

Hers proves after all to be a familiar Jewish revelation, discovering that one's personal story is actually the same as the story of a people. However, as a postemancipation universalist vision, it also expresses a specifically modern Jewish consciousness. Yezierska's pronouncement implies that her own Jewish story is after all a minor one among the tales of the world. To many assimilated Jews that means the Jewish story was most interesting and gratifying in the chapters covering events long ago; in the modern era, everyone else's story is more important than one's own. Perhaps that contributes to the contemporary focus on the Holocaust among even assimilated Jews, and it may have contributed to the somewhat earlier passion for Zionism. In the destruction of European Jewry and, to a narrower extent, in the formation of a modern Jewish nation, Jews and non-Jews could perceive Jewish experiences uncontestably significant amid the chronicles of modern civilizations.

Absorbing universalism was a consequence of the Haskalah, the Jewish branch of the Enlightenment movement, dating from the last decades of the eighteenth century. Is this cultural maturity, nobility of vision, or stifling of one's own past? To say, "I am not a Jew, but everyone": Is that nobly self-effacing, or does it hide identity, the ideological equivalent of cosmetic surgery? Driven by the conviction that improvements in the lives of Jews would follow from casting off the traits of sectarian difference and adopting modern European languages, manners, and secular learning, Jews often attempted to integrate themselves totally into societies in which they lived previously without full legal rights. Benjamin Harshav has observed that many Jews came to believe that "the real road to equality led through entering the dominant Christian society. Individual Jews assimilated or converted to Christianity and entered the Gentile economic, political, and cultural structures."[3] Although others effected more positive transformations within Judaism, Harshav shows, they did so in ways that implicitly or explicitly declared themselves freed from the historically evolved conceptions of what being Jewish entailed. The newly liberated or defined selves sometimes articulated the cultural language or self-conceptualizations of earlier biblical Jewish models; however, they frequently strove for more contemporary, cosmopolitan accents. (This difference would have political analogues, for example, in the Zionist tension between developing a state upon the religious and social teachings of Judaism or developing a state guaranteeing a national home for Jews but otherwise a nation like all other nations.) Amending the Haskalah Jew's self-identification as a French or German citizen "of the Mosaic faith," many later Jews would choose to define themselves principally by a national identity although "Jewish by birth" or "ethnically Jewish."

Again, it is important to recall that the Jewish responses to cultural alienation or exclusion should be taken as paradigmatic, not unique. The light-skinned Jamaican-born writer Michelle Cliff named the process of recovering her connection with her black ancestors "Claiming an Identity They Taught Me to Despise."[4] Her "they" includes her family members who found it easier and preferable to "pass" as white. One form of passing is through physical assimilation; mental assimilation is another. As has been observed before and by others, a paradox of Jewish culture (notwithstanding its alleged particularism) is that Jews, inheritors of a prophetic tradition, have so often taken on the universalist role of the prophet in the modern world to give testimony and redemptive speech to others. It may be more gratifying or ennobling to speak for "all of humanity," than for "Jews like me." However, the writer's bond with community is lived through style and the store of stories forming one's cultural inheritance.

In "Dream-Vision" Tillie Olsen writes of an elderly Jewish woman, the narrator's mother, one of that generation of twentieth-century immigrants from czarist Russia, who long ago turned her back on all religion, rejecting oppressive traditional structures. This mother has a vision transforming the Christmas tale by means of her own maternal connections with babies. In place of the magi appear "old country women of her childhood" singing a lullaby for a baby "breathing the universal sounds every human baby makes, sounds out of which are made all the separate languages of the world." The episode lets us glimpse creation before Babel, sound as not only potential but common, rather than divided or divisive. This dream child embodies, as the narrator's mother says, "the human baby before we are misshapen; crucified into a sex, a color, a walk of life, a nationality . . . and the world yet warrings and winter."[5] The Christian story of Jesus's birth is thus accepted for its supposed universality through being reinterpreted (in an essentially midrashic manner) by a Jew who grasps the emotional relevance of solstice rituals and finds profound wisdom in the nativity tale. This same Jew, however, has discarded any Jewish obser-vance—Chanukah, for instance. One could cite countless similar examples, textual and historical, in which the universal is not merely added to the Jewish but replaces it. Does one know of many non-Jews who so early smother their own particularism (Christian or otherwise) to embrace Judaism's humanistic universality? Or is their verbal embrace of Jewish tradition more likely smoth-ering, obliterating it by subsuming it into someone else's particularism?

These passages suggest that we can understand exile as including a form of internal exile, exile from one's particular group or cultural identity. Unlike examples we will consider in the final chapters, Yezierska and Olsen are not deprived of public language. Even the mother in Olsen's story is at last given her say. However, although they are Jews who write and speak, they seem to exile themselves from Jewish speaking. Universalism authorizes their speech. They allow themselves to write as long as they do not claim Jewishness as either subject or point of view.

That both authors are female and feminist is relevant. The relationship be-tween Judaism and feminism has long been problematic, particularly for Jewish feminists, who may feel ambivalent about reconciling priorities. One may ponder, am I at this point principally a feminist who is also Jewish and therefore concerned with sensitivity toward Jewish issues within feminist thought and activism, or am I principally a Jew trying to shape the practice and thought of Judaism in the light of my feminist understanding of behavior and concepts?

The answer is not simply private. It may determine in what community one speaks, in what community one is heard.

But neither is feminism determinative. Absorption of Christian mythology is not narrowly a product of feminist alienation from traditional Judaism: that can be evinced from numerous other works of art by male Jews. Sholem Asch's trilogy of novels on the life of Jesus and Chagall's famous painting depicting Jesus as a prayer shawl–wrapped shtetl Jew on the cross are merely examples. Philip Roth's story "The Conversion of the Jews" plays provocatively with the conceptual division between Judaism and Christianity. Centering on a Jewish boy who will not accept his mother's ethnocentrism or his rabbi's rationalism, Roth creates in Ozzie Freedman a character whose ideas and attitudes are profoundly Jewish and yet whose rhetoric proves to be either universalist or Christian.

The Jewish Ozzie emerges through his alienating conflicts with the authorities around him. An inveterate questioner, Ozzie refuses to accept passively his mother's obsession with Jewish people rather than general humankind or to accept the rabbi's glib accommodation of religion to sociology and logic. A victim of his exasperated mother's impatience with his persistent disputes of Rabbi Binder's religious-school talks, this scion of a martyr people demands that his mother "never hit anybody about God." An instinctive believer in miracles, he also refuses to accept his rabbi's dismissal of Jesus on grounds of natural laws: Ozzie insists that God rules nature and is not ruled by it, consequently "God can do Anything," even "make a child without intercourse." In passionately pursuing his convictions on these issues, he risks martyrdom by climbing to the synagogue roof like Moses going up to Mount Sinai; the whole community, including his two principal antagonists, gathers below him. From there he thunders down his insistence that they accept his commandments, acknowledging God as capable of doing "anything," promising not to do anyone violence on account of religion.

Along with the Jewish text, however, runs a Christian text. The Christian Ozzie insists that all kneel to make their pledge, an un-Jewish worship posture, and although he first presses only God's omnipotence, he then "made them all say they believed in Jesus Christ—first one at a time, then all together." The narrator describes it as "the catechizing." When Ozzie descends from his substitute mountaintop into a world he has converted to believe in God's absolute power, the boy steps "into the center of the yellow net that glowed . . . like an overgrown halo."[6] Petty tyrant in the tradition of the furious, short-tempered near-legendary rabbis glowing with religious intensity, a zaddik, Ozzie is also ringed with the halo of Christian symbology, rather than radiant from within like Moses when he descends from the mountain.

The author's confrontational title seems to rejoice in the ambiguity, which is thorough. For although the behavior of the rabbi and all the faithful Jews around him might appear dismaying and blasphemous, a Jewish principle holds that saving a life takes precedent over virtually all religious commandments. By threatening his own life, or appearing to, Ozzie has compelled all of them to a lesser violation. On the other hand, the surnames also shape the issues of the story. To see this as the conflict of the rabbi as Binder versus the universalist child as Freedman is to see it as a confrontation between narrow and confining strictures—not just of religion in general but of a particular religion, Judaism—and the emancipation of free thought, reaching out to encompass all of humanity and a god of miracles, a god who makes Christianity possible. If Ozzie is an Isaac refusing to be a martyr ("Be a martin!" the other children shout in urging him to jump from the roof), he also refuses the testimony of faith expected of Isaac by his father, Abraham, the binder. (The Mount Moriah episode, so often termed "the sacrifice of Isaac" in Christological readings, is known to Jews as the *akedah*, the binding.) Nor is the contest a draw. One side bows to the other, and the champion comes forth to accept his halo.

A contemporaneous story by one of Roth's older peers, Bernard Malamud, can help sharpen our grasp on the temptations of universalism. "The Lady of the Lake" is so unsubtle in its symbolism, in fact all but allegorical, that the author did not include it in his own selected stories; nonetheless, it illustrates a point. The protagonist, an American Jew named Henry Levin, has traveled to Lake Maggiore hoping for a romantic adventure. There, he meets and falls in love with a hauntingly beautiful young Italian woman, the tantalizing and aristocratic but wistful inhabitant of a secluded island estate. Returning his affection, she oddly inquires whether he is Jewish; he, however, has passed socially with an assumed name, adopting an air of false gentility as if he were trying hard to be worthy of a place in a Henry James story. Persistently probing, she even asks him whether the seven mountain peaks of the horizon look like a menorah, a word he pretends not to know so as not to be tricked into revealing an identity that would spoil his chances with her. And again he denies her direct question. At last, of course, desperate to marry her, Henry is rebuffed. She and her father are not nobility but merely caretakers, and, furthermore, they are Jewish survivors of Buchenwald; too late he sees the numbers tattooed on her chest. She had been reluctant to reveal this to him directly, hopeful that he would respond affirmatively to her. "I can't marry you," she announces. "We are Jews. My past is meaningful to me. I treasure what I suffered for."[7] Because she has put the issue in such terms, Henry cannot even offer a belated admission.

Malamud has played the Holocaust as a trump card here. He is not the only Jewish writer of the latter half of the twentieth century to perceive that phenomenon as definitional for Jewish identity; to deny one's Jewishness (Judaism being another issue) after the destruction of European Jewry is to erect a false boundary that merely cuts one off from other Jews without making one safe. Henry has assumed a false surname because "Levin" tags him with a Jewishness that is part of a past he feels to be too narrow for him in his new role of cosmopolitan traveler. He feels, we are told, "tired of the past—of the limitations it has imposed upon him."[8] Emancipating himself from the limitations of the past through that adopted name and the pretended non-Jewish identity accompanying it, he loses the one person who could have transformed his life. The surname he had bestowed upon himself was "Freeman."

Commitments to humanity as a whole are certainly part of Jewish ethical teachings; Jewish religious tradition calls us to wider moral involvements. Some sages have criticized Noah ("righteous *in his generation*") for being too narrowly engrossed with saving his own household, rather than pleading with God to show mercy as did Abraham and Moses. The burden that Jonah tried to shirk by sailing toward Tarshish rather than preaching to Nineveh was that of trying to save the lives of sinners whom he thought of as enemies. Cultural experience, moral integrity, doubtless at times guilt and self-repression (and even self-hatred) have often moved Jews to universalism at the expense of their own ethnic or religious concerns. Such motives were among the influences on Jews active in labor, civil rights, and human rights movements (for instance, the Jewish civil libertarians who have defended the rights of American Nazis to demonstrate in public). Passionately, eloquently, often effectively they spoke for the rights of a class or for the interests of a principle, rather than the concerns of their own group. Without disparaging the principles of the individuals or the value of the causes, one might recognize a disparity. There are Jews who find their public voices most readily when not speaking as or for Jews. There are Jews in exile from Jewish speech.

Who, however, is not exiled from language when we recognize, as sooner or later we each recognize, what we cannot, dare not, will not say? Computer simulators speak of virtual reality, the suggestion of full-dimensional experience achieved by complex computer-generated modeling of invented spaces and objects. Through language we connect with, "virtually" touch one another; and we bring into living space our ideas and observations. Or we choose silence, refrain from touching, acknowledging, admitting. Judith Herzberg, a modern Dutch Jewish poet, has written about acquaintances evading and avoiding communicating the truth of an abusive relationship,

> When I ask: why don't you leave?
> she'd say if she were honest, but she isn't
> she says, so I don't ask.

On the personal level (but it could also be the political level) this stanza admits silent complicity. Strikingly, the one who claims not to be honest is the one who admits verbally that she is not. Instead of meeting frankness, we puzzle through a seeming syllogism reminiscent of Zeno's paradox of the liar. On what basis do we believe anyone's candor? The equilibrium of the relationship is destabilized by the disparity between the hypothetically spoken question that is actually suppressed and the honest answer that is evaded by being given. The final stanza traces the implications within silences to which the two speakers leave themselves.

> Then she could say oh meaning
> that's what you'd like, and I could say no
> and think yes and not be able to explain.[9]

These are not silences of suppression or repression; more specifically, they are the silences of what cannot fully be said, within which is hidden the unspoken text.

Herzberg acknowledges in another poem the power within a lie—"unsharing of thoughts"—to be "destructive," "dangerous," "worse and much more dead" than dying itself. Her speaker urges forthrightness: "if I don't trust what I know / you'll be a stranger."[10] Together with others of her works, this poem notes the capacity of false words, as much as withheld words, to alienate. Discreet about connecting her personal past to her poetry, Herzberg does not explicitly explore that past; her translator says she does not exploit it. Knowing that she survived the German occupation in hiding while her parents were taken to concentration camps, knowing that she divides her time now between the different linguistic and cultural environments of Amsterdam and Tel Aviv, one may suspect that underlying her poetic sensitivities is the special awareness of someone acquainted with hiding, not saying, feeling alienated by not trusting what one knows, eeking out the meanings within the unsaid passages. Her poem "1945" speaks of "having heroes to tea" but "They didn't have a thing / to say" because they could not cope "with such peace."[11] Heroes, they yet have been disarmed by war; survivors, they are disabled in the country of language.

Exile is not a uniquely Jewish experience. Meliboeus's lament in Vergil's First Eclogue—"we must give up our country's sweet fields, . . . we have to move on. . . . I shall sing no more songs"—may sound to the Bible-reader very much like the Jewish lamentation that arose during Babylonian captivity, "How shall we sing songs of Adonai in an alien land?"[12] Regarding exile, however, one might say that Jews have special, although not unique, expertise. Jews have written the book on exile. It is a polyglot text, and each shift of language records awareness of the struggles and losses that have accompanied and sometimes overwhelmed the gains. Jewish responses to our innumerable expulsions, flights, and migrations bear witness to the nature of every exile from place and from language.

Henry Roth's *Call It Sleep*, a superb novel of an immigrant child's youth in pre–World War I Brooklyn, captures the cultural dislocation and attests to the energies contained within the exile's circumstances. Roth's literary silence following this book probably communicates the consequences of losing those energies with the dissipation of bilingualism and diglossia through the passage of time and changes in the ethnic community. In a fine essay on this novel, Hana Wirth-Nesher summarizes the protagonist's linguistic situation:

While Yiddish is the spoken language of the home, . . . Hebrew and Aramaic are also foreign tongues, the sounds being as incomprehensible to his ear as they would be to that of the English-speaking reader. Yet they are part of his home culture, because they are central components of his Jewish identity. Thus, David is bilingual and multicultural, his bilingualism consisting of Yiddish and English, and his multiple cultures consisting of Yiddish as home and everyday life, English as the street and the culture to which he is assimilating, and Hebrew and Aramaic as the mysterious languages, the sacred tongues, that represent mystical power to him and that initiate him into the Jewish world. Moreover,

Yiddish, Hebrew, and Aramaic are all languages of his Jewish culture, while American English, the language of the author's primary literacy, is the language of the "other" in that it is the language of Christianity.[13]

As this description indicates, the languages show David as not merely divided between two cultures (American and Jewish) but at least three, for his Jewish environment is itself split between the secular (experienced at home through the mother tongue) and sacred (engaged in the religious school through the holy tongue). Also present is yet another language, the gentile Polish language in which his mother and aunt can speak of their past to one another while concealing it from him even as he overhears them.

Roth brilliantly conveys the linguistic negotiations to the reader as well. Words or snippets of phrases from various of these languages dot the English text, usually, though not always, translated or paraphrased but always transliterated; even the reader of Yiddish or Hebrew will sense disorientation.

The languages each carry their own emotional pitches as well as level of diction. The Yiddish of the home sounds eloquent, sometimes even elegant, yet passional; the English of the street by contrast is crude, frequently comical, often almost inarticulate, brutal. The former allows its native speakers subtle command over silences and restraints; in the latter, barely learned, they must fumble to express unnuanced facts. As Wirth-Nesher writes, sometimes "the English text read[s] as if *it* were a translation."[14] Alice Walker applies a similar strategy in her story "Everyday Use." Her narrator, a rural southern black woman, addresses the reader wittily in the prose of an educated person, though professing no more than a second-grade schooling. Only when she speaks in the story's dialogue do we hear the lack of formal education. Meeting such a person only in public conversation, we likely would not suspect the verbal fluency that Walker reveals through the narrator's unarticulated thoughts. Walker's stylistic device distinguishes between lack of education and lack of intelligence. Roth uses the differences between the inner and outer social tongues to differentiate between the significant and the mundane. Alfred Kazin has observed that Roth stretched the characteristics of each tongue to heighten Yiddish's cultural value.

By using Yiddish-English homonyms Roth suggests the cultural dislocations. Sometimes even comical (such as when David's aunt inadvertently pronounces the anodyne *cocaine* so that it sounds like the Yiddish *kockin*, "defecate"), they mark the immigrants' heightened sensitivity to the sounds and meanings of words but also their confusion. Nadine Gordimer, reflecting on difficulties of communication between immigrant black mineworkers and immigrant Jewish shopkeepers in the small South African mining town in which she grew up, noted their high level of frustration with one another. One critic has termed Roth's "the noisiest book ever written," and reading the street episodes in particular is likely to confirm that impression, for characters typically converse by shouting at one another. Furthermore, Roth's general omission of speech prefixes (regardless of what it might owe technically to modernism) runs together those bellowed exchanges in fast-paced cacophonous vollies. In keeping with the conventional wisdom that one communicates best with foreigners by yelling, regardless of whether or not they know one's language, these immigrant children and children of immigrants shout because the language of the street and of the land is not the language of their normal expression. Roth's book implies that access to speech can be distinguished from access to language. Painfully, one realizes that Roth's literary silence coincides with his gaining of adroitness in the literary language he has pursued to find a modulated public voice.

Irena Klepfisz's dramatic monologue "Fradel Shtok" explicitly addresses the crisis affecting a writer attempting to bridge a linguistic gulf.[15] The poem is based on some of the few known events in the life of the real poet named in the title. Shtok came to the United States from Galicia in Eastern Europe as a seventeen-year-old in 1907; at twenty-nine she published a collection of her works in Yiddish, and eight years later a volume in English. Not long afterward she was in a mental institution, where she died around the age of forty.

Klepfisz's angle of vision on Shtock's repression is informed by her own linguistic anxiety over speech and composition. Klepfisz was born in Warsaw in 1941 and was hidden by her mother during the war (her father was killed on the second day of the Warsaw ghetto uprising). She arrived in the United States at the age of eight, already competent in Polish (her first language and the language that hid her Jewish identity) and conversant in Swedish from a postwar stay in Sweden. Although becoming fluent in the Yiddish of her daily environment in the United States, she was virtually silenced as an English essayist by the tutelary hands marking the technical errors of grammar and spelling in her public-school compositions. Poetry, she found in an era of free verse, allowed her the poetic license to create as best she could without the anxieties attending the need to be judged correct in usage. After publishing two volumes of poems entirely in English, in her early forties Klepfisz began working in the other direction. Writing poems that speak with the two voices of English and Yiddish to raise the issue of language as a key to identity, she understands that for a multilingual speaker a choice of language constitutes more than merely a range of lexical options. In the words of Czeslow Milosz quoted as the epigraph to "Fradel Shtok," "Language is the only homeland."

As Klepfisz grasps Shtock's mental state, language and place are simply versions of one another, not only on the large scale but even—perhaps especially—on the small scale, "the distance from here / to the corner or between two sounds." It is indeed on the small scale that the dislocations in place and language are likely to become most disorienting. No traveler is likely to mistake New York City for her hometown in Galicia; the slippage occurs when the resonances or residences carry too many familiar evocations:

> Think of it: *heym* and *home* the meaning
> the same of course exactly
> but the shift in vowels was the ocean
> in which I drowned.

The poem's extended counterpoint between place and language traces Shtock's bewilderment in wandering down the street, like the victim of a collision, traversing a neighborhood where the entryways seem "slightly familiar" but "you can't place it / exactly." That topographic disorder corresponds with her phonic disorder in hearing "the vowels / shifting" and "the subtle / change in the guttural sounds" turning speech into "nothing more than babble." Klepfisz's characteristic spaces within lines to serve for punctuation and rhythmic emphasis usually seem like vocal suspensions that allow a reflective traversal across the syntactic units. In this work, especially in the last line quoted, where extra spaces separate each word, those pauses suggest more strongly the breakdown of the subject's powers of understanding and communication, leading to the point at which she must admit to herself that she truly is lost. From the physical and verbal confusion it is a small step to the psychologically cognitive disorder in the last stanza, when she does not recognize until too late that after she accedes to these voices welcoming her through the doorway, she will hear behind her the asylum's door lock. By the end of the poem her exile in the word will be complete. Yet more poignantly, the nature of the word itself has become ambiguous, and the ways in which she is lost have formed into a maze from which she has no escape.

"Water without a Tongue," a poem by the Yiddish writer Malka Heifetz Tussman, who came to America in 1912 from the Ukraine when she was sixteen, delineates what else might be found on the exile's route. Writing of an experience less destructive than Shtock's, she describes instead something reminiscent of Yezierska's, the experience of becoming inconsequential.

> The sea
> ripped a rib
> out of its side
> and said:
> Go,
> lie there,
> be for me a sign that I am
> great,
> mighty am I.
> Go,
> be for me a sign.
>
> The canal lies at my window
> Mute.
>
> What could be sadder
> than water
> without a tongue?[16]

Crucial to the poem but difficult to translate is the lexical sense of the Yiddish *loshn*, the poem's last word, meaning tongue as a physical organ, as speech, and as language (e.g., native tongue). Further, the last words of the second and third stanzas may play on the Yiddish phrase *shtum-loshn*, "sign language." On a level of diction that can even less easily be translated, the Yiddish words for sea (*yam*) and sign (*simn*) come from the language's Hebrew component, whereas those for canal (*kanal*) and water (*vaser*) derive from German. Consequently, in the original, *sea* and *sign* may resound with biblical reverberation; set against these, *canal* does actually imply something meager, motionless, without resonance, and the water lies not just soundless but uncommunicative. The canal "outside my window" expresses through its sign language not only the greatness of the sea but also the quietness of a backwater, removed from its ocean of verbal context.

That enforced isolated dumbness may be seen as expressing the problem of the Jewish writer in general and more particularly the Yiddish writer in America, whose branch of the sea is now only an artificially created, minor tributary, the presence of which meagerly betokens the great breadth and depth of the Yiddish sea. Tussman, we might note, taught in a Yiddish school in Milwaukee and subsequently lived in California, obviously not isolated from other Yiddish speakers but nonetheless detached from a society whose world-view was shaped through the Yiddish language and culture. Ernest Hemingway claimed that news does not really seem to matter for expatriates, wherever they are. Tussman indicates that the immigrant's language ceases to resonate.

Tussman's text suggests how being reduced to cultural sign language specially affects the female writer. The quiet canal is specifically associated with her by being located "outside my window" (as if this backwater is her sole connection with that sea). That canal, furthermore, is characterized in the opening lines as "a rib torn out from [the sea's] side," almost inevitably recalling not the first but the second story of woman's creation, in Genesis 2:21–22, from Adam's rib, a story making Eve a sort of tributary derivation from Adam. The canal, though grammatically masculine, is culturally feminine, quiet and subsidiary, sadly lacking a tongue or language for wider discourse, mere water without substance, effect, or majesty. It is a modest branch in the Yiddish *mame-loshen* distantly evoking memory of the great but remote sea of Hebrew letters, that vast and mighty realm traversed by generations of men who were lettered in the *loshn-koydesh*, the "holy tongue," and therefore capable of (as the saying goes) swimming in the sea of Talmud. The canal makes no sound that carries; it has no tongue in which to speak.

In a wicked story called "Envy; or, Yiddish in America," Cynthia Ozick centers on the frenzy of one Edelshtein, an aging, impoverished Yiddish poet (probably modeled on Mani Leib) desperate for someone to save his works from oblivion by translating them. His bête noir (transparently Isaac Bashevis Singer) is a much-translated, enormously popular Yiddish writer named Ostrover, whom Edelshtein both envies and despises. Confronting a potential translator who has spurned his own work, the poet challenges her esteem for Ostrover by ridiculing the other's universal appeal.

"Ostrover's the world. A pantheist, a pagan, a goy."

"That's it. You've nailed it. A Freudian, a Jungian, a sensibility. No little love stories. A contemporary. He speaks for everybody."

"Aha. Sounds familiar already. For humanity he speaks? Humanity?"

"Humanity," she said.

"And to speak for Jews isn't to speak for humanity? We're not human? We're not present on the face of the earth? We don't suffer?"

Edelshtein longs to confront the lovers of Western civilization with a question: "Suppose it turns out that the destiny of the Jews is vast, open, eternal, and that Western Civilization is meant to dwindle, shrivel, shrink into the ghetto of the world—what of history then?" Instead, he can muster to the woman who will not translate him only the declaration, "I didn't ask to be born into Yiddish. It came on me."[17] Centered in a language whose life seems to be fading along with the environment in which it flourished, Edelshtein's Yiddish poetry seems doomed. He can save it only by reshaping it to fit the ideologically amorphous and deracinated public gravitating to Ostrover, a Yiddish writer who has escaped the impediment of seeming Jewish.

Near the end of the story Edelshtein gives in to the inducement to dial a Christian messianic number advertised in the telephone booth. The voice at the other end argues, "Christ released man from Judaic exclusivism. . . . Christianity is Judaism universalized. Jesus is Moses publicized for ready availability. Our God is the God of Love, your God is the God of Wrath." Ludicrously yet not inaccurately, Edelshtein grasps the nature of his enemy: "The whole world is infected by you anti-Semites! . . . On account of you I lost everything, my whole life! On account of you I have no translator!"[18] Truths dwell within the bathos and hyperbole. Anti-Semitism seared into ashes two-thirds of the world's Yiddish speakers between 1939 and 1945; assimilation and indifference or hostility to an old-world tongue associated with life in shtetls, ghettos, and tenements reduced Yiddish to the status of dried fish wrapped in newspaper. His life's work is water lacking a tongue, a disregarded tributary of the great sea of art.

Tussman's poem, like a parable in its unstated meanings, soundlessly seems to whisper of several silences implicitly protested, and Ozick's work bellows its protest against the silencing through Edelshtein's frantic, impotent rantings. Only now, as the native speakers and native writers of Yiddish are falling silent before time, are translations published of selected works of such essential poets as Abraham Sutzkever, Kadia Molodovsky, Tussman, Yankel Glatshtein, and Moyshe-Leib Halpern, and a score of other splendid artists remain available only in anthologies, albeit now in some bilingual collections with extensive samples of their works.[19]

The muted are in vast and good company. Tillie Olsen noted the significance of "women's silence of centuries; the silences of the rest of humanity. Not until several centuries ago do women writers appear. Sons of working people, a little more than a century ago. Then black writers . . . more and more writer-mothers. Last of all, women writers, including women of color, of working class origin, perhaps one generation removed; rarest of all, the worker-mother-writer."[20] Even as one welcomes the speaking roles for those who have seemed merely silent extras on history's stage, we may strain our ears to catch the sounds of the eloquent ones who have struggled in the past to find words and bring them forth, always an adventure and a task of risk. By dedicating *Silences* to those "who begin to emerge into more flowered and rewarded use of our selves," Olson remembers that "by our achievement [we are] bearing witness to what was (and still is) being lost, silenced." Remembering how many stories are left untold, using whatever gifts of language we have seems both a privilege and an obligation both to language and to silences. To cite Adrienne Rich again, words are not merely neutral, nor can the one who uses them claim neutrality. One chooses between speech and silence, yet even to choose "is verbal privilege."[21]

Is that privilege the writer's alone? What of the verbal privilege exercised by readers and teachers who let the words lie silent in unopened and unacknowledged books, allow the tongues to fall silent along with their languages and texts? The Talmud tells us, *ta sh'ma*, "Come and hear."

8

One-Way Conversations

> What is a Jew in solitude?
> What is a woman in solitude, a queer woman
> or man?
>
> —*Adrienne Rich*

ANYONE WHO HAS BEEN to Granada, known in Moorish times as *Granat'-al-Yahud* (Granada of the Jews), will probably recall seeing in a downtown square the massive statue depicting Queen Isabella "the Catholic" handing to Columbus the royal charter for his expedition. That event occurred in 1492, following the expulsion of Jews from Spain; confiscated Jewish property helped finance the enterprise. Not far away, a far less imposing, more recent statue might be found serendipitously or hunted out by an avid visitor. On the corner of a side street near one of the former Jewish quarters stands the effigy of a solitary man in simple medieval Arabic garb, a rolled scroll pointed toward the sky in his uplifted left hand. This monument pays tribute to Judah ben Saul ibn Tibbon, a twelfth-century Granada-born scholar (later a resident of Greece) whom historians have given the sobriquet "the Translator." By profession a physician like many Jewish intellectuals (Maimonides, for instance), ibn Tibbon translated from Arabic (in which they were written) into Hebrew works by great Jewish scholars of the time, such as Saadia Gaon, Bahya ibn Paquda, and the poet-philosopher Judah ha-Levi.

Ibn Tibbon was not an isolated figure, despite the impression of the statue: among his descendants who followed him into both medicine and letters, his son translated Maimonides extensively, and a grandson, who was also an astronomer, translated Euclid and Averroes. While unquestionably an illustrious family, the ibn Tibbon clan merely represents a rich Jewish tradition of translating cultural and scientific works among the major contemporary languages of Europe. Adept in Hebrew, Arabic, Latin, and vernacular tongues, the Jewish (and converted Jewish) translators brought to Christian Europeans writings by Plato and Aristotle that had been preserved in Arabic copies, the Koran, studies in astronomy, cartography, and mathematics vital for the expeditions of Columbus and his followers, as well as Jewish ethical, philosophical, and religious writings from the great medieval efflorescence of Jewish thought. These translations provided the means of cultural transmission among civilizations.

The contrasting sculptural images, close enough to one another for us to feel Isabella's shadow behind us as we pay respects to ibn Tibbon's legacy, make visible the contradictory passions of the secular and sacred, temporal and eternal. The seated Christian monarch places in the hands of her kneeling subject the parchment that will confer terrestrial authority to possess and dispossess at will. The Jewish scholar holds aloft instead of a scepter of dominion the scroll of teachings extended to the world, pointed toward heaven. These designs are equivalent to the symbolic figures of Ecclesia and Synagoga on gothic cathedral facades that Franz Rosenzweig allegorized so differently from the church that commissioned them. In contrast to the triumphant Ecclesia, representing the church, with gaze directed to the physical world that she rules with sword and scepter, the blindfolded Synagoga has fixed her mind inward on the eternal truths about the divine and the end of time.

To Jews, that conceptualization may be gratifying. Still, the monumental cathedrals stand; the Jewish quarters have disappeared, often for the worst of reasons, along with the Jews and their synagogues. Ibn Tibbon's modest statue and terse inscription loiters out of the way, up the urban equivalent of Malka Heifetz Tussman's silent canal, gesturing to a culture that passes by him unaware, and nothing about the monument speaks of his mission or his faith. That silent figure betokens the stifling of a once-vital, transforming conversation among cultures in which Jews (though never on equal standing) were essential participants, for their own contributions and as intermediaries between people without a common language.

Pondering European history with an awareness of both Jewish and non-Jewish cultures, one becomes conscious of the fracture line running through the phrase "Judeo-Christian tradition."[1] That expression manifests Christianity's attempt to assimilate a Jewish biblical tradition into its own past. Perhaps the term also expresses Jewish cravings to be accepted as integral to what is usually termed Western civilization. Listening carefully, however, one cannot help being aware of hearing two separate voices, like two stereo speakers that are out of phase. The voices do not blend, they do not always complement one another, and one of them often cannot be heard at all.

To speak of Jews as marginalized, as the Other, as the outsider silenced in Europe is not simply a rhetorical strategy. English Jews were literally expelled in 1290 and not officially readmitted until Cromwell's commonwealth more than 350 years later. Jews were also cast from their homes in regions throughout France in 1306, 1322, and 1394. Spain's much larger and seemingly more influential Jewish community was ordered to choose between conversion or exile in 1492, and five years later in Portugal thousands who had been given no choice fled after forced baptism. In a metaphorical way, however, Jewish thought had been expelled much earlier and remained in exile for centuries from the mainstream of Europe's cultural and intellectual development.

Consider a set of paradigmatic examples as metonymous for the impact of such a cultural expulsion on the Christian consciousness of Jews—the artist Andrea Mantegna's depictions of Hebrew writing in four of his paintings. The first instance in fact is a nondepiction. Early in the 1460s the artist painted what is now known as the Uffizi Triptych. The right panel portrays (according to most interpretations) the infant Jesus being presented for circumcision in a magnificent Renaissance-style edifice, perhaps representing the Temple. Within the arches on the wall, lunettes depict as seemingly gold leaf bas-relief two scenes from Jewish scriptures that were typologically interpreted in the Renaissance as prefigurations of Jesus's mission: the binding of Isaac and the presentation of the Ten Commandments. In the latter, Moses holds up to our view a large rectangular tablet. The face of the tablet, however, is blank. Given the painting's rich architectural detail, one cannot argue aesthetic simplicity as a motive, and (given the conventional option of representing the commandments simply by roman numerals) one cannot rest simply with the nonetheless revealing likelihood that Mantegna did not know Hebrew letters. It appears instead that Jesus's advent obviates the need for the Jewish text.

Mantegna's later works sharpen the issues through cultural stereotypes and through cultural developments. One of the portrait masterpieces of the Italian

Renaissance is his *Ecce Homo,* painted in the Este family's learned humanistic court of Mantua, and signed and dated by the artist in 1500.[2] A soberly suffering Jesus crowned with thorns is depicted full face between grotesque-featured tormenters. The one on the right of the painting wears a turban, probably signifying "Levantine" to the contemporary viewer and not incidentally linking this presumably Jewish accuser to the troublesome Turks. The figure in the left foreground is topped by a turretlike cap inscribed in billboard fashion with a lengthy text in quasi–Middle Eastern characters, undoubtedly meant almost literally to label this character as a Jewish denouncer of Jesus. If one is able to get close enough to look at the writing, one discovers that the letters are not real but are actually vaguely Greco-Semitic-Arabic squiggles that probably are intended to signify Hebrew (again, perhaps with an admixture of graphic arabesques for contemporary reasons). Some modern studies of Mantegna, unwittingly confirming the artist's strategy and influenced by the work's subject but without linguistic grounds, even confidently claim that the text is Hebrew.[3] However, in this painting, "Hebrew" equates with gibberish. The presence of Latin quotations from the Vulgate New Testament in scrolls at the top of the work underscores the Hebrew language's easy dismissal.

If we know that the headdress's inscription is mock Hebrew, we can then grasp that the cartoonishly hideous figure designated as a Jew, not simply by the situation but specifically by the parody text on his headpiece, is no Jew. Rather, he is a stereotype: stereotyped physically, and stereotyped textually by the gobbledygook passing for his language. The pseudo-Hebrew marking his headpiece seems appropriate to label him as pseudo-Jew, a stock character hauled out of a storehouse of deformed European racial images, a murderous stage Jew of Malta, a Shylock unredeemed and unredeemable.

That the imagery and orthography of this picture have been shaped by a tendentious Christian program seems plausible given how Mantegna represents Hebrew in two other works from about the same time. A remarkable, monumental (though small) composition from 1495, now in the Cincinnati Art Museum, depicts two characters, painted on canvas in distemper and gold to resemble a bronze relief, in animated discussion over an apparently Hebrew text on partially unrolled scroll. This somewhat enigmatic work (whose figures have also been identified as Tarquinius and sibyl, Sibyl and Prophet, and even—as in Cincinnati—Esther and Mordecai) may be connected to a Christological motif. If it pairs sibyl and prophet, it brings together across a text the representative personae from the two faiths that from a Christian viewpoint are about to be superseded in history by the prophesied redeemer whose coming is supposedly foretold in the scrolls of the Jewish Bible presumably under discussion in the painting. Nonetheless, no polemic seems implied in Mantegna's treatment of either figure, and there are no visual evocations of a specifically Christian context against which to judge them. Perhaps the respectful treatment of the pagan and Jewish prophetic figures seems particularly appropriate if the typological reading of the painting is correct. (Although Christianity of course accepts the Ten Commandments, Moses in the earlier Uffizi composition was treated as forerunner giving laws, not prophet of the messiah.) In this piece, which is devoid of contempt for the Jewish figure, the representation of Hebrew lettering on the scroll is noticeably more credible (although it is still not genuine Hebrew), despite being dated five years earlier than the *Ecce Homo*. It is impossible that the artist would have known more about the look of Hebrew lettering in 1495 than in 1500, and the dates of the pictures seem unquestionable. The difference surely results from polemical purposes rather than erudition.[4]

Mantegna perhaps saw a Hebrew scroll among the antiquities collected by the urbane humanistic court in Mantua; he might also have inferred the appearance of a Jewish scroll from (for instance) fragments of Roman ones. The one depicted in this painting at least looks convincing from a distance of six feet. Still, the appearance of the "letters" is only evocative rather than denotative. So an artist today might represent other non-Western languages through characters suggesting the visual forms of Arabic, Japanese, Sanskrit, or Chinese, very likely without great concern for linguistic or even orthographic accuracy. Mantegna clearly felt that he could adequately imply that a text was in Hebrew without troubling to be sure that he painted any actual Hebrew letter, which he did not. Implicit, surely, is the idea that few of his viewers would know the difference, and fewer still would care.

This is not merely a matter of a visual artist's insouciance toward text. Even apart from the relationships between literature and the visual arts so often articulated in the Renaissance (evinced paradigmatically in the visual and verbal artistry of Michelangelo), one can be sure that no painter, learned or otherwise, would think of representing a text in nonsense Latin or, more to the point, in concocted false shapes supposedly standing for Greek letters. An artist would have ready models of Greek letters within that cultural environment. More important, an artist would have the cultural acclimatization to "see" Greek letters, to look at, comprehend, differentiate, and represent those letters accurately, knowing that the most significant segment of the work's viewers would be able to judge that accuracy and would expect accuracy. Greek was a weight-bearing cornerstone of the humanistic curriculum; Hebrew was not.[5]

The crucial difference caused by audience attitude and knowledge is revealed by a fourth Mantegna work, his famous allegory of *Pallas Expelling the Vices,* painted apparently between 1499 and 1502, certainly later than the sybil and prophet, and probably later than the *Ecce Homo.* This large work bears an explanatory text in three languages—Latin, Greek, and Hebrew—presumably composed by one of Isabella d'Este's resident scholars, likely Paride de Ceresara, displayed on scrolls ornamenting the scene. (Although not at all necessary to explain the legend being portrayed, the use of all three languages doubtless advertises the court's erudition while it also suggests the story's timeless moral relevance.) Here at last Mantegna, perhaps under Paride's tutelage, shows not only an exquisite Greek script but also genuine Hebrew letters. The accuracy and completeness of the Hebrew, of course, is a separate matter for which the painter is certainly not accountable; Paride was known for his abilities in Latin and Greek, but his knowledge of Hebrew seems less certain. Nonetheless, for this picture at least one viewer who mattered knew the language well enough to care that the supposed Hebrew was actually Hebrew, at least orthographically.

In this instance Hebrew makes a more or less genuine appearance in the Renaissance context. Such was not often the case. (The tetragrammaton fares better, so to speak, in visual representations.) There would be other and better Renaissance Hebraists, of course, though the entries into Hebrew are consistently through Christian doorways, even when the Christianity owes much to neoplatonic philosophy. Evidence of the visual arts, however, indicates how rare in the Renaissance is the accurate depiction of Hebrew letters (of—to stress the point—Jewish characters) when compared with the omnipresent familiarity with Latin that afforded literate people access through their church-based education to Roman culture. In addition, Hebrew letters were much less common than Greek letters, examples of which abounded on fragments of classical coins, statuary, and inscriptions, all beloved of the antiquity-collecting Renaissance patrons and scholars as well as in editions of the classical authors and of course the Greek New Testament. Revival of interest in Hebrew during the Reformation and Counter-Reformation, as well as the easy relations between religious communities in Amsterdam during Rembrandt's time, obviously altered matters.

The causes of these inequities in cultural knowledge clearly are complex. One cannot simply say that anti-Semitism or disdain for Jews accounts for artists' relative ignorance of Hebrew letters among the principal ancient languages to which Christian Europe paid attention. What makes that ignorance worth noting is that these same artists had within relatively easy reach, sometimes in a nearby street or *calle*, contemporaries who actually knew those letters, prayed daily—both in their homes and on their ways—using them, daily studied texts written in them, taught them to their children, and indeed used them as the main tools and building blocks of an ongoing civilization, though ghettoized and in many places fallen on hard times.

Despite often seeming obsessed with Jews and with Judaism during what the scholar Frank E. Manuel has called "the long history of Christianity's wrangling with Judaism,"[6] Christianity has for the most part been engaged in either a monologue or a debate about the place and survival of Jews and Judaism rather than a conversation with Jews and Jewish culture. Manuel's fascinating study of that history warns against too hastily simplifying it. It seems fair to say nonetheless that over the centuries the Jewish voice has rarely been heeded for what it might have of broad value to say to the Christian or secular community, whereas non-Jewish voices have continually been heard and have sometimes intervened intellectually, theologically, or politically in discourses of the Jewish community.

Whether Hebrew and Judaism are still consigned to the fringes or even to the wilderness beyond the borders of our cultural life may be judged by considering the usual content of courses in Western civilization or, perhaps more strikingly, in medieval literature and even medieval philosophy. Teachers (regardless of their religious or ethnic background) who would not deem their courses complete or their students properly introduced to these areas without covering Aquinas or Anselm, Augustine or John Chrysostom or John of the Cross, may never in their careers even mention (for instance) Judah ha-Levi or Maimonides or Isaac Luria. Notwithstanding a detailed grasp of the structure of the *Summa Theologica*, they may be totally unaware of the entirely different but nonetheless complexly conceived organization of the Talmud, so much more responsive than Aquinas to mnemonic needs and associative connections as well as to issues often touching on immediate practical legal or social dilemmas.[7]

In Jewish interpretive traditions over the past nineteen centuries, Jewish scholars have reacted protectively to the intellectual and spiritual threat posed by Christian appropriation of Jewish teachings, particularly regarding the messiah, and to the religious and physical threat posed by Christian polemics against Jews and Judaism. Included in these latter categories are such phenomena as the "debates" between Jewish and Christian scholars as to which is "the" true religion. Frequent in the late Middle Ages and Renaissance, typified by the notorious "Disputation of Tortosa" (1413–14), they were always initiated by the church, which had the temporal power to compel Jewish participation as well as the religiotemporal power to decree which side "won" the so-called debate.

Silence was a privilege not granted to Jews, and, therefore, compulsory speech took place under circumstances both censorious and futile. These public gatherings had the form of debates, but in the balancing of powers they more resembled the occasions when Jews were compelled to attend conversionary sermons in Christian churches. At such sermons, only one party spoke while the other side remained silent; in the disputations, both sides spoke, but one was in effect silenced. The body of Christian belief strove to assimilate part of the body of Jewish belief, although rejecting the remaining tissue of faith and practice. Medieval and Renaissance Christianity silenced Jewish teachings, sporadically through suppression but more often through ventriloquistic possession, as Jewish texts were contorted to validate Christian beliefs. Jewish scholars in the same period felt compelled to tend the boundary conceptually separating Judaism from all other religions, including Christianity. Therefore, Christian beliefs and biblical interpretations enter Jewish texts primarily through allusive markers of what lies just on the other side of acceptably Jewish praxis and testimony once one crosses beyond the mezuzah.

As a minority and subject community, Jews necessarily have heard exogenous ideas and reacted to what they have heard, though the negative and positive responses alike have been those of members of a minority and often subject population rather than those of free and independent consumers strolling voluntarily through the marketplace of ideas or cultural insiders dwelling within neighborhoods of common beliefs. The traffic, furthermore, has been largely in one direction, heavily weighted toward imports. It is no wonder that in years past many found their means to productivity through "emigration" by conversion into the dominant religiocultural environment (among Europe's best-known, Heinrich Heine, Felix Mendelssohn, Gustav Mahler). Like that of a marginalized economy, inherently rich in undervalued or ignored commodities, Judaism has only rarely been able to export its own cultural tradition to the dominant culture, with exceptions to test the rule like Benedict de Spinoza, who lived on the fringe of Judaism, or Moses Mendelssohn, the cosmopolitan and preeminent Jewish philosopher of the Enlightenment whose descendants (including his talented grandchildren, Felix and Clara) converted to Christianity.[8]

Emmanuel Levinas, writing in France in 1959, described a relationship between the state and religious institutions certainly not unique to his time and place. "There is in fact a sense of inequality," he asserted, "between Christianity—which even in the secular state, is present everywhere—and Judaism, which does not dare show its face out of doors, held back as it is by scruples about being indiscreet." Assumed commonality of shared religious experiences and outlooks are so much a part of the body politic that "they float around in it like lymphatic matter. The churches are integrated into landscapes that always seem to be waiting for them and to sustain them. We give no more thought to this Christian atmosphere than to the air we breathe. The juridical separation of Church from state did nothing to dispel it." Christian holidays and days of rest, he noted, determine the "rhythm of legal time," as much as Christian churches "determine towns and sites." Furthermore, the cultural life of art, music, literature, and ethics is suffused by Christian motifs and morality, often embedded in polished stylistic achievements compelling esteem (and in the academies, we might add, leading to canonization).[9]

Remarking even briefly on the chronicle of Jewish-Christian relations may suffice to suggest the asymmetry of silences and communication characterizing that chronicle and to suggest how great the effects might have been for each party. One might be inclined to regard the issue under discussion as simply that of a democratic approach to academic discourse. Presuming that anyone might have something worthwhile to say, equal access to the floor allows everyone to be heard.

Regardless of the debatable merits of such a viewpoint, the issue in fact seems rather different. The silence that absents Jewish writings from canonical educated discourse may be seen as one variety of the artificial restriction of canonicity (by racial, sexual, class, and religious priorities) that has only recently been challenged. A much deeper critical grasp of cultural history could be gained were we capable of mapping discourses and silences in the colloquy of cultures. It would be more than interesting to see, for instance, not only how Arabic cultures influenced what is generally thought of as the West but also how and when, in counterpoint with an exploration of the West's influences on the Arabic world. We do not even have all the elements of a full account of the conversations and the silences in the discontinuous conversation between Jewish traditions and the several non-Jewish traditions that developed in Europe from classical antiquity onward. We can come closer to a detailed description of how Jews and Christians talked about or learned from the other by studying the influence of the kabbalah on Renaissance humanists or of the Enlightenment on Jewish culture and society.

A different but also useful kind of knowledge accrues from studies of the image or the legal status of the Jew at a particular time and place. Yet more broadly we need to grasp to what extent people are oblivious of one another or consciously divided at given periods, to comprehend what cultural developments or social experiences they do not share. This idea seems important enough to warrant urging the point, to speak of silences and to make a presence of absence, even though it is not possible here to offer more than a cursory suggestion of how the muting of Jewish culture within the pre-Christian and Christian environments can be traced in art and what some consequences of that muting might have been. Except relatively late in Roman history, Jewish texts and civilization attracted no mention in the literature of the classical world on whose geographic and conceptual margins Jewish civilization dwelt. Jewish writings, by contrast, necessarily preserved much greater awareness of the Grecian and Roman cultures that presented great challenges, invitations, and obstacles to Jewish self-rule, Jewish religion, and Jewish cultural integrity. The Chanukah story of the Maccabees is merely the most widely known record of the multifaceted conflict between Judaism and a dominant pagan Grecian culture; the last years of the last Jewish kingdom were played out, as every Jew and every Christian knows, under Roman rule.

Under foreign domination, the double dangers, one externally defined and the other internally, were oppression and assimilation. An alien force embodied an inescapable presence for Jews, making the "other" central to their experiences. To the dominant power, however, the Jews constituted a marginal otherness on the boundaries of their empires. Jewish settlements may have had some political, military, and economic significance, but the existence of Jews as a people and as a culture was insignificant to that dominant society's beliefs and culture and consequently irrelevant to its understanding of itself.

Granted that much of postclassical Western literature has been occupied with the Bible, nonetheless the Jewish Bible (the Old Testament to Christians but known in Hebrew as the Tanakh) has figured only selectively through stories and characters significant as dramatic, pictorial, symbolic, or Christian typological material. The canonical Tanakh of Western literature encompasses most of Genesis and Exodus through the revelation on Mt. Sinai and the giving of the second tablets of the covenant, as well as the desert wanderings in paradigmatic summary. It incorporates little from the remaining books of the Torah (that is, Leviticus, Numbers, and Deuteronomy); selected stories from the "Writings" or hagiography (in Hebrew, Ketuvim), for instance, parts of the tales of Jonah, Samson, Solomon, and David; extensive selections from the prophets, especially those critical of Jewish failings or arguably messianic in outlook; and quotable extracts from many of the psalms.

Christian tradition also takes in, appropriates, or even misappropriates (according to one's outlook) Jewish interpretative strategies such as midrash and kabbalah. These contribute not only in theological but in artistic circles as well; the last three major works of John Milton (*Paradise Lost*, *Samson Agonistes*, and *Paradise Regained*) can be understood as clearly in the midrashic mode, imaginative articulations of motives and emotions occurring in the silences within laconic biblical texts, Hebraic and Christian.[10] Milton's poems also demonstrate the manner in which Jewish writings took their places within a Christian literary culture, to be subsumed into the Christian interpretive context and thereby assimilated.

One figure admired if not assimilated by Christians and Muslims was Moses, whom Milton termed "that shepherd who first taught the chosen seed." Moses became the central Jewish heroic and religious figure to Jews and non-Jews because of his direct relationship with God, his leadership in liberation, and his transmission of the Torah. However, we might also question whether Moses is not more acceptable to non-Jews than his brother, Aaron, as a focal Jewish figure because Aaron the high priest seems a purely endogenous figure. Jews are not enjoined to imitate Moses (since there has never been a prophet like him, according to the Torah) but rather Aaron : the Talmud instructs us to be among the disciples of Aaron, loving peace and pursuing it. In good moments as well as bad, he exists wholly within his relationship to the Jewish community. Moses, though seemingly as much a part of that community as his brother is, also appears to be on its fringe. An outsider in so many ways, he goes off by himself to Midian, to Horeb, to Mount Sinai.

Perhaps this is one of the figurative meanings contained within the story of Moses being cast into the water in his reed basket, sent to safety outside the Jewish community and raised in the Egyptian court milieu. Moses knows the exogenous society and has had the opportunity to become acculturated to it. He not only escaped being killed in an environment hostile to Jews, but he also escaped being completely repressed. No wonder he was so attractive a figure for African Americans during and after the years of slavery.

Slaying the brutal Egyptian overseer turns out to be a double self-revelation. Moses reveals that despite his privileged upbringing among the Egyptians, politically he is one of "us," and not one of "them." He also reveals that psychologically he is not like us. In positive terms, he has escaped the so-called ghetto mentality of passively enduring injustice; in negative terms, he has shown impatience with the divine will and has put the community at risk because he has not developed the oppressed survivor's wary strategies for enduring rather than rebelling suicidally. The dilemma of response posed by Moses' behavior becomes a familiar one in Jewish history, repeated during each *ḥurban* in the conflict between Jews who favored active resistance and those who believed that even defensive violent actions were either irreligious or ruinously impractical. Such a dichotomy is replicated in the split between the typical Israeli concept of Israel as a strong autonomous Jewish state equal with the other nations of the world and a supposedly submissive diaspora still afflicted with the subjugated mentality of enduring one's lot among the nations of the world rather than standing up for oneself as Jew.

Moses' liminality subsequently becomes clear through his rapid shifts from defender to critic of the Jews. He will save them from Pharaoh's wrath and more importantly from God's as well as Moses' own, yet he will nonetheless excoriate, harangue, and denounce them with intense passion. This dichotomy does not mean that Moses fits the category of the identity-denying, self-conscious, self-hating Jew. Still, his sermons against his people's failings compile an extensive catalogue of faults that could be described as a rhetorical quarry for anti-Semites as well as for Jewish self-criticism. Freud's Moses, one recalls, is not even a Jew but a rebellious Egyptian who assumed command of this rabble horde of déclassé outsiders as a way of keeping alive the great monotheistic culture of Ikhnaton that the more traditional of the Egyptians themselves had defeated and suppressed. Though Freud's argument has a more complex genesis, it supports interpreting Moses as a leader who is not quite one of the people whom he leads, someone sufficiently independent and critical of them to be recognizable from the outside as an outsider.

Complementary to the social, political, and economic ghettoization of the Jew prior to the Enlightenment—and in various times and places subsequent to the Enlightenment—has been the intellectual ghettoization of the Jew. This phrase should not be taken to entail merely the passive, self-deprecatory outlook that has been termed by some modern Jews the "ghetto mentality." It extends beyond the issues of Jewish self-image and the image of Jews before non-Jews. It encompasses a broader phenomenon, the artificial restriction of opportunities for Jewish intervention in the general history and intellectual construction of the modern world.

During the historical contest of wills and unequal contest of might fought over the privileges of speech and silence, the multivolume, monumental Talmud occupied a significant and complex place. (Although there are two somewhat different versions, known respectively as the Babylonian and the Jerusalem Talmud, the name generally designates the former, the more complete and influential Talmud Bavli.) To the traditional Jew, the Talmud constitutes the oral Torah, approaching in importance the written Torah (the Pentateuch, or first five books of the Hebrew Bible), of which it is deemed an essential explanation. The philosopher Emmanuel Levinas has phrased the relationship between the two bodies of texts in a way that succinctly captures the Talmud's significance for traditional Judaism: "The Old Testament does not prefigure the New; it receives its interpretation from the Talmud."[11] According to tradition, Moses received on Mount Sinai the interpretive commentary clarifying the laws and precepts embodied in what became the written Torah. That commentary, transmitted orally and elaborated by generations of scholars, became codified and written in stages during the second through sixth centuries of the Common Era, when the continuing growth of Talmudic analyses combining with the decentralization of Jewish culture following the fall of Jerusalem impelled the transcription of the oral tradition. Studying Talmud became part of the basic educational background of any literate Jewish male. The work was a constant source of both practical communal guidance and intellectual training for rabbis, scholars, and indeed any Jew with at least a pretense toward education or learning; its teachings formed the foundation of Jewish religious practice and mutual obligation.

Of all Jewish religious texts, the Talmud was the one toward which the Christian church had the most hostile response.[12] The Talmud itself was tried and convicted of heresy by ecclesiastical courts (for example, in Paris in 1240). Copies were subsequently confiscated, expurgated, and obliterated. The most notorious episode, of incalculable damage to Jewish communities at the time and with residual scholarly impact today, was the seizure and burning of wagonloads of Talmud manuscripts (as well as prayer books and other theological works, some condemned because they contained Talmudic passages) by order of King Louis IX of France on June 17, 1242. Similar spoliation spread from Rome throughout northern Italy in 1533 and occurred yet again in Poland in 1757.

Of all of Judaism's writings, the Talmud has remained into our own time a particular target of anti-Semitic demonizers. Close at hand, for instance, sits a vicious monograph called "The Talmud Unmasked," reprinted in 1985 by a right-wing Christian fundamentalist group. Originally written in Latin by a Roman Catholic priest and published in Russia in 1892 bearing an archbishop's imprimatur, this farrago was drawn principally from material appearing in that notorious nineteenth-century czarist fraud "Protocols of the Elders of Zion," which trumpeted the supposed international Jewish conspiracy to torture and kill Christians, use their blood to make matzo, and conquer the world. It can be found on the open shelves of university libraries.

Although the partial censoring of the Talmud derived from allegations that selected passages were deprecatory toward Christianity, the Church's attempt at completely silencing the Talmud within not just Christian but Jewish discourse as well was driven by the belief that the work's entire spirit was inimical to Christian faith. Predicated on at least the hypothesis of self-governing and self-regulating sacerdotal and tort systems and directed toward refining the implications of biblical teachings regarding ritual, observance, and social obligations, the Talmud embodied what Pauline Christianity regarded as Judaism's superficial legalism and excessive concern for the letter of the law as opposed to Christianity's superior grasp of the spirit of the law. In this framework, therefore, Talmudic Judaism did not merely differ from Christianity; it was deemed an impediment to the spiritual growth offered to Jews by Christianity. Some

Church theologians and preachers (among both categories, a number of converted Jews) seem to have made their careers by arguing against the Talmud, which scarcely any of their readers and a far smaller percentage of their auditors could possibly have known directly.

The Talmud remains singular. The Hebrew Bible, with its teachings about creation and divine revelation and perhaps most of all its glimmers of messianic promise, was essential to Christianity; midrashic and, eventually, kabbalistic writings were amenable to Christian adaptation or interpretation, as was even the Jewish prayer book. By contrast, the Talmud was the one major category of Jewish text that was not assimilable.

It also would have been inaccessible for technical reasons to virtually all Christians, other than male converts from Judaism or particularly ambitious and dedicated scholars. Encyclopedic in length, it was not translated fully into any language until Lazarus Goldschmidt single-handedly translated it into German between 1897 and 1935. At that date the historically aware mind must pause in stupefaction. A German-language Talmud was completed in 1935, the year in which Germany passed the notorious Nuremberg Laws segregating Jewish from Aryan Germans: What does this not tell us about Jewish devotion to the text!

The Talmud comprises sections in Hebrew (the Mishnah, the earlier core of teachings) and Aramaic (the Gemara, the compilation of later explications of the Mishnah). Although the two languages are related, they are further apart than mere dialects. Engaging the Talmud has meant, for its students, involving themselves in a multilingual conversation whose languages (Mishnaic Hebrew, Aramaic, the varieties of Hebrew from intervening centuries, and their own vernacular) express different eras in Jewish history. In addition, the Mishnah and Gemara are each written in their own highly abbreviated and virtually encoded styles, filled with technical terms and phrases, more characterized by the textual interstices than the webbing of statements. It is a puzzling, cryptic, at times paradoxical work that Jewish tradition wisely dictates should not be learned by one person as an individual enterprise. Instead, students probe the text together in pairs and in groups, immersed in colloquy or dispute with one another over the perplexities presented by the text, assisted by a more learned Talmudist whose first task is to initiate pupils into the traditional methodology of Talmudic inquiry.

The Talmud's textual and logical obscurities were not designed for obfuscation or covertness. Its written form was a mere concession to the expansion of material over time and the dispersion of Jewish communities. The Talmud was not termed "oral Torah" out of whim; the written text was intended as a permanent study and reference guide for a work that lived orally, through dialogue and dialectic, but also through practical application as a code of practice and governance in many situations. The silences of the Talmudic text were openings to be filled by discussion of its students, potential inferences and connections to be made in theory and practice by rabbis or rabbinic courts guiding the lives of individual Jews and the relations of Jews with one another. Studying and being guided by the Talmud distinguished the Jew from the non-Jew more clearly than did adherence to any other form of religious writing.

Consequently, stifling the Talmud did not obliterate the distinction between Jews and Christians, because Jews continued to practice Talmudic Judaism, though sometimes hampered by the loss of books. Instead, censorship suppressed the most distinctively Jewish voice (until perhaps recently) from participating in the broad, centuries-long European cultural and intellectual discussions of logical methodology.

In one superficial respect this is ironic, for the Talmud could be regarded as the most scholastic, virtually Thomistic, of Jewish texts. Elaborately and topically organized, the Talmud's system, like Aquinas's, can best be understood from the inside by someone totally immersed in it and devoted to its byways. Indeed, Freud, a Jew who despised both scholasticists and Talmudists, perceived a connection between the two intellectual modes.[13]

However, heard properly, Talmudic discussion sounds totally unlike scholastic disquisition. In contrast to the rigidly constructed, highly determined, monologic exposition characteristic of patristic writing, Talmudic discourse unfolds through a concatenation of dialogic questions, challenges, false leads, hypothetical inquiries no sooner raised than discarded, assertions and objections, associative analogies. The result is a sometimes-heated debate carried on back and forth across the page and across the centuries as generations of scholars attempt to grasp or refute the thinking of others, regardless of chronology or reputation. That process of argumentation and testing paradigms through hypotheses was (ideally) continued across the desks of the students who learned Talmud by entering into the Talmudic method of disputation. Susan A. Handelman has analyzed how rabbinic analytic processes differ from what she calls the Greco-Christian tradition that has dominated Western logic and philosophy, and she has also pointed out ways in which recent literary critical thought seems indebted to the influence of rabbinic texts on and through Freud, Jacques Derrida, Levinas, Edmond Jabès, and Harold Bloom.[14] Levinas himself, involved in both the Hebraic and Hellenic traditions, evoked the latter in distinguishing the dialogic nature of the Talmud: "It is a dialogue where there is no Socrates facing a young man. Shmuel is not Socrates, neither is Rav. Both have the clarity, the modesty and the irony of Socrates."[15] The key word is *both*, for the Talmud records disputes in which every participant is potentially the decisor, every disputant an authority to be reckoned with, every authority sooner or later found wanting.

During the many centuries when institutes of higher education—and sometimes any education—were supported by churches or states that excluded Jews from schools, study of the Talmud and attendance at yeshivas (academies for advanced Jewish studies) afforded Jewish males their only higher education and perhaps their most sustained involvement with intellectual pursuits and a life devoted to learning. For centuries, rabbis becoming fanciful about the reward of the afterlife have represented it as a grand Talmudic academy in which one can partake of the highest levels of sophisticated reasoning. Added to the fancy is undoubtedly a considerable measure of special pleading for the rewards of Talmudic study; still, the fable must have spoken of an experience appealing enough to justify its invention. Also suggestive is the tradition that one of Elijah's tasks will be answering all of the Talmud's unresolved cruxes. In other words, we have devoted ourselves for centuries to studying compendia that bear their unanswered questions unabashedly and think their puzzles not too trivial to engage the attention of the messiah's herald. At the end of *The Rise of David Levinsky,* Abraham Cahan's novel depicting a successful immigrant Jew's ambivalence toward his material prosperity in America, David recalls the few early years he spent as a youth studying in the heder in Europe as more than a happy time; it was a time when he experienced his best and truest self. Despite his financial successes, he feels embarrassed by losing contact with that intellectual environment.

The consequences for European intellectual life, not merely in the Middle Ages but through the present day, of excluding the voices of the Talmud from the center of critical discourse has inestimable consequences, obviously including the marginalization of Jewish intellectual contributions, which are not the same as the intellectual contributions of Jews. Less obviously but still profoundly, the consequences also include skewing the character of respected scholarly inquiry to admit the abstractly constructed monologue (tending to be ideologically authoritarian) or, at the creative fringe, the Socratic dialogue in which one is virtually never in doubt as to whose is the voice of truth. Even though the Talmud's discussions often lead to an unequivocal halakah (literally Hebrew for "the way to walk," a consensual rule for Jewish practice), such a process, which demands we listen to so many voices, often leads to ambiguous results—"Some sages say . . ." but "Others agree instead with . . ."

True, from especially the late nineteenth century onward, a sizable body of Jews, whether more practical minded or more Westernized, has regarded the Talmud as a bizarre, fusty relic of medieval ghettos, pored over by petty-minded legalists. Notwithstanding this attitude, still today some special panache is likely to be accorded in the Jewish community to someone who has actually studied Talmud. To summarize, the Talmud was a work to be instructed in, debated with, analyzed, learned from, and governed by; yet learning Talmud was also a major Jewish model of what paradise would offer.

Again, what individual Jews might have found available to them as exceptions to the rule or as converts is not at issue. Nor is Jews' freedom to participate in the culture of Christian Europe. Certainly, many Jews must have been attracted by some of what they saw and heard, as would any person of taste and sensitivity or any person impressed by magnificent displays of opulence and power. Walk the streets of Spain's Segovia or Toledo or Cordoba to seek out the poignant despoiled remnants of their once lovely small synagogues whose walls are ornamented by Hebrew texts chiseled into the stones and plaster, and then turn to the mountainous brilliant edifices of the cathedrals, still in use, filled with art and artifacts and often resonating with splendid organs, testimony to the wealth and might of church and state. How striking the contrasts and how obvious the Church's physical dominance and appeal to wonderment. Yet there were limits, fairly narrow limits indeed, as to how much of this European and Christian cultural discourse could have been appreciated by Jews merely as viewers, readers, or auditors.

Today, for example, albeit with a far wider range of cultural experiences available, consider the amount of European music (classical as well as traditional) rooted in church ritual, no matter whether the church is Catholic, Protestant, Anglican, or Eastern Orthodox. Notice how much of Europe's architectural monuments are ecclesiastical or royal, the sanctuaries of powers often inimical as well as alien to Jews. Recall how much of European literature from classical times to the Enlightenment was linguistically closed or theologically antipathetical to Jews. Observe how many of the timeless paintings and statuary (most of which were in churches or palaces anyway) were iconographically alien to Jews. Contemplate even today from a Jew's viewpoint any exhibit of classical, medieval, Renaissance, or baroque European art and imagine the reaction to the Minervas (while the unfigurable Shekhinah remains absent), to the St. Sebastians studded with arrows (but where are the Jewish martyrs of centuries of anti-Semitic riots?), or to the St. Jeromes studying in the wilderness with the protection of their friendly lions (but never do we see pairs of rabbis disputing over a page of the Talmud).

We are in truth there, although hidden. Jews actually are omnipresent in European art, but they are unrecognized because they have been so thoroughly de-Judaized. Jews, one remembers with a jolt, are hidden subjects of all those literally countless Annunciations and Nativities, Presentations and Assumptions of the Virgin, Crucifixions and the Resurrections. Surely the artists themselves forgot that they were painting Jews or were indifferent to the historical veracity; some would have been aghast at the idea. European art flourished for centuries by masking, underneath ethnically purified gold or russet ringlets, Teutonic gauntness, or cream complexions, those two Jews who were at the center of its spiritual and ecclesiastical culture and whose Jewishness that culture erased: a pregnant Jewish bride, a Jewish mother and her infant son, the iconoclastic Jew in his early thirties dying nailed on a Roman cross. To contemplate cultural history in this way is to recognize why the artistic richness of Europe until modern times felt unwelcoming from a Jewish standpoint, even when it was not explicitly hostile.

Although not often acknowledged explicitly, these are rather obvious issues. The less obvious and perhaps more significant one is the enforced absence from most of the history of the European intellectual scene of a Jewish intellectual heritage, articulated from a Jewish vantage point and within a methodology honed over centuries within Jewish intellectual communities that were, if not actually integrated into the general community, at least geographically coterminous with it. The non-Jewish environment, whether Christian, secular, or Muslim, continually pressed in upon Jewish life, which rarely had openings to affect the content or form of the total environment of which they were and were not a part. Jews (unlike Buddhists, for instance) were physically active on the European scene; unlike Muslims, Jews did not combat Christian temporal power or even religious power outside of the Jewish community itself. These facts make the marginalization of European Jewry especially startling in retrospect.

The extended effect on the understanding of Judaism outside a practicing Jewish community can be glimpsed from Levinas's 1959 reply to an address by a distinguished Catholic Church historian on the shared spiritual foundations of the Mediterranean civilizations. The Jewish scholar demurred,

> When he described the gestation and birth of the three monotheisms and their reciprocal collaboration, Father Daniélou completely left out the element that remains essential to those of us who are Jews: the constitution of the Talmud. . . . If there had been no Talmud, there would have been no Jews today. (It certainly would have saved the world a lot of problems!) Or else, we would have been the survivors of a finished world. This is the suggestion that, in spite of everything, persists in Catholic thought. We reject, as you know, the honor of being a relic. Was Father Daniélou's discourse entirely free from this suggestion? In order to demonstrate Judaism's contribution to the legacy of humanity, it confined itself to Jews without Judaism. He quoted only the descendents of Jews.[16]

We need not enter into arguing current relations between these two communities of faith, or questioning how each today understands the other's traditions and self-concepts little more than thirty years after Levinas's speech. In the long history in some sense shared by Judaism and Catholicism, the mid–twentieth century seems rather a late date for a Catholic theologian to grasp the significance of the Talmud for Jewish religious identity. We also need not consider how widely the Talmud is read in contemporary Jewish communities, either as an intellectual exercise or for religious guidance, even though there is evidence suggesting a recent increase in adult Talmud study by both women and men.[17] The Talmud's teaching, Levinas means, sets the Jewish interpretation of the Bible and the Jewish concept of a religious community apart from the Christian. Jewish religious practice and observance derive in large measure from the Talmud. Even the authority that Jews have granted the Talmud in applying the Bible's teachings means that the Jewish notion of religious and biblical tradition will differ from the Christian. Rather than accepting a view of Judaism as essentially like Christianity but without having Christ, Levinas argues that Judaism should be understood as having the Talmud—not a central lack but a central presence that others have ignored.

The extended effect of that slight on the educational process can be gauged from a typical but nonetheless arresting polemic in an essay by George Steiner, a Jew whom no one could accuse of being uncommitted to Jewish issues or oblivious to active or covert anti-Semitism. Yet consider the canon he evokes in *Language and Silence* two years after Levinas's speech examined above, when Steiner asserts that, "Classic and medieval philosophy were wholly committed to the dignity and resources of language, to the belief that words, handled with requisite precision and subtlety, could bring the mind into accord with reality. Plato, Aristotle, Duns Scotus and Aquinas are master-builders of words, constructing around reality great edifices of statement, definition and discrimination. . . . They share with the poet the assumption that words gather and engender responsible apprehensions of the truth."[18] Anyone who has read even a page of Talmud, Philo, Maimonides, or Saadia Gaon (to keep within the classical and medieval context), is likely to be struck by the appropriateness of Steiner's words to such writings (among others) and to be startled by his silent disregard of the Jewish philosophers and theologians, both those who adhere to his standard and those who understand that developing their insights obliges them to something other than "constructing around reality great edifices of statement."

Writing of Pharisaical Judaism's legacy, Emmanuel Levinas posits a rhetorical question about the segregation of Judaism (even if not of Jews) from the development of European culture. In his striking words, "We may well ask whether ideas that cannot break through to the masses . . . can still determine the progress of the world, and whether Christianity was not the last and only entry of Judaism into World History."[19] Even more striking is the fact that his reply to those questions, although seemingly negative, unfolds as tacitly affirmative through its almost evasive reconceptualizing of the main issues.

Levinas suggests an essentially subterranean influence of Judaism through "the intrinsic value of truth," the ability of the "revealed idea" to live outside "the history in which it was revealed," and the possibility for truth to burst forth "volcanically" through "abrupt irruptions."[20] That is to say that Judaism has contributed to world history outside of the rise of Christianity but not in ways visibly identifiable with Judaism, although an opportunity for some explicitly Jewish entry may arise at some time in the future. As if in mockery of anti-Semites' fantasies of omnipresent Jews who secretly control everything, Levinas posits an apparently absent Judaism that affects the world but does so invisibly. Despite the attraction of nonsectarian universalism implied in Levinas's argument, one might well argue that such invisibility has benefited neither Jews nor non-Jews. Silence has been forced, not chosen.[21]

So Emil Fackenheim observed that,

> Jewish testimony, albeit to the nations, was between God and Israel alone, if only because to hold otherwise would have led to despair. Thus the Jews behind medieval ghetto walls could not seriously believe that the nations on the other side knew or cared about their faithfulness or faithlessness to the Torah; nor could the martyrs of Worms and Mayence seriously think that the crusading mobs would be moved by their martyrdom. And while it is a documented fact that countless pious Jews died at Auschwitz with the *Shema Yisrael* on their lips, no less documented is the fact that, while the Nazi murder machines on occasion broke down, the murderers themselves did not.[22]

We have begun to grasp that issues of cultural audibility (for this is the critical core, rather than cultural achievement) affect all other aspects of our social, psychological, and political lives. Jews, familiar stereotypes apprise us, are loud, noisy, and pushy. Might we not turn such allegations around? Do they not mean that the conversation and public demonstrativeness of Jews sound offensive because the presence of Jews is resented? For surely this canard has been fabricated out of the same material by which women are stereotyped as talkative and their conversation denigrated as gossip or chat. Communication, whether undertaken for denotative or expressive purposes, is reductively perceived as chatter when its source is devalued. Experiments show repeatedly that in groups of both men and women, women speak less than men yet are interrupted more frequently. That women are more talkative than men is simply verifiably false. That they are perceived to be more talkative suggests the unstated but apparently prevailing notion that women, like Victorian children, should be seen, not heard. The difference in regard to Jews, of course, is that the Jew's body (for reasons that Sander Gilman has suggestively explored) is also seen as offensive.

Jewish discourse, so long as it is biblical or intellectual, may be more broadly accepted or even envied as manifestation or pure moral force or intellect at work. What is likely to be resented is the actuality of Jewish presence in the social environment. Jews may seem more acceptable when they are heard than when they are seen, but only when they are heard in a disembodied context. When they are heard socially, they are thought to be too loud, and when they are heard politically, they are thought to be too prominent. Arguments about the site and design of the U.S. Holocaust Museum (which opened in Washington, D.C., in 1993) suggest the pervasiveness of such attitudes. An influential architectural critic on the district's Fine Arts Commission objected to the size, color, and physical alignment originally proposed, insisting that the building "take a 'distinctly secondary position' to the other memorials on the Mall," and that (even at the loss of exhibit space) it not protrude further than the neighboring Bureau of Printing and Engraving. In particular, he complained about the proposal to tear down a building on the other side, in which case the Holocaust Museum "and its striking Hall of Rememberance will forevermore exist in direct sightline with the Washington Monument as well as the Jefferson Memorial, and will rival both. This, I submit, is wrong."[23]

The resentment of assertiveness by Jews about Jewish issues seems to hold true on the international as much as the national scene. Without ignoring or minimizing numerous other factors, some measure of international resentment of Israel can probably be ascribed to hostility toward Israeli assertiveness. What appears in the behavior of other countries as understandable pursuits of national interests is taken, when it comes from Israel, as arrogance or pushiness.

It does not seem implausible that the repeated brutalization of the Jewish communities of Europe through our present time has been possible partly because Jews were made to seem expendable from European civilization or even parasitical upon it; consequently, the educated classes too frequently responded to pogroms with (at best) silence. Actively malicious anti-Semitism was obviously the crucial ingredient, but it took root in a culture willing to believe that Jews as Jews, which is to say Jews embodying Judaism as a religion and an intellectual practice, had nothing that Christian Europe would find worth hearing. Not a Jew but a modern Christian theologian, J. Coert Rylaarsdam, wrote, "Over the centuries Christians have generally lived with the tacit assumption that a 'good Jew' is either a dead Jew or a Christian. So, alternately, they have consented to the death of Jews and prayed for their conversion."[24] Heine, a Jew who converted to make his way in the world, observed that a society that burns books will eventually burn people. He was not only being prophetic; he knew what had happened to the Rhineland Jews during the Crusades of the Middle Ages. We might carry forth his thought to say that a society that discards a culture will end by discarding the people who have embodied it.

·

9

The Lead Plates
of the Rom Press

FIRST, AN ANECDOTE from an American junior high school more than thirty-five years ago. Two hulking bullies, too old still to be among the other ninth graders and improbably convincing embodiments of the stereotypical gentile thug of Jewish folklore, had established reputations for gratuitous physical harassment of some of the Jewish students. One afternoon, cornering a Jewish boy alone in an empty school corridor, they first contented themselves with verbal menacings and the occasional provocative shove. Then the quieter one, with a gesture the full significance of which he would likely never comprehend, snatched from the Jewish boy's shirt pocket a cheap ballpoint pen and "hid" it on top of some steam pipes just below the ceiling. (The silently eloquent admission of "pen envy" would have worked just as well as both a visual and phonemic pun had he found a pencil instead.)

His taking away the means to control the word, despite that action's veiled symbolism of castration or unmanning, seemed preposterously futile to the victim even amid his apprehension. Perhaps it could have felt so even to the perpetrator, could he have been moved to examine it. He did not want to steal the pen; he made no conscious attempt to possess it for himself, much less appropriate whatever it represented. He merely attempted to deprive the despised yet envied Jew of whatever powers that pen seemed to represent. Those powers must have included (even if he could not have said so directly) that of having a future different from any for which he himself could hope or dare to aspire. He would not have been widely enough read to know that Goebbels, supervising one of the earlier Nazi book-burning orgies twenty-odd years before, had celebrated the final solution to "Jewish intellectualizing."

The pen's abduction—surely it was something other than a theft!—was pathetically inept, befitting the entire episode of intimidation. Unimpeded by his two tormentors looming over him, the owner of the pen reached above the pipe, retrieved the implement, and replaced it in his pocket. A few grumbling mumbles passed to negotiate his safe departure, but the only words that remained in his recollection were those muttered by the more loquacious of the two when the purloined pen was silently and quickly retrieved, for they were a phrase seeming to say all that might be said of motive and meaning: "Oh, he's a smart Jew!" Smart; rearmed.

One might compare Vladimir Horowitz's recollection of how he escaped anti-Semitic harassment as a student in Kiev early in this century. Horowitz, who became one of the world's greatest pianists, did not take top places in his academic examinations, as many of his fellow Jews had done. Consequently (as he told the critic and biographer Harold Schonberg), his gentile classmates, who intensely resented the successful Jewish students, liked the young musician because "I was a Jew who was not smart."[1] His mastery of the language of the keyboard became his triumph. There, he was smart.

Such anecdotal recollections trivial in themselves remind us of the power of language, particularly in empowering those socially, economically, or politically powerless. So it was for Frederick Douglass, whose remarkable accounts of his stratagems for covertly learning the letters of the alphabet and then relating them to words form some of the most memorable pages of his autobiography. Having been alerted by his master's hostility to the danger inherent in a slave learning to read, Douglass grasped a connection between his education and his freedom. His story also records that the dangerous nature of his enterprise was widely perceived in the antebellum South, and the secret Sabbath school he established to spread the knowledge of the word was soon discovered and suppressed as subversive. In different ways Helen Keller's comprehension of the meaning of language became the crucial step in allowing her to function fully as a person, and Maya Angelou's avid absorption of language as a traumatized child dwelling in her preferred silence but with the words and music of others in her ears and before her eyes equipped her with the means to find her individual strengths, as well as a lifelong love of languages.

By contrast, the tormenting suppression of power along with words is manifested in Eva, the grandmother in Tillie Olsen's "Tell Me a Riddle." During the story Eva recalls her past as a poor Jewish girl in czarist Russia. Taught to read by the dearest friend of her youth, an aristocratic young Russian woman subsequently executed for her part in the 1905 revolution, Eva cherished reading both for pleasure and intellect. She bitterly recalls her husband's stifling of her personal development in their youths through his insistent entreaties not to read, to put the book away, to have sex with him. She, who had associated reading with political activism, was then forced to treat reading and living as antithetical. Putting the book away meant being induced instead to sex and sleep and childbearing, a long life of physical hardships and commitments to the lives of her husband and children, during which she became silent by preference because the hunger for words had been closeted within her.

Framing the issues of power and speech in solely Jewish terms would be convenient but misleading, as we have seen. Alan Tate, introducing his version of the Latin "Pervigilium Veneris," speculated: "Perhaps in the Amyclae, the people of the town of that name in Latium who were called *tacitae* and who, when menaced by an enemy, could not speak for help and were destroyed, we may see an image of all 'late' people. . . . Is the poem not telling us that the loss of symbolic language may mean the extinction of our humanity."[2] Whether the language lost is symbolic language seems doubtful in this instance. However, the story does attest that language is one lifeline to aid. In our own time we have learned to recognize that this is true of our psychological as well as political needs.

Other classical stories show the reverse process by which loss of humanity leads to the attempt to obliterate symbolic language. Such an idea seems suggested in the myth of Philomela, raped and deprived of speech when her assailant (her brother-in-law, for this story also exposes incestuous rape) cut out her tongue. As metaphor, the legend powerfully expresses the silencing of women generally and rape victims particularly. Even the revenge that she and her sister, Procne, almost achieve is defeated. Like Procne, Philomela is divinely transformed into a bird; her tale is thereby transformed into a discourse by but not about her. Vocalizations attest to her presence but cannot communicate her story. That story can only be told by people who have not lived it.

Shakespeare's related narrative of Lavinia in *Titus Andronicus* expresses greater confidence in the human resourcefulness to communicate, even as he displays more frankly the human capacity for barbaric cruelty.[3] Lavinia, her hands also cut off to prevent her from writing what happened to her, discloses it nonetheless by using her stumps to turn pages in a volume of Ovid until she can show the story of Philomela, and Lavinia names her attackers by writing their names on the ground with a staff held in her tongueless mouth. Muted, Lavinia breaks through the imposed silence to make the book of poetry and the book of nature tell her tale. The words stifled in her force their way out through what remains of her body; arms that cannot write can turn a writer's pages, and a mouth that cannot speak can hold a surrogate pen. She, her father, and her uncle, driven by passions for disclosure, find ways to expose the almost silenced truth. Survivor of a horror from which eloquence could not save her, Lavinia tells a survivor's tale with as much eloquence as is needed: what happened, who did it.

Such testimony is not confined to Wittgensteinian equivalencies, a word for a fact. Speaking of a horror demands explanation or justification, not for the horror but for continuing to speak. In his diary recording the Nazi destruction of the Vilna Ghetto and its inhabitants, Herman Kruk attempted to answer the questions of his fellow death camp inmates,

> Why do you write in such hard times? —
> Why and for whom? . . .
> . . . For, anyway, we won't live to see it?

Kruk's reply is twofold: "I write because I must write—it's a consolation in my horror time. / For future generations, I leave it as a trace."[4] The impulse to record comes from inner necessity and commitment to the future to be a witness; "I, a prisoner, . . . recorded, fixed faithfully." For the author, finding consolation merely in the act of writing is equally important. Out of the writing comes "a hope for a miracle" because the process itself implies commitment to a future, perhaps even for oneself. The writer goes on "Drunk on the pen trembling in my hand." Drunk on the pen—so it is not hope, pride, or imagination but the physical act of writing that produces the uplifting frenzy. We who come forward need the language that acts as a fixative, gluing experience to the page, stopping its half-life decay before all is lost. This we will value more highly, and we may be right if we believe that what serves to hold experience before the eyes of eternity is meritorious because of it. The "leaves of horror" hold the record of "what I could not live to tell." Kruk, with thousands of other captives from the Vilna ghetto, was murdered at Kloga, Estonia, a day before the Soviet army arrived. Only the pages of his diary remained for the record.

"I write because I must write. . . . For future generations, I leave it as a trace." Those words could be formulated by any writer. Perhaps what is most striking on reflecting about Kruk's testimony is what it does not say, for he omits the natural middle element. Both the most noble and most venal writers would admit that they write expecting an audience in their own time. True, many would claim that they write only for themselves, but other than the rarest exception—Emily Dickinson notably, who chose public literary silence to protect the great eloquence of her ample body of privately held poems—they put their works before the public and hope for readers. Kruk had no means of reaching his contemporaries who needed to read him because they were ignorant of what was occurring; he had nothing to say to his contemporaries who were able to read him but knew as well as he did what had happened and what they were enduring. He had not given up life: "Maybe a miracle will liberate me." However, his silence about the present readership eloquently expresses individual and collective isolation; it seems a foretaste of their mutual doom.

The miracle of liberation saved the text itself, not its author. That diary's survival was at least one miracle. Another was the survival of any of us who would care to read it and claim that it matters. At the same time, for the persistence of national and ethnic and religious bigotry and hatred that we continue to experience, the word *miracle* is impossible, but we seem to lack a satisfactory term for anything so improbable and monstrous after what we saw of these in our own times. Language, in which we live and through which the lives of others live, is pushed to the limits by such experiences and there it stops.

Manès Sperber recalled the encomium to God cited at the beginning of the second chapter of this book, "Were the sky made of parchment." For him, five decades after learning it in a Galician shtetl early in this century, this testimony of language's inability to encompass the ineffable had taken on a new context. "I come back to the resonance of these phrases," he wrote, "whenever I bring myself, once again, to the realization that we will never succeed in making the *hurban*—the Jewish catastrophe of our time—understood to those who will live after us. The innumerable documents . . . the diaries, chronicles and records—all these millions of words remind me that 'even if all the firmament. . . .' "[5] The documents have been written. Some have been read by some people and spoken of by many others. We can add to them other necessary records—the wretched chronicles of the slave trade, with the horrific middle passage and its aftermath, or the recording of the Armenians' sufferings, the tales of Stalin's gulags. We can even note the terrible silences: the public neglect of the Nazi destruction of the Romany (the gypsies), the rape and murder of women by marauding soldiers all over the world. Is it accurate to say that the words of evidence have fallen on deaf ears, so that the testimonies are like the silences?

They may be, but we know that silence is equivocal. We often feel compelled by Muriel Rukeyser's command, "answer the silence of the weak: / Speak!"[6] At other times, silent resistance or dissent must suffice. José Faur, analyzing a Talmudic story of the Hadrianic persecutions of Jewish authority, derives the meaning that our choices are multiple, though finite. One canny sage spoke equivocally about the benefits of Roman rule, with words that could be taken as praise or ironic mockery and was honored by the Romans with the post of head spokesman. Another, as noted for his eloquence, kept silent. "R. Yosé's refusal to speak constituted a most eloquent outcry protesting the impossibility of speech. The Romans understood this quite well. He was sentenced and banished," Faur notes. A third directly attacked each presumed benefit mentioned by the first speaker and had to go into hiding to evade his resultant death sentence. The fourth principal collaborated. Thus we find here the four paths open to the sage, according to Faur's commentary: "(1) diplomacy (cunning); (2) silence; (3) confrontation; and (4) collaboration with the adversary." He observes that confrontation may lead to silencing, and diplomacy (evading confrontation) may also be regarded as a form of silence. Although his discussion deals with verbal expressions, it applies equally to the options for action.[7]

A poem by the Polish-born Israeli poet who called himself Sh. Shalom (born Sholem Shapiro) sets a pragmatic context for silence, in his case silence as cunning. Describing Jewish efforts to cultivate the Galilee after Israeli independence while facing harassing attacks from marauding guerrillas, "Hazzorim baleylot" ("Sowers by night") records the self-protective silence of farmers who want only to sow and harvest their grain.[8] Farming by night under the dangerous protection of the moon (whose light both aids and jeopardizes them), they have taken precautions to work as quietly as possible: "*lo kol lanu v'lo hegeh*" (we do not speak, make no sound). The poet continues, "*lo mammash l'farsot suseynu v'galgaley eg'loteynu r'fudim*" (the horses' hooves seem without substance and our wagon wheels are cushioned). Amid silence, the declaration of their identity (given as if a password to the guardian moon) sounds falsely grandiloquent, especially because the announcement "*anashim ivrim anaḥnu*" (we are Hebrew men) immediately precedes the statement that "we" are voiceless. The damped wheels are described, furthermore, with the word *r'fudim*, which may suggest *rafeh* (weak) and *r'fedim* (weak ones). Implications of impotence and timorousness are reinforced by the poem being directed not to God but to the feminine night. However, the meaning of the poem undermines that appearance. Cultivating the land appears quietly heroic, or at least georgically admirable, under these circumstances. The silence that might be taken as timid avoidance of a direct confrontation or attack is a sign of strength, because it permits the workers to survive and indeed prevail. If this is femininely passive, it is also femininely strong. The poet's words reveal the ruse and along with it the success. This is the underdog's strategy, using the weapon of apparent weakness to endure and triumph.

This victory of Shalom (the poet's true given name and his chosen pseudonym, meaning "peace") is pragmatic. Cultivating the land is more vital than battling. Of course, plowing and planting this land has to be understood as more than merely useful because it means helping fulfill a biblical mandate to dwell in the land of Israel and make it fruitful as well as more generally to build a nation instead of simply tending one's private property.

In Moyshe-Leyb Halpern's "Sacco-Vanzetti" the silent helplessness of the political system's victims becomes a regal dignity attesting to a moral victory. At first, acceptance of death seems merely a passive response to life's tribulations. "One must only be quiet for a time [*Men darf nur ruik ẓayn a vayl*] / And like a typhus patient bow your head to one who shaves it." In preparation for their execution, their stillness assumes a noble character transfiguring the meaning of this event. Correspondingly, the poet transforms the metal band that will connect their skulls to the electric chair into a macabre crown, indeed, "a wonder-crown" (*a vunder-kroyn*) "in this desolate world."

> *A kinig—ven dos gantse folk afile veynt arum ẓayn tron—*
> *darf schvaygen, ven men kroynt im.*

> A king—even while all the people weep around his throne—
> Should be silent when he is crowned.[9]

Taking the crown of silence necessarily means being silenced; it can be made to mean rising above the world's turmoil. Even silence accrues meaning from its context, for, as is true of speech, neither its denotations nor connotations are absolute.

Silence can even express overt defiance. We know this from the sullen withdrawals of children and lovers that psychologists describe as passive aggressive. Politically, however, silent withdrawal—refusing to vote or to fraternize with the enemy—may be an oppressed population's last defense against its oppressor. A notable example is a French resistance work from the Second World War, *The Silence of the Sea* (*Le silence de la mer*) by the writer known as Vercors (Jean Bruller). In this novella, a cultured German officer has been billeted on a French family consisting of an elderly writer (the narrator) and his young niece, both of whom respond to his presence by according him the silent treatment. From the viewpoint of the writer of this story, the fictive writer's refusal to speak is an appropriately literary form of resistance if not of actual rebellion. Indeed, the pseudonymous "M. D.," in the preface to the wartime edition smuggled into France, specifically contrasted the honorable *ecrivains du silence*, the French "writers of silence," with the Nazi collaborator Drieu la Rochelle and other busy fascist sympathizers or hacks conspicuous for their noise (*par leur bruit*). The writers of silence comprised those who were suppressed or banned as well as those who used their words for subversive purposes and the others who voluntarily stopped writing to make their silence a weapon (*n'écrivant que pour rendre leur silences plus éclatant que leurs mots*).[10] Illustrating silence's ambiguity, "M. D." protects the writers of silence in the most appropriate way possible, by pointedly keeping silence about their names.

Because silence can be a form of passive resistance, the strategy unites the girl and the sedentary older writer. They share a conceptually feminine strength through the nexus of her gender, his occupation, and their ages; neither of the French characters can be a direct combatant, yet each avoids collaborating or weakening. The essentially feminine nature of their silent resistance is implied by the monologically loquacious German officer's interpretation of what he has experienced. Although neither the uncle nor the niece speaks to him, he seems conceptually uninterested in finding symbolic meaning to silence of the older man. However, he sharply responds to the similitude between the *demoiselle silencieuse* and *le silence de la France*, between the silent maiden and the silence of (grammatically and allegorically feminine) France, both of which he is vainly determined to overcome: *Il faudre vaincre ce silence. Il faudra vaincre le silence de France,* "Her silence must be vanquished. France's silence must be vanquished."

The text implies that the German's interminable monologue is an oral form of imperialistic occupation, carried on without care to extract a word, a sign of assent, even a look (*car pas une fois il ne tenta d'obtenir de nous une réponse, un acquiescement, ou même un regard*).[11] His determination to overcome the girl's silence as well as France's is revealed as the personal analogue to the forcible possession of the territory that he desires not only to control but to compel into yielding to him, a barely covert metaphor of sexual domination. Having asserted his determination that the resisting victims must be made to capitulate, he passes judgment on his announcement: "*Cela me plaît*" (This pleases me). Vercors's exposure of territorial occupation shows coercive discourse to be a form of coercive intercourse.

This work evinces how powerlessness, gender, and status can make silence a powerful political weapon, perhaps the moral weapon of last resort for those otherwise politically unarmed; it also clarifies the concept that silence, femininity, and powerlessness may be bound together as parts of one ideological construct. From the narrator's perspective, the voluntary muteness in which he and his niece persist is their main weapon, augmented by its kinetic equivalent, immobility, which weighted down that silence, turned it to lead (*alourdissaient ce silence, rendaient de plomb*).[12] Silence becomes a lead bullet to use against him.

A metaphorically analogous trope governs the poem by the Yiddish poet Abraham Sutzkever, "The Lead Plates of the Rom Press." In it, he imagined himself and his fellow fighters from the Vilna ghetto melting down the printing plates from the great Vilna edition of the Talmud into bullets to use against the Nazis. Transforming the speaking text into silence is the intermediary stage in making it a weapon.

From the eighteenth century onward, Vilna had been the most important northern European site of traditional Jewish learning. The edition of the Talmud printed there by the Rom family's publishing house—the so-called Vilna *shas* (*shas* being an acronym for the term "Six Orders" designating the Talmud itself)—became the standard scholarly text. Metonymically, in Sutzkever's poem it represents the entire Jewish tradition of scholarly pursuits. It also stands for the Jewish devotion to books in lieu of secular power or capabilities. For the battling ghetto fighters, turning the printing plates into bullets means casting off intellectualism to fight for their lives. As Sutzkever phrased this, *"mir, troymer, badarfn itst vern soldatn"* (we, dreamers, had to become soldiers).[13]

That metamorphosis also entails redefining the meaning of Jewish history.[14] Sutzkever's poem, in evoking the Maccabean battle for the Temple and the survival of Judaism, obviously does not reject the entire Jewish past and identity in favor of mere secularism. Rather, he joins an ancient conflict in Judaism itself over the essence of Jewish life, a conflict expressed in the doubleness within our observance of Chanukah. One element derives from priestly Judaism centering on territory and Temple, polity and priesthood; it celebrates the courage and military success of the Maccabees, whose revolt was initiated by a priest, Mattityahu. The other element, arising from the rabbinic Judaism that gained predominance after the destruction of the Second Temple and the expulsion of Jews from the land of Israel, honors observation of the nonsacerdotal commandments and devoting oneself to learning, prayer, and piety — personal acts that one can undertake anytime within a community existing anywhere. The former view of Chanukah is accounted in the story of Judah Maccabee's military victory (in the first and second books of the Maccabees, excluded from the Hebrew Bible as a late and merely violent chronicle but preserved in the Apocrypha); it is honored in the second major benediction and the special prayer of thanks recited for Chanukah. The latter interpretation is signified through the Talmudic story about the miracle of the oil (not recorded in the books of the Maccabees) and honored by the focal ritual and first benediction for the holiday, the lighting of the special Chanukah menorah.

Sutzkever's heroic fighters feel that they are joining both strands together as they shoot, but they are joining them in a way that melts down and absorbs the rabbinic tradition of study, prayer, and miracles, allowing the emergence of the other tradition so desperately needed on this occasion, the tradition of the Maccabee warriors. *"Un mir hobn vider geefnt dem shtempl"* (And we broke the seal again), so that the leaden text can be transformed into bullets, poured as the Temple's sanctified oil had been in ancient days into golden holy-day candelabras (*gildene yom-toyv-menoyres*), a line from Babylonia, (*a shura fun Bovl, a shura fun Poyln*), a line from Poland. A people's identity is transformed as much as objects by this process. Frieda W. Aaron has observed that this passage demands that the " 'dreamers' must now strike a blow at the very 'soul' of diaspora culture," by melting down "the coveted literary record of the diaspora," from Babylon to Poland. Only in that way can they "defend the honor, if not the survival, of that culture."[15]

The process of transformation is even implied lexically. Using the Hebrew-based, liturgically resonant word for strength or courage, Sutzkever affirms, "*di yiddishe gvure, in verter farhoyln*" (Jewish might, concealed in words) will declare itself with a shot. By using *gvure* in this context, the author recalls the prayer recited on Chanukah giving thanks for the *gevurot*, the courageous deeds of might that resulted in victory. The poem's imaginative alchemical process takes these Yiddish dreamers of Vilna from *shura* to *shos*, from a textual line to a shot. The journey's significance is further underscored verbally because *shas* is spelled in Hebrew with the same two consonants as *shos*. Indeed, in this poetic fiction, *shas* becomes *shos*. That transformation makes a new vision of the Jew explode upon the world; that vision, however, is actually an old reality restored. The poem's ultimate ironic twist is that the entire episode expresses a poet's fantasy. We can say, therefore, that the poet turns that *shos* back into *shura*. The (Talmudic) text seemingly becomes a cartridge shell that turns again into a (poetic) text.

The celebration of might accruing from the bullet is not uttered in a vacuum. Rabbinic tradition teaches that violence disqualifies prayer: "He who prays unto God with hands soiled from violence is not answered . . . because it says, 'And when you spread forth your hands . . . I will not hear because your hands are full of blood.' "[16] We Jews knew, therefore, how to pray and how to study texts. We gave no attention to getting a nation or an army or learning to defend ourselves physically. Imagining turning those printing plates of the Talmud into bullets, Sutzkever destroys that rabbinic culture to turn it into something useful in the violent world that continually turns its terrors against Jews.

In taking the metaphor of the weapon, perhaps we write human experience in characteristically masculine metaphors. Gloria Anzaldúa imagines her creative process through a different but still violent set of images, marked not only by their gender connections but also by their cultural associations. "This vampire which is my talent does not suffer other suitors. Daily I court it, offer my neck to its teeth. This is the sacrifice the act of creation requires, a blood sacrifice. For only through the body, through the pulling of flesh, can the human soul be transformed. And for images, words, stories to have this trans-

formative power, they must arise from the human body—flesh and bone—
and from the earth's body—stone, sky, liquid, soil." While expressing the
transformative (rather than destructive) power of language, Anzaldúa also
recognizes the destructive potency in creating. However, her imagery (characteristically female, according to some theoretical constructs) emphasizes the
self-sacrificial and the biological. Even the metaphor of herself as vampire's
victim can be seen as a typically female cultural role. This particular use of the
metaphor, which derives directly from Nietzsche's characterization of art's
relationship to the artist, encourages us to see the artist as both feminine and
victim. They are mutually bound under the power of an inescapable, preying
presence that demands nothing less than the lifeblood.[17]

The notion of blood sacrifice, of course, connects this way of thinking with
both Amerindian (especially Aztec) and Christian (especially Catholic) ritual
and imagery. It seems in this way un-Jewish. So too does the idea that images
must come from the natural bodies of human beings and the earth, a concept
that seems artistically self-evident but conflicts directly with the biblical injunction against setting up images of anything that is on or above or below the sky
and earth and the related affirmation that we are made in God's image.

Yet surely there is a subjective truth to this, experienced by all creative
artists. Herein lies the terror of creating out of nothing. For the religious
person this may be differentiated from commenting on the religious text by
studying and interpreting it. One creates out of nothing because all is vanity,
that is, nothingness; one makes images and stories not out of Torah, not out of
the timeless divine word, but out of the insubstantiality of physical matter and
our own imaginations. And one is driven to do this by a hard taskmaster.

But for the artist, this taskmaster dwells within, seemingly inescapable.
Thus, the paradoxes: Does the artist struggle more against the self than against
the other? In struggling with the self, is one really struggling with the other
that is within? One turns language against one's enemy or against oneself. For
the creative artist or any writer, both are one because we have internalized the
oppositional. Milton felt it obsessively from early in his life:

> How soon hath time the subtle thief of youth
> Stol'n on his wing my three and twentieth year!
> My hasting days fly on with full career,
> But my late spring no bud or blossom shew'th.[18]

The phrase "full career," meaning at top speed, ironically glances at the paucity of his own achievements in art and the absence of any other clear pursuit for his life. A half dozen years later he will begin his elegy "Lycidas" ruing his own unripeness for the poem he feels constrained by "sad occasion" to bring forth "with forced fingers rude." That is not purely a literary strategy but a reflection of his persistent conflict between necessary public commitments and internal private misgivings about his readiness for the greatness without which writing appears pointless. If, as he says in the closing words of the earlier poem, "my great task-master's eye" commands the prospect of all that he does or achieves, his phrasing may imply that the master has set the task and is the master of the task. Because the twelfth line of this sonnet refers to "time . . . and the will of heaven" and we know Milton's poetry to have been deeply influenced by his Christian convictions, readers usually take that "great task-master" to be God. Need it be so, we may be permitted to ask? Two centuries later Thoreau would observe in *Walden* that although having a southern overseer is bad, being enslaved to oneself is worse. Whether Milton thought of the poem's task-master as the master of the universe, he felt that master's gaze within himself.

To raise this ambiguity necessitates recalling the Decalogue's prohibition of worshipping other gods and making graven images. We have considered ways in which creativity risks intruding upon the divine precincts of creation. It may also involve a different transgression. In opening ourselves to the powerful creative and formative urges, we admit the presence in us of that inspiration (literally, the breathing in) that has been termed a *daimon*, a spirit-demon-divinity powerful and demanding, seemingly given to its own rules and its own transgressive inclinations.

There is another way to imagine the burden of creativity. Maybe Anzaldúa's text suggests that in the process of writing, one's self becomes another enemy to combat? For within us is stasis, resistance to the struggle to define and express, resistance to the effortful transformation that occurs as latency gives way? Arrayed against us inside are our own incapacities, fears of failure, fears of the test that every venture into language represents, and fears of what Hélène Cixous called the "transgression" of "speaking—even just opening her mouth."[19] However, fear on one side is answered by resentment on the other. As Anzaldúa protests, "To be a mouth—the cost is too high—her whole life enslaved to that devouring mouth. *Todo pasaba por esa boca, el viento, el fuego, los mares y la Tierra*. Her body, a crossroads, a fragile bridge, cannot support the tons of cargo passing through it. She wants to install 'stop' and 'go' signal lights, instigate a curfew, police Poetry. But something wants to come out."[20] The birthlike process of verbal creativity represents it as a virtually irrepressible natural urge against which border guards prove powerless, even those that one wants to put in place for self-protection. Perhaps the art is a burden, but it is not unspeakable. Quite the reverse.

Any writer likely feels the inner compulsion; many are also conscious of the external obligations. What does one tell, and to whom, and to what end?

> Speak for   sing for   pray for
> everyone in solitary
> every living life.[21]

Rukeyser challenges us to commitment. However, to be offered the gift of speech and not to be heard is the writer's and prophet's equivalent of the myth of Sisyphus. The terrible need to reveal what had taken place already and what was still taking place in Nazi-dominated Europe compelled a small number of Jews and non-Jews in the early 1940s to address British and U.S. government offices, the International Red Cross, and Jewish agencies. Almost everywhere, these accounts were dismissed as propaganda, ignored as incidental, or suppressed as detrimental to the Allies' military aims. Even to those people for whom one picture would be worth a thousand words, aerial photographs of Auschwitz produced only silence. The newsreels of skeletal survivors, mounds of corpses, heaps of eyeglasses and human hair, crematoria with human remains still unconsumed, visual relics of what had occurred—these pictures at last spoke for their thousands of words, spoke and stopped speech. As Emil Fackenheim replied to those for whom the silence of Jewish theology after Auschwitz signaled that God was dead, "Might it not be a well-justified fear and trembling, and a crushing sense of the most awesome responsibility to four thousand years of Jewish faith, which has kept Jewish theological thought, like Job, in a state of silence, and which makes us refuse to rush in where angels fear to tread, now that speech has become inevitable?"[22]

Only the ensuing silence allowed enough quiet for the accounts and chronicles to add their words. Through those texts we became more than observers. Of course, we would always be less than, other than, participants; for such an experience, those who were not there will always be outsiders. Through such testimonies of victims and perpetrators, witnesses and liberators, judges and scholars, we gain a sense of the innerness of experience, the texture of life and thought, without which merely looking at the images—with whatever depth of feelings—takes us to the borders of pornography, as if one were invited to come and see the horror. The texts, even when artlessly written, inscribe people who have not merely seen but experienced.

Redeeming language through commitment may be the only way for the pious writer to experience language or silence piously. The virtuous Lady of Milton's "Masque Presented at Ludlow Castle" ("Comus"), lost at night in the woods, correctly perceives that her ear is "My best guide now," not only because it is still accurate in the physical darkness; it is also less likely than her sight to be deceived. Deluded into following the sybaritic enchanter, Comus, to his palace, she has been fooled initially by his humble appearance, but she hears through his seemingly subtle verbal seduction. In replying, she suggests that words and silence alike acquire moral status through place, circumstance, and usage.

> I had not thought to have unlocked my lips
> In this unhallowed air but that this juggler
> Would think to charm my judgement, as mine eyes
> Obtruding false rules pranked in reason's garb.
> I hate when vice can bolt her arguments,
> And virtue has no tongue to check her pride.[23]

Through the Lady's speech Milton implies that we are responsible at least to ourselves for our ventures into dialogue with "him that dares / Arm his profane tongue with contemptuous words"; we are also accountable to ourselves if we encounter impiety silently. She knows as well, notwithstanding the full flight of her eloquence and morally impelled imagination, that her speech will fail to take its auditor with it.

> Fain would I something say, yet to what end?
> Thou hast nor ear, nor soul to apprehend
> The sublime notion, and high mystery.[24]

Young though she is, she is not so naive as to believe that her eloquence itself will dissuade the evil-intentioned or persuade the low-minded. She might indeed agree with the rabbi renowned for his preaching who replied angrily when praised for speaking beautifully, "God forbid that I should ever 'talk well.'" The lady's contempt for Comus's decadence extends to his language:

> Enjoy your dear wit, and gay rhetoric
> That hath so well been taught her dazzling fence,
> Thou art not fit to hear thyself convinced.[25]

Vice and fancy-footed rhetoric, both feminine personifications according to the Lady's speech, have become Comus's pupils and do his bidding. She will not join them. Her thrust, "Thou art not fit to hear thyself convinced," says more than that he is not worth her time. It attests that being persuaded by the truth is morally gratifying and therefore a privilege one must deserve. If one attempts to persuade the likes of Comus, failure is inevitable.[26] What then? The Lady must be rescued by a veritable deus ex machina leading on stage her two brothers with drawn swords. The sword comes into the world, the Talmud tells us, because of justice and righteousness delayed or denied. If not the word, the sword; if not the sword, the knife. Casca's "Speak hands for me" calls forth the blades that bring down Caesar.[27]

Words may be vain, silence may be the voice of despair, the grip of art may be, like Hamlet's ghost, "from heaven or from hell." We are presumptuous when we think that our words construct more than a tower of Babel, but that belief may be what saves us. To quote Muriel Rukeyser once again, "What would happen if one woman told the truth about her life? / The world would split open."[28] Conviction impels our speaking and writing. Prayer's only absolute requirement according to Jewish teachings is *kavvanah* (focus, purposefulness, devotion). As with prayer—*l'havdil* (to separate between sacred and profane)—so with speech. We pray and speak from the intensity of that commitment; our power stops at the boundaries of the act of speech. But words venture on.

Jews believe that our utterances need to be shaped by the words of Torah and the stillness within the divine. The chronicles of our relations with the sacral attest to the importance of articulated commitments forming a covenantal relationship; obedience to the *mitzvot*, the body of commandments, is central to our part of the covenant. It links us to God and to one another, in whom we are commanded also to acknowledge the image of the divine. Such connections involve us in ongoing conversations or dialogue with one another and with God. The topics of those conversations include how to be holy while also in the world and how to be human among other humans while also being an individual. Our words and deeds, the mystics tell us, will contribute to or detract from the process known as *tikkun olam,* binding together the scattered fragments of the once-unified creation. We live and speak and keep silent as individuals and as peoples, but words and deeds alike have missions transcending our personal desires or fates. We are made of and by words, and we are also filled with silences. Thus, we are made in the divine image, and, thus, silence and speech as well will outlast any one of us to eternity. These facts have been known to fill some with despair and sickness unto death, but to live within a covenantal relationship with the sacral means to commit oneself trustingly or timorously to the spoken as well as the unutterable, to (Ps. 19) the words of the mouth and the meditations of the heart, linked like mortise and tenon to each other.

The story is told that when the Romans burned rabbi Hanina ben Teradyon, they wrapped him in the scroll of the Torah, the teachings of which he had persisted in expounding. While the flames consumed them both, he proclaimed to his horrified pupils, "The parchment burns, but the letters fly away."[29] Hopefully, we read this as affirming that though the corporeal substance will be annihilated, the word cannot be obliterated. In shadowed moments we may wonder instead whether those letters, charred wisps rising through the scorching air, only waft away jumbled, mute, unspeakable.

We who have lived in the latter half of the twentieth century have known of cruelties terrible enough to make anyone who must speak of them wish that "unspeakable" were not a mere copper token. Words fail us, although they may be all that we have. And still they may even turn on us, like vipers' brood. We have surely had too many opportunities to admire Cleopatra's canny analysis of the promises of another, craftier politician, "He words me."[30] Where are the words that disarm? How do we construct the silence that will draw around us as an impervious shield? And if we ever manage to do that, can we safely emerge again?

Words cannot choose to be on our side. If we care about words and the life behind them, we want to heft them knowingly and feel in them the divine correlation between the word and the reality. We strive for the word well measured by righteousness and mercy and also for the silence sustainable by piety and decency. We crave words of fire, words of light, on our cold, dark journeys, but also the stillness of *shalom* in our homes and on our ways, the peace in which, after the fire, we can hear the still, small voice. We long for the word whose gleaming edge is the sword of justice and the word weighty as the hammer that will turn the sword into a ploughshare. Even more, we may yearn for the silence when the most perfect union dissolves the distinction between I and thou so that even dialogue becomes superfluous.

Wishing for all this and knowing that still we are left only with words or silence, we may come to cherish them and to respect them both, when used honestly and responsibly, as the last gifts of conscience. We have heard the lies and the betrayals, the denunciations and scorn, heard the silence of connivance and indifference; we have also heard the spoken testimonies and mute resistance. The Hasidic rabbi told his inquiring pupils that this was the lesson of the telegraph: that every word is counted and charged for—all, all. And we exiles in the word, all poets, all Jews, stand for the charge, valuing the cost, committed to believe that words should be counted, fearsome though the toll may be. We know also—the lesson of the telephone!—that even the silences are reckoned. Who could deny praying, even if one does not pray, that both our words and silence count, that neither may be that of ashes in the mouth.

Notes

Introduction

1. Sander Gilman, *Jewish Self-Hatred: Anti-Semitism and the Hidden Language of the Jews*, 14. Gilman's detailed study is especially relevant to the role of language in forming self-perceptions and constructing stereotypes from the late Middle Ages to our own time.

2. Compare this observation from the senior resident historian at the U.S. Holocaust Memorial Museum: "At least part of the reason for the neglect of the latest research in books and courses on the Holocaust is that in most American universities, the Holocaust has been considered, incorrectly, as an aspect of Jewish history and thus segregated in Jewish-studies programs in departments of ethnic studies or religion" (Sybil Milton, "Re-Examining Scholarship on the Holocaust," *Chronicle of Higher Education,* 26 April 1993, p. A52).

3. Tillie Olsen, *Silences.*

4. John Cage, *Silence.*

5. André Malraux, *The Voice of Silence: Man and His Art.*

6. Ihab Hassan, *The Literature of Silence: Henry Miller and Samuel Beckett,* 216–18.

7. George Steiner, *Language and Silence.*

8. This study will use the terms *ḥurban, Shoah,* and *Holocaust* as seems appropriate to the context. The first, the traditional Hebrew term for destruction, places the Nazis' annihilation of European Jewry within a historical pattern including the destruction of the First and Second Temples. The second designates the event as a disaster and implies its uniqueness by distinguishing it from earlier destructions. The third, given broad currency through Elie Wiesel's work, appropriates the biblical term designating a sacrificial burnt offering. Although it is the most widely used, it is problematic partly because it too characterizes the events as unique, not as the culmination of a long

history, and partly because its original religious meaning seems so inappropriate. The latter, of course, exactly suited Wiesel's ironic point, his protest against divine silence (a point that one need not accept).

9. André Neher, *The Exile of the Word: From the Silence of the Bible to the Silence of Auschwitz.*

10. Max Picard, *The World of Silence.*

11. David Wolpe, *In Speech and in Silence.*

12. José Faur, *Golden Doves with Silver Dots: Semiotics and Textuality in Rabbinic Tradition,* 145.

13. Arthur Green, *Tormented Master: A Life of Rabbi Nahman of Bratslav,* is an outstanding study; pp. 290–320 are especially relevant to these issues. Elie Wiesel, in *Souls on Fire: Portraits and Legends of Hasidic Masters,* has written of the Bratslaver and Kotzker *rebbes* in ways that have strongly influenced my views of them; however, one might also note with caution Wiesel's inclination to regard his subjects as if they had, like him, outlasted the Auschwitz gas chambers and emerged spiritually rent.

14. Elie Wiesel, *Somewhere a Master: Further Hasidic Portraits and Legends,* 201.

15. Neher in *The Exile of the Word* (pp. 34–47) undertakes a remarkable taxonomy of the Hebrew biblical words related to silence.

16. Arthur Green, *Seek My Face, Speak My Name,* 61.

17. Gilman, *Jewish Self-Hatred,* 15.

18. Benjamin Harshav, *The Meaning of Yiddish,* 97.

19. Jacques Lacan, *Speech and Language in Psychoanalysis,* 39; French text of "*Fonction et champ de la parole et du langage,*" in Lacan, *Écrits,* 276.

20. Green, *Seek My Face,* 61.

21. Lacan, *Speech and Language,* 42.

22. Sue Levi Elwell, "Rosh Hashanah Sermon (1987)." In *Four Centuries of Jewish Women's Spirituality: A Sourcebook,* ed. Ellen M. Umansky and Dianne Ashton, 273.

Chapter 1: Speaking of Silences

1. Hélène Cixous, "Sorties," in *The Newly Born Woman,* ed. Cixous and Catherine Clement, 92.

2. John Milton, *Paradise Lost,* 9.11.20–21 and 7.1.38, in *John Milton.*

3. Osip Mandelshtam, untitled poem beginning "Zvuk ostorozhnyj," in *Modern Russian Poetry,* ed. Vladimir Markov and Merrill Sparks (N.p. [Scotland]: Macgibbon and Kee, 1966), 263, my translation. This was the opening poem in Mandelshtam's first published volume.

4. The first two quotations are from Norman O. Brown, *Love's Body,* quoted by Hassan, *Literature of Silence,* 218. The second pair are from D. H. Lawrence, *Apocalypse,* also quoted by Hassan, 3.

5. Georg Trakl, "Nachtlied," *Dichtung und Briefe*, 1:68; my translation.

6. Elie Wiesel, *The Testament*, 304–5.

7. Barbara Newman, "Lynn Seymour," in her *Striking a Balance: Dancers Talk about Dancing* (Boston: Houghton Mifflin, 1982), 235.

8. Walt Whitman, "Song of Myself," section 24, in *Leaves of Grass*, ed. Malcolm Cowley (New York: Viking, 1959), 48.

9. Olsen, *Silences*, x.

10. Edmond Jabès, *From the Book to the Book: An Edmond Jabès Reader*, 211.

11. Eugenio Montale, "L'anguilla," in his *Selected Poems* (New York: New Directions, 1965), p. 156.

12. Faur in *Golden Doves* (pp. 115–18) discusses this concept in Jewish scribal tradition and thought, noting that "the blank spaces between the letters . . . is essential for writing" because of not only practical but also hermeneutical considerations.

13. The Heidegger issue is raised and most fully documented by Victor Farías in his *Heidegger and Nazism*. The principal philosophical questioning of the meanings of Heidegger's "silence" is by Jean-François Lyotard, *Heidegger and "the jews."*

14. Franz Kafka, *Letter to His Father* (New York: Schocken, 1966); Nadine Gordimer, "Letter from His Father," in *Something Out There*, 39–56. For a discussion of the relationship between these works in terms of Gordimer's literary priorities, see Andrew Vogel Ettin, *Betrayals of the Body Politic: The Literary Commitments of Nadine Gordimer*, 132–34.

15. Gordimer, "Letter from His Father," 43.

16. Ibid., 56. Franz Kafka had written that "a book should be like an axe for the frozen seas inside us" (Franz Kafka, *Letters to Friends, Family, and Editors*, 16).

Chapter 2: A Sea of Ink

1. I am grateful for David Wolpe's citation of this passage in *The Healer of Shattered Hearts: A Jewish View of God*, 56. The poem, "Akdamut," written in Aramaic by Rabbi Meir ben Isaac of Orleans, appears in the liturgy for the scriptural reading on Shavuot (Pentecost). The translation is my own.

2. Edmond Jabès, *Le Livre des Questions*, 132, my translation. I have also consulted the English translation of this passage in *From the Book to the Book*, xxv.

3. Gloria Anzaldúa, *Borderlands/La Frontera*, 72.

4. Bertrand Russell, Introduction to Ludwig Wittgenstein, *Tractatus Logico-Philosophicus*, 8.

5. Martin Buber, *I and Thou*, 3, 136.

6. Neher, *Exile of the Word*, 235.

7. Ibid., 85.

8. Ibid., 210–26.

9. Wiesel, *The Testament*, 345.

10. Ibid., 210.

11. Wittgenstein, *Tractatus*, 68, propositions 4.0311 and 4.03, respectively.

12. Ibid., 150, propositions 5.621 and 5.63.

13. Ibid., 188, proposition 7.

14. Rosenzweig did evaluate with polemic acerbity contemporary Zionist theories for the new Hebrew in his essay "Classical and Modern Hebrew," in Nahum H. Glatzer, ed., *Franz Rosenzweig*, 263–71.

15. Ibid., 298.

16. Buber, from *Israel and the World*, in Bernard Martin, ed., *Great Twentieth Century Jewish Philosophers: Shestov, Rosenzweig, Buber*, 324.

17. Faur, *Golden Doves*, 29.

18. Green, *Seek My Face*, 72.

19. Susan A. Handelman, *The Slayers of Moses: The Emergence of Rabbinic Interpretive Tradition in Modern Literary Theory*, 4.

20. Glatzer, ed., *Franz Rosenzweig*, 216.

21. Louis Jacobs, *Jewish Mystical Testimonies*, 220–21 (translation slightly revised).

22. Maimonides, *Guide for the Perplexed*, cited in Abraham Joshua Heschel, *God in Search of Man: A Philosophy of Judaism*, 122–23.

23. Joseph B. Soloveitchik, *The Lonely Man of Faith*, 73–74. Soloveitchik points out that the Hebrew word root spelled *aleph-mem-resh* means "to think" as well as "to say."

24. David Hakohen, *Hishtaḥavi u-birkhi* ("Silence and Praise"), in *The Penguin Book of Hebrew Verse*, ed. T. Carmi, 396–97, slightly revised.

25. Aaron Zeitlin, "Tekst," my translation from the Yiddish in *Onions and Cucumbers and Plums: Forty-six Yiddish Poems*, ed. and trans. Sarah Zweig Betsky, poem no. 3.

26. *Pirkei de Rabbi Eliezar*, 10, cited by Alon Goshen-Gottschein, "Creation," in *Contemporary Jewish Religious Thought*, ed. Arthur A. Cohen and Paul Mendes-Flohr, 114.

27. Ross Brann, *The Compunctious Poet: Cultural Ambiguity and Hebrew Poetry in Muslim Spain*, 30, quoting Menachem ibn Saruq against Dunash ben Labrat. Brann discusses this linguistic dispute and its aftermath on pp. 28–40; further, his entire book is relevant to the status of Hebrew in this diaspora environment. An excellent description of the impact of Arabic on medieval Hebrew metrics may be found in Benjamin [Hrushovsky] Harshav's "Prosody, Hebrew" in the *Encyclopedia Judaica*, 24–33, and (in briefer form) in his introduction to *The Penguin Book of Hebrew Verse*, ed. T. Carmi, 63–64.

28. Glatzer, ed., *Franz Rosenzweig*, 251. One should not miss the canny ambiguity poised in Rosenzweig's naming of Mendelssohn without a given name: the composer Felix was a convert to Christianity, his grandfather Moses the greatest German Jewish philosopher of the Enlightenment and so a symbol of cultural assimilation.

29. Lawrence Kushner, *The Book of Letters: Sefer Otiyot*, 4.

30. Wolpe, *Healer*, 144, citing Gittin 56b.

31. Ibid., 108, citing Megillah 16b.

32. Rachel Adler, "The Jew Who Wasn't There: *Halakhah* and the Jewish Woman," in *On Being a Jewish Feminist*, ed. Susannah Heschel, 12–18; Nessa Rapoport, "The Woman Who Lost Her Names," in *The Woman Who Lost Her Names*, ed. Julia Wolf Mazow, 135–42. Tova Rosen has written a fine essay analyzing earlier literature through a feminist framework, "On Tongues Being Bound and Let Loose: Women in Medieval Hebrew Literature."

33. Among the examples: Rabbi Lynn Gottlieb, "The Secret Jew: An Oral Tradition of Women" and "Spring Cleaning Ritual on the Eve of Full Moon Nisan" in *On Being a Jewish Feminist*, ed. Heschel, 273–77, 278–80. Susan Starr Sered, *Women as Ritual Experts: The Religious Lives of Elderly Jewish Women in Jerusalem* (N.Y.: Oxford Univ. Press, 1992); Rabbi Nina Beth Cardin, *Out of the Depths I Call to You: A Book of Prayers for the Married Jewish Woman* (Northvale, N.J.: Jason Aronson, 1991); Penina V. Adelman, *Miriam's Well: Rituals for Jewish Women around the Year* (Fresh Meadows, N.Y.: Biblio Press, 1986); and the texts in Umansky and Ashton, eds., *Four Centuries of Jewish Women's Spirituality*.

34. "Notes toward Finding the Right Question," in Heschel, ed., *On Being a Jewish Feminist*. See also the discussion by Judith Plaskow, *Standing Again at Sinai*, esp. 149–54.

35. Plaskow, *Standing Again at Sinai*, 138. Plaskow's entire discussion of theological language and the images of God, pp. 121–69, is important, especially her sections on fear of paganism (pp. 147–54) and on the continuing need for anthropomorphic imagery (pp. 160–67).

36. Ibid., 143–44.

37. *Kol Haneshamah*, the Shabbat Eve prayer book developed by the Reconstructionist movement, offers notably creative liturgical approaches to these various issues.

38. Midrash Rabbah, Bereshith, 8.1.

Chapter 3: Letters in Love with Letters

1. Faur, *Golden Doves*, 135.

2. Jabès, *Le Livre des Questions*, 109.

3. Benjamin Harshav and Barbara Harshav, eds., *American Yiddish Poetry: A Bilingual Anthology*, 78–79, my transliteration; translation slightly revised.

4. Wolpe, *In Speech and in Silence*, 114.

5. Cited in Gunther Plaut, ed., *The Torah: A Modern Commentary*, 1519.

6. Marthe Robert, *As Lonely as Franz Kafka*, 31.

7. Ibid., 151–52.

8. Audre Lorde, "The Transformation of Silence into Language and Action," in her *Sister Outsider: Essays and Speeches*, 42–43.

9. *Cassell's New German Dictionary*, rev. Karl Breul (New York and London: Funk and Wagnalls, 1906), 313.

10. Benjamin Harshav, *The Meaning of Yiddish*, especially 137–50.

11. Isaac Deutscher, *The Non-Jewish Jew and Other Essays*, ed. Tamara Deutscher (New York: Hill and Wang, 1968), 44–46.

12. Glatzer, ed., *Franz Rosenzweig*, 307.

13. Gilman, *Jewish Self-Hatred*, 102–3.

14. So, for instance, Susannah Heschel notes: "Reform called over a hundred years ago for complete equality of men and women with Judaism, not out of a commitment to women, but in order to modernize Judaism by removing embarrassing vestiges of 'orientalism' from its public religious services." From her introduction to *On Being a Jewish Feminist*, xxvii.

15. *Cassell's New German Dictionary*, 314.

16. David Margolick, "At the Bar," B10.

17. Gerald Stern, *Leaving Another Kingdom: Selected Poems*, 21.

18. Marina Tsvetaeva, "Poema kontsa," in her *Izbrannaye proizvedeniya*, 356 (Moscow and Leningrad: Biblioteka Poèta, 1965), my translation, assisted by Marina Raskin; a translation of the full work appears in Tsvetaeva, *Selected Poems*, trans. Elaine Feinstein and Angela Livingstone (Oxford: Oxford University Press, 1971), 48–79.

19. Jabès, *Le Livre des Questions*, 109.

Chapter 4: The Silence of Potentiality

1. Martin Buber, *Tales of the Hasidim: The Early Masters*, 315.

2. Jerome Rothenberg et al., eds. *A Big Jewish Book: Poems and Other Visions of the Jews from Tribal Times to the Present*, 101–2.

3. Neher, *The Exile of the Word*, 43.

4. Faur, *Golden Doves*, 51.

5. Neher, *The Exile of the Word*, 9.

6. Cage, "Composition as Process," in *Silence*, 22–23.

7. Green, *Seek My Face*, 26–27.

8. *The Zohar*, 2b, 3b–4a; 1:9, 15. The gloss is on the word *b'hibaram*, distinguished at this place in the Torah scroll by the use of a small letter *hey* (= h). By transposing that letter and the *alef*, one turns the word into *b'abraham:* that is, "by their creation" becomes "by Abraham."

9. Jacobs, *Jewish Mystical Testimonies*, 87–97.

10. See for instance the midrashic interpretation of Genesis 1:31 by Rabbi Abbahu, *Midrash Rabbah, 8:6–7, Genesis*, vol. 1, 23–24.

11. A. R. Ammons, "Coon Song," in his *Collected Poems, 1951–1971*, 87–89.

12. Jabès, quoted by Waldrop, in *From the Book to the Book*, xxv.

13. Green, *Seek My Face*, 18, 102.

14. Henry Roth, *Call It Sleep*, 441. The fine afterword by Hana Wirth-Nesher, especially pp. 454–60, offers a rather different analysis of the religious motifs and finds even more pessimistic implications in the novel's concluding engagements with languages and stylistics.

Chapter 5: Limen / Meₓuₓah

1. Chaim Potok, *The Gift of Asher Lev*, 33.

2. Masao Miyoshi, *Accomplices of Silence: The Modern Japanese Novel*, xv.

3. Ibid., 178–79.

4. Ibid., xv.

5. Ibid., 179.

6. Etty Hillesum, *An Interrupted Life: The Diaries of Etty Hillesum, 1941–43*, 143.

7. Ibid., 124–25.

8. Etty Hillesum, *Letters from Westerbork*. This remarkable letter also appears in Hillesum, *An Interrupted Life;* the quoted passages appear on pp. 258, 263, with minor variants in punctuation.

9. Ben-Zion Bokser, *The Jewish Mystical Tradition*, 110–11.

10. See for example Brann, *The Compunctious Poet*, 32–33, and the criticism cited there. Carmi, ed., *The Penguin Book of Hebrew Verse*, 280, prints each hemistych as a separate line for reasons of layout; thus, the two sections appear as eighteen and eight lines, respectively.

11. Dimitri Obolensky, ed., *The Penguin Book of Russian Verse*, 132–33.

12. Adrienne Rich, "Twenty-One Love Poems: No. 7," in her *The Fact of a Doorframe: Poems Selected and New, 1950–1984*, 239.

13. Milton, "The Reason of Church Government," in *John Milton*, ed. Orgel and Goldberg, 166–67, 172–73.

14. Anzaldúa, *Borderlands*, 73–74.

15. Hillesum, *An Interrupted Life*, 124.

16. Bokser, *Jewish Mystical Tradition*, 143–44, quoting from Chayyim Vital's *Eitₓ ha-Chayyim*.

17. Green, *Seek My Face*, 163, and bibliographic note, 243–44.

18. Irena Klepfisz, "Bashert," in *A Few Words in the Mother Tongue*, 192.

19. Maya Angelou, *I Know Why the Caged Bird Sings*, 73.

20. Dolly A. McPherson, *Order Out of Chaos: The Autobiographical Works of Maya Angelou*, 147–48.

21. Angelou, *Caged Bird*, 81–82.

22. Bella Akhmadulina, "The Noise of Silence," in *The Garden: New and Selected Poetry and Prose* (a bilingual ed.), 93–95. The citations that follow are to "[The Secret]," 23; "The Coffee Imp," 9; and "The Garden," 5, respectively. "The Garden/The Guardsman" appears on pp. 103–5.

23. My translation from Amir Gilboa, "*Ba'aletet*," in Carmi, ed., *The Penguin Book of Hebrew Verse*, 562.

Chapter 6: Compulsion for the Word

1. Hassan, *Literature of Silence*, 203, quoting from a letter to Anaïs Nin.

2. Green, *Seek My Face*, 64.

3. Hillel Halkin, introduction to Sholem Aleichem, *Tevye the Dairyman and the Railroad Stories* (New York: Schocken, 1987), xxxvi–xxxvii. Harshav, *The Meaning of Yiddish*, 102–7, has an insightful analysis of the Yiddish characteristics in Tevye's speech patterns.

4. Sholem Aleichem, "Shprintze," in Halkin, *Tevye the Dairyman*, 96.

5. Harshav, *The Meaning of Yiddish*, 107.

6. Peter Gay, *Freud, Jews, and Other Germans: Masters and Victims in Modernist Culture*, 55–56.

7. Soloveitchik, *Lonely Man of Faith*, 67, 38.

8. *Midrash Rabbah* 1:10, in *Midrash Rabbah*, ed. and trans. H. Freedman and Maurice Simon, 1:9.

9. Mishnah Sanhedrin 11:1.

10. Thus the Zohar suggests, 1:11b; *The Zohar*, 1:48–49.

11. William Shakespeare, *King Lear*, in *The Riverside Shakespeare*, act 1, sc. 1, line 50. All subsequent text references are to this edition.

12. E.g, *Bava Metzia*, 4A.

13. Adin Steinsalz, *The Talmud: The Steinsalz Edition, a Reference Guide*, 259.

14. John Milton, *Paradise Lost*, bk. 5, lines 117–18.

15. Mishnah Ḥagigah 21:1.

16. Rich, "Cartographies of Silence," in her *The Fact of a Doorframe*, 232.

17. Rich, "Twenty-One Love Poems: No. 20," ibid., 246.

18. Ingeborg Bachmann, "Exil," in her *Werke*, 1:60; my translations.

19. Mark Anderson, "Introduction: Poet on the Border," in Ingeborg Bachmann, *In the Storm of Roses: Selected Poems*, ed. and trans. Mark Anderson, 12–13.

20. Bachmann, "Wahrlich," ibid., in *Werke*, 1: 174, my translation.

21. Bachmann, "Keine Delikatessen," ibid., 1:86, my translation.

22. Anderson, "Introduction," to Bachmann, *In the Storm of Roses*, 12.

23. See for instance Emmanuel Levinas, *Difficult Freedom*, and the analyses of this

idea in Robert Gibbs, *Correlations in Rosenzweig and Levinas*, 156–75, and Susan A. Handelman, *Fragments of Redemption: Jewish Thought and Literary Theory in Benjamin, Scholem, and Levinas*, 263–65, 309–12, 328–29.

24. Katherine Washburn, Introduction to Paul Celan, *Last Poems*, xxxiv.

25. See Steiner's essay "Schoenberg's *Moses und Aron*," with particular reference to the composer's Judaism, in Steiner, *Language and Silence*, 169–82, esp. 170–71.

26. Donald Jay Grout, *A History of Western Music*, 656.

27. Paul Celan, "Was es an Sternen bedarf," in *Lichtzwang*, 48, my translation.

28. Edmond Jabès, *Elya*, quoted in Rothenberg et al., eds., *A Big Jewish Book*, 13.

29. *Bereishit*, 53b, in *The Zohar*, 1:169.

30. Franz Rosenzweig, *The Star of Redemption*, 336.

31. Neher, *Exile of the Word*, 43–44.

32. Glatzer, ed., *Franz Rosenzweig*, 255. See also Rosenzweig's "Sociology of the Whole: The Greeting," in his *Star of Redemption*, 321–23, or in Glatzer, ed., *Franz Rosenzweig*, pp. 308–9 (translated as "Sociology of the Multitude: The Listening).

33. Wiesel, *Somewhere a Master*, 175–76. This chapter concludes with Wiesel's historical and theological consideration of silence's meanings as suggested by the Hasidic school of Worke and the modern experiences of Jews in Europe (pp. 199–201).

34. *Midrash Rabbah*, 38:11 in *Midrash Rabbah*, 1:310, translation slightly revised.

35. Gay, *Freud, Jews, and Other Germans*, 55.

36. Primo Levi, "Cantare," in his *L'osteria di Brema*, 13.

37. Sidra DeKoven Ezrahi, *By Words Alone: The Holocaust in Literature*, 18.

38. Levi, "Alzarsi," in his *L'osteria*, 21.

39. Elements of parataxis in Levi's prose are discussed by Pietro Frassica, "Aspetti della narrativa italina postbellica (Beppe Fenoglio e Primo Levi)."

40. Sander L. Gilman, "Primo Levi: The Special Language of the Camps and After," interestingly studies Levi's treatment of Yiddish, Hebrew, and Italian as attempts to reconstruct Jewish language and civilized language for himself against the camp jargon in which "Everything had an affective dimension that transcended the meaning of the words themselves" (p. 22).

41. Cesare Segre has said that the Polish word produces "una specie di richiamo all'apocalisse che continua a pendere su di noi," and noted the "ricorso al plurilinguismo per evocare la stridula commistione di lingue che caratterizzava il Lager." See Segre, "Primo Levi nella Torre di Babele," in *Primo Levi as Witness*, ed. Pietro Frassica, 87.

42. Primo Levi, "Afterword: The Author's Answers to His Readers' Questions," in his *Survival in Auschwitz*, 376. This passage is also cited by Alexander Stille, "Primo Levi and the art of memory," in *Primo Levi as Witness*, ed. Frassica, 103.

43. Sigmund Freud, *The Question of Lay Analysis*, quoted in Gay, *Freud, Jews and Other Germans*, 54.

44. Rich, "Twenty-One Love Poems: No. 20," in her *The Fact of a Doorframe*, 246.

45. Nadine Gordimer, "A Journey," in her *Jump and Other Stories*, 146.

46. Shakespeare, *The Tempest*, in *The Riverside Shakespeare*, act 1, sc. 2, lines 363–64.

47. Grace Paley, "Listening," in her *Later the Same Day*, 210.

Chapter 7: Exiles from Their Words

1. Anzia Yezierska, "America and I," in *America and I: Short Stories by American Jewish Women Writers*, ed. Joyce Antler, 72.

2. Rich, "A Valediction Forbidding Mourning," in her *The Fact of a Doorframe*, 136.

3. Harshav, *The Meaning of Yiddish*, 120. Harshav's discussion of the "Modern Jewish Revolution" (pp. 119–38) is especially pertinent to the connections between language and identity.

4. Michelle Cliff, *Claiming an Identity They Taught Me to Despise*.

5. Tillie Olsen, "Dream-Vision," in *Shaking Eve's Tree: Short Stories of Jewish Women*, ed. Sharon Niederman, 122.

6. Philip Roth, *Goodbye, Columbus and Five Short Stories*, 169–71.

7. Bernard Malamud, *The Magic Barrel*, 132.

8. Ibid., 104.

9. Judith Herzberg, "Disturbing the Peace," in her *But What: Selected Poems*, 108.

10. Ibid., 102.

11. Herzberg, "1945," ibid., 62.

12. I discuss Vergil's treatment of exile in this poem in Andrew V. Ettin, *Literature and the Pastoral*, especially 96–104 and 161–63.

13. Hana Wirth-Nesher, Afterword to Roth, *Call It Sleep*, pp. 448–49; essay originally published as "Between Native Tongue and Mother Language in *Call It Sleep*."

14. Ibid., 452.

15. Klepfisz, "Fradel Shtock," in her *A Few Words in the Mother Tongue*, pp. 228–29.

16. My translation from Malka Heifetz Tussman, "Vasser on loshen," in *The Penguin Book of Modern Yiddish Verse* (bilingual ed.), ed. Irving Howe, Ruth Wisse, and Khone Shmeruk, 499.

17. Cynthia Ozick, *The Pagan Rabbi and Other Stories*, 95–96.

18. Ibid., 99–100.

19. Among the anthologies, the most notable is Harshav and Harshav, eds. and trans. *American Yiddish Poetry*, with bilingual selections from seven poets, an essential introduction, and pertinent illustrations. Howe, Wisse, and Shmeruk, *The Penguin Book of Modern Yiddish Verse*, is also bilingual and offers a much broader selection but with far fewer offerings from each writer. Volumes devoted to individual poets include

Moyshe-Leyb Halpern, *In New York: A Selection*, trans. and ed. Kathryn Hellerstein (Philadelphia: Jewish Publication Society, 1982); A. Sutzkever, *Selected Poetry and Prose*, trans. Benjamin Harshav and Barbara Harshav (Berkeley: University of California Press, 1991); and Malka Heifetz Tussman, *With Teeth in the Earth: Selected Poems*, ed. and trans. Marcia Falk (Detroit: Wayne State University Press, 1992).

20. Olsen, *Silences*, 262.

21. Rich, "North American Time," in her *The Fact of a Doorframe*, 325–26.

Chapter 8: One-Way Conversations

1. Frank Manuel, *The Broken Staff: Judaism through Christian Eyes*, 1, traces this phrase to narrow applications by Ernest Renan and Mark Pattison, and Manuel believes that it did not come into popular usage in its modern sense until after World War II. There is no listing of it in the Oxford English Dictionary.

2. This work is now in the collection of the Institut de France, Museé Jacquemart-André, in Paris.

3. So, for instance, Niny Garavaglia, *The Complete Paintings of Mantegna* (New York: Harry N. Abrams, 1967), 118.

4. I am aware of Tietze-Conrat's opinion that Mantegna was responsible only for the design of the piece as well as of Kristeller's and Venturi's belief that it comes from the master's studio, not from his hand. However, most authorities consider it a genuine Mantegna, and I see no justification for doubting that attribution. If the work was executed by another artist, that obviously mars my theory about Mantegna but not the larger point raised in the next paragraph, that Hebrew accuracy was generally immaterial.

5. Manuel, *The Broken Staff*, writes that late in the Renaissance, "The trilingual man became a humanist ideal" (p. 32). My contrary generalization, albeit unfairly broad, rests on my phrase "weight-bearing cornerstone." Focusing as he does on Christian scholars studying Jewish texts, Manuel understandably stresses that Hebrew was more widely known and Judaism more intensely studied than is generally assumed. I would reply that it was at best the short leg of that trilingualism; on the whole it did not acquire Latin's or even Greek's status as an essential language. We would agree that knowledge of Hebrew did not necessarily correlate with respect for Judaism or tolerance (much less acceptance) of Jews.

6. Ibid., 13.

7. Handelman, *The Slayers of Moses*, 170, writes, "The history of philosophy, then, is ultimately an argument between Jews and Greeks," and she notes the relevance of Matthew Arnold's contrast between Hebraism and Hellenism. Although I do not dispute the conceptual validity of these antitheses, I would argue that in historical reality

Jews, Judaism, and Hebraism are all terms deserving quotation marks because they have not been allowed to speak as equals on their own behalf. The dominant Hellenism and Hellenistic Christianity have defined them and their roles, circumscribing them into categories subsumable within the dominant tradition or subservient to it.

8. On Spinoza, see, for example, Yirmiyahu Yovel, *The Marrano of Reason.*

9. Levinas, "How is Judaism Possible," in *Difficult Freedom,* 246–47.

10. Milton's knowledge of Hebrew and familiarity with Jewish theology has been explored by, among others, Harold Fisch, "Hebraism, Milton's," in *A Milton Encyclopedia,* ed. William B. Hunter, Jr. (Lewisburg, Pa.: Bucknell University Press, 1978), 3:162–70 and bibliography, 9:62.

11. Levinas, "Jewish Thought Today," in *Difficult Freedom,* 161.

12. See, for instance, Adin Steinsalz, *The Essential Talmud,* 81–85.

13. Sigmund Freud, *Moses and Monotheism,* 17, protests, "It is not attractive to be classed with the scholastics and Talmudists who are satisfied to exercise their ingenuity, unconcerned how far removed their conclusions may be from the truth," a remarkable statement considering the date (1937) as well as the scholarly context in which he made it.

14. Handelman, *The Slayers of Moses.*

15. Quoted by Gibbs in *Correlations,* 168.

16. Levinas, "Israel and Universalism," in *Difficult Freedom,* 175.

17. Two factors contribute to the increase in the study of Talmud. One is a general revival in traditionalism among Jews, as well as among other religions. Another is the wider accessibility of the Talmud, principally through Adin Steinsalz's translation of the difficult text into modern Hebrew and its subsequent publication in English, providing both a literal and a freer interpretive translation (along with the original text) that allows for mutual study without an experienced Talmudist present. The remarkable sales figures for Steinsalz's user-friendly, elegant, expensive volumes likely attest to a combination of feelings, including interest, envy, and guilt, in their purchasers.

18. Steiner, "Retreat from the Word," in *Language and Silence,* 39.

19. Levinas, "Judaism and the Feminine," in *Difficult Freedom,* 30.

20. Ibid.

21. A remarkable music recording, fittingly called *Silenced Voices: Victims of the Holocaust* (Northeastern NR 248-CD), ends with a "Duo for Violin and Cello" by Gideon Klein, who began it in 1941 and left it unfinished at his death in a concentration camp about three years later at the age of twenty-six. The performance stops abruptly at the end of an inconclusive phrase two-and-a-half minutes into the second movement, when Klein's artistic voice fell silent.

22. Emil Fackenheim, *God's Presence in History: Jewish Affirmations and Philosophical Reflections,* 94. The final remark is based on an observation by Simon Wiesenthal.

23. Edward T. Linenthal, "Contested Memories, Contested Space: The Holocaust

Museum Gets Pushed Back," 49, 52. This article provocatively examines the forces at work in shaping the eventual design and placement of the museum.

24. Quoted by Fackenheim in *God's Presence in History*, 99, n.6, quoting in turn from A. Roy Eckhardt, *Elder and Younger Brothers* (New York: Scribners, 1967), 171.

Chapter 9: The Lead Plates of the Rom Press

1. Vladimir Horowitz quoted in Harold S. Schonberg, *Horowitz: His Life and Music* (New York: Simon and Schuster, 1992), 47.

2. Allen Tate, *Collected Poems: 1917–1976*, 147–48.

3. I have argued elsewhere that this play criticizes the values of Roman culture so admired in the Renaissance. See Andrew Vogel Ettin, "Shakespeare's First Roman Tragedy."

4. Herman Kruk, *Vilna Ghetto Diary*, trans. from Yiddish by Barbara Harshav, intro. by Benjamin Harshav (New Haven: Yale University Press and YIVO, forthcoming). I am grateful to the Harshavs for making this text available to me.

5. Quoted in Fackenheim, *God's Presence in History*, 72.

6. Muriel Rukeyser, "Bubble of Air," in *Out of Silence*, 61.

7. Faur, *Golden Doves*, 144–45.

8. Hebrew text from Ruth Finer Mintz, ed. and trans., *Modern Hebrew Poetry: A Bilingual Anthology*, 199–201; my translations.

9. Yiddish text from Harshav and Harshav, eds. and trans., *American Yiddish Poetry*, 438; my transliteration and translation.

10. Vercors [Jean Bruller], *Les silences de la mer*, 14.

11. Ibid., 34.

12. Ibid., 25.

13. The Yiddish text for Sutzkever's poem is that of Howe, Wisse, and Shmeruk, eds., *The Penguin Book of Modern Yiddish Verse*, 678; translations are my own. A fine discussion of the poem's background and composition appears in David G. Roskies, *Against the Apocalypse: Responses to Catastrophe in Modern Jewish Culture*, 250–51.

14. Roskies, *Against the Apocalypse*, 250–51 and 345 n.70, notes that this stanza appeared first in 1945, two years after the poem's first publication. It presumably represents the poet's deliberate development of a longer historical context than the fictive event of the Vilna resistance that it describes. Roskies also affirms from interviews that the episode, taken by many readers to be true, was Sutzkever's poetic invention.

15. Frieda W. Aaron, *Bearing the Unbearable: Yiddish and Polish Poetry in the Ghettos and Concentration Camps* (Albany: State Univ. of New York Press, 1990), 170.

16. Soloveitchik, *Lonely Man of Faith*, 76–77.

17. Anzaldúa, *Borderlands*, 75.

18. Milton, sonnet 7, in *John Milton*, 34.

19. Cixous and Clement, *The Newly Born Woman*, 92.

20. Anzaldúa, *Borderlands*, 74. Anzaldúa frequently chooses to leave her Spanish untranslated, as here. *Todo pasaba por esa boca, el viento, el fuego, los mares y la Tierra:* "Everything passes through this mouth—wind, fire, the seas and the Earth."

21. Rukeyser, "The Gates," in *Out of Silence*, 161.

22. Fackenheim, *God's Presence in History*, 71–72.

23. Milton, "A Masque Presented at Ludlow Castle," lines 171, 756–61, in *John Milton*, pp. 49, 64.

24. Ibid., lines 780–81, 783–85; pp. 64–65.

25. Ibid., lines 790–92, p. 65.

26. I hope that this phrase will recall for some readers somewhat appropriately the motto of the campaign for the Equal Rights Amendment: "Failure Is Impossible."

27. Shakespeare, *Julius Caesar*, in *The Riverside Shakespeare*, act 3, sc. 1, line 76.

28. Rukeyser, "Käthe Kollwitz," in *Out of Silence*, 132.

29. Avodah Zorah 17a; the story is recounted in the martyrology ("*Eleh ezk'rah*") of the Yom Kippur *musaf* service.

30. Shakespeare, *Antony and Cleopatra*, in *The Riverside Shakespeare*, act 5, sc. 2, line 191.

Bibliography

Akhmadulina, Bella. *The Garden: New and Selected Poetry and Prose.* Ed. and trans. F. D. Reeve. New York: Henry Holt, 1990.

Ammons, A. R. *Collected Poems, 1951–1971.* New York: Norton, 1972.

Angelou, Maya. *I Know Why the Caged Bird Sings.* New York: Bantam Books, 1971.

Antler, Joyce, ed. *America and I: Short Stories by American Jewish Women Writers.* Boston: Beacon Press, 1990.

Anzaldúa, Gloria. *Borderlands/La frontera.* San Francisco: Aunt Lute Press, 1987.

Bachmann, Ingeborg. *In the Storm of Roses: Selected Poems.* Ed. and trans. Mark Anderson. Princeton, N.J.: Princeton Univ. Press, 1986.

The Bahir. Trans. Aryeh Kaplan. York Beach, Mass.: Samuel Weiser, 1979.

Bakhtin, Mikhail. *The Dialogic Imagination.* Ed. Michael Holquist, trans. Caryl Emerson. Austin: Univ. of Texas Press, 1981.

Beckett, Samuel. *Eh Joe and Other Writings.* London: Faber and Faber, 1967.

Betsky, Sarah Zweig, ed. and trans. *Onions and Cucumbers and Plums: Forty-six Yiddish Poems.* Detroit: Wayne State Univ. Press, 1958.

Biblia Hebraica Stuttgartensia. Stuttgart: Deutsche Bibelgesellschaft, 1977.

Bokser, Ben-Zion. *The Jewish Mystical Tradition.* New York: Pilgrim Press, 1984.

Brann, Ross. *The Compunctious Poet: Cultural Ambiguity and Hebrew Poetry in Muslim Spain.* Baltimore: Johns Hopkins Univ. Press, 1991.

Buber, Martin. *I and Thou.* 2d ed. Trans. Ronald Gregory Smith. New York: Charles Scribner's Sons, 1958.

———. *Tales of the Hasidim: The Early Masters.* Trans. Olga Marx. New York: Schocken, 1947.

Cage, John. *Silence.* Middletown, Conn.: Wesleyan Univ. Press, 1961.

Carmi, T., ed. and trans. *The Penguin Book of Hebrew Verse.* New York: Penguin, 1981.

Celan, Paul. *Last Poems.* Ed. Katherine Washburn, trans. Katherine Washburn and Margueret Guillemin. San Francisco: North Point Press, 1986.

Cixous, Hélène, and Catherine Clement. *The NewlyBorn Woman*. Trans. Betty Winger. Minneapolis: Univ. of Minnesota Press, 1986.

Cohen, Arthur A., and Paul Mendes-Flohr, eds. *Contemporary Jewish Religious Thought*. New York: Charles Scribner's Sons, 1987.

Cliff, Michelle. *Claiming an Identity They Taught Me to Despise*. Watertown, Mass.: Persephone Press, 1980.

Epstein, Isadore, ed. *The Soncino Talmud*. London: Soncino Press, 1955.

Ettin, Andrew Vogel. *Betrayals of the Body Politic: The Literary Commitments of Nadine Gordimer*. Charlottesville: Univ. Press. of Virginia, 1993.

——. *Literature and the Pastoral*. New Haven: Yale Univ. Press, 1984.

——. "Shakespeare's First Roman Tragedy." *ELH* 37 (1970): 325– 41.

Ezrahi, Sidra DeKoven. *By Words Alone: The Holocaust in Literature*. Chicago: Univ. of Chicago Press, 1980.

Fackenheim, Emil. *God's Presence in History: Jewish Affirmations and Philosophical Reflections*. New York: Harper, 1970.

Farías, Victor. *Heidegger and Nazism*. Trans. Paul Barrell et al. Philadelphia: Temple Univ. Press, 1989.

Faur, José. *Golden Doves with Silver Dots: Semiotics and Textuality in Rabbinic Tradition*. Bloomington: Indiana Univ. Press, 1986.

Frassica, Pietro. "Aspetti della narativa italiana postbellica (Beppe Fenoglio e Primo Levi)." *Forum italicum* 7 (1974): 365–80.

——, ed., *Primo Levi as Witness*. Fiesole: Casalini Libri, 1989.

Freud, Sigmund. *Moses and Monotheism*. Trans. Katherine Jones. New York: Vintage, 1967.

Gates of Prayer / Shaarei Tefilah (prayer book). New York: Central Conference of American Rabbis, 1975.

Gay, Peter. *Freud, Jews, and Other Germans: Masters and Victims in Modernist Culture*. New York: Oxford Univ. Press, 1978.

Gibbs, Robert. *Correlations in Rosenzweig and Levinas*. Princeton, N.J.: Princeton Univ. Press, 1992.

Gilman, Sander. *Jewish Self-Hatred: Anti-Semitism and the Hidden Language of the Jews*. Baltimore: Johns Hopkins Univ. Press, 1986.

——. "Primo Levi: The Special Language of the Camps and After." *Midstream* 35 (1989): 22–30.

Glatzer, Nahum H., ed. *Franz Rosenzweig: His Life and Thought*. New York: Schocken, 1972.

Gordimer, Nadine. *Jump and Other Stories*. New York: Farrar Straus Giroux, 1991.

——. *Something Out There*. Harmondsworth: Penguin, 1984.

Green, Arthur. *Seek My Face, Speak My Name*. Northvale, N.J.: Jason Aronson, 1992.

——. *Tormented Master: A Life of Rabbi Nahman of Bratslav*. New York: Schocken, 1979.

Grout, Donald Jay. *A History of Western Music.* New York: Norton, 1960.

Handelman, Susan A. *Fragments of Redemption: Jewish Thought and Literary Theory in Benjamin, Scholem, and Levinas.* Bloomington: Indiana Univ. Press, 1991.

———. *The Slayers of Moses: The Emergence of Rabbinic Interpretive Tradition in Modern Literary Theory.* Albany: State Univ. of New York Press, 1982.

Harshav, Benjamin. *The Meaning of Yiddish.* Berkeley: Univ. of California Press, 1990.

———. "Prosody, Hebrew." *Encyclopedia Judaica,* 1981. A shorter version appears as the introduction in Carmi, ed., *The Penguin Book of Hebrew Verse.*

Harshav, Benjamin, and Barbara Harshav, eds. and trans. *American Yiddish Poetry: A Bilingual Anthology.* Berkeley: Univ. of California Press, 1986.

Hassan, Ihab. *The Literature of Silence: Henry Miller and Samuel Beckett.* New York: Alfred A. Knopf, 1967.

Hertz, J. H., ed. *The Pentateuch and Haftorahs.* London: Soncino Press, 1965.

Herzberg, Judith. *But What: Selected Poems.* Trans. Shirley Kaufman with Judith Herzberg. N.p.: Oberlin College Press, 1988.

Heschel, Abraham Joshua. *God in Search of Man: A Philosophy of Judaism.* Cleveland: World Publishing, 1959.

Heschel, Susannah, ed. *On Being a Jewish Feminist: A Reader.* New York: Schocken, 1983.

Hillesum, Etty. *An Interrupted Life: The Diaries of Etty Hillesum, 1941–43.* New York: Washington Square Press, 1985.

———. *Letters from Westerbork.* Trans. Arnold J. Pomerans. Introduction by Jan G. Garlandt. New York: Pantheon Books, 1986.

Hoffman, Lawrence A., ed. *Gates of Understanding.* N.p.: Central Conference of American Rabbis, 1977.

———, ed. *Gates of Understanding 2: Appreciating the Days of Awe.* N.p.: Central Conference of American Rabbis, 1984.

The Holy Scriptures According to the Masoretic Text. Philadelphia: Jewish Publication Society, 1955.

Howe, Irving, Ruth Wisse, and Khone Shmeruk, eds. *The Penguin Book of Modern Yiddish Verse.* New York: Viking, 1987.

Jabès, Edmond. *From the Book to the Book: An Edmond Jabès Reader.* Trans. Rosemarie Waldrop. Hanover, N.H.: Wesleyan University Press, 1991.

———. *Le livre des Questions.* N.p.: Gallimard, 1963.

Jacobs, Louis. *Jewish Mystical Testimonies.* New York: Schocken, 1977.

Kafka, Franz. *Letter to His Father.* New York: Schocken Books, 1966. Orig. pub. as *Dearest Father.* New York: Schocken Books, 1954.

———. *Letters to Friends, Family, and Editors.* Trans. Richard and Clara Winston. New York: Schocken Books, 1977.

Klepfisz, Irena. *A Few Words in the Mother Tongue.* Portland, Ore.: Eighth Mountain Press, 1990.

Kol Haneshamah (prayer book). Wynecote, Pa.: Reconstructionist Press, 1989.

Kruk, Herman. *Vilna Ghetto Diary*. Trans. Barbara Harshav. New Haven: Yale Univ. Press, 1993.

Kushner, Lawrence. *The Book of Letters: Sefer Otiyot*. New York: Harper and Row, 1975.

Lacan, Jacques. *Écrits*. Paris: Éditions de Seuil, 1966.

——. *Speech and Language in Psychoanalysis*. Trans. and ed. Anthony Wilden. Baltimore: Johns Hopkins Univ. Press, 1981. [Orig. pub. as *The Language of the Self: The Function of Language in Psychoanalysis*.]

Laytner, Anson. *Arguing with God: A Jewish Tradition*. Northvale, N.J.: Jason Aronson, 1990.

Levi, Primo. *L'osteria di Brema*. Milano: All'insegna del Pesce d'Oro, 1975.

——. *Survival in Auschwitz*. Trans. Ruth Feldman. New York: Summit Books, 1986.

Levinas, Emmanuel. *Difficult Freedom*. Trans. Seán Hand. London: Athlone Press, 1990.

Linenthal, Edward T. "Contested Memories, Contested Space: The Holocaust Museum Gets Pushed Back." *Moment* 18 (June 1993): 46–53, 78.

Lorde, Audre. *Sister Outsider: Essays and Speeches*. Trumansburg, N.Y.: Crossing Press, 1984.

Lyotard, Jean-François. *Heidegger and "the jews."* Trans. Andreas Michel and Mark Roberts. Introduction by Daniel Carroll. Minneapolis: Univ. of Minnesota Press, 1990.

McPherson, Dolly A. *Order Out of Chaos: The Autobiographical Works of Maya Angelou*. New York: Peter Lang, 1990.

Malamud, Bernard. *The Magic Barrel*. New York: Farrar, Straus, Giroux, 1977 (originally published 1958).

Malraux, André. *The Voices of Silence: Man and His Art*. Trans. Stuart Gilbert. Garden City, N.Y.: Doubleday, 1953.

Manuel, Frank. *The Broken Staff: Judaism through Christian Eyes*. Cambridge: Harvard Univ. Press, 1992.

Margolick, David. "At the Bar." *New York Times*, 9 October 1992, p. B10.

Martin, Bernard, ed. *Great Twentieth Century Jewish Philosophers: Shestov, Rosenzweig, Buber*. N.p.: Macmillan, 1970.

Mazow, Julia Wolf, ed. *The Woman Who Lost Her Names*. New York: Harper and Row, 1980.

Midrash Rabbah. Ed. and trans. H. Freedman and Maurice Simon. London: Soncino Press, 1951.

Milton, John. *John Milton*. Ed. Stephen Orgel and Jonathan Goldberg. Oxford: Oxford Univ. Press, 1990.

Mintz, Ruth Finer, ed. and trans. *Modern Hebrew Poetry: A Bilingual Anthology*. Berkeley: Univ. of California Press, 1966.

Miyoshi, Masao. *Accomplices of Silence: The Modern Japanese Novel.* Berkeley: Univ. of California Press, 1974.

Neher, André. *The Exile of the Word: From the Silence of the Bible to the Silence of Auschwitz.* Trans. David Maisel. Philadelphia: Jewish Publication Society, 1981.

Newman, Barbara. *Striking a Balance: Dancers Talking about Dancing.* Boston: Houghton Mifflin, 1982.

Niederman, Sharon, ed. *Shaking Eve's Tree: Short Stories of Jewish Women.* Philadelphia: Jewish Publication Society, 1990.

Obolensky, Dimitri. *The Penguin Book of Russian Verse.* Harmondsworth: Penguin, 1962.

Olsen, Tillie. "Dream-Vision." In *Shaking Eve's Tree,* ed. Sharon Niederman, 119–23. Philadelphia: Jewish Publication Society, 1990.

——. *Silences.* New York: Delacorte Press, 1978.

——. *Tell Me a Riddle.* New York: Dell, 1961.

Ozick, Cynthia. *The Pagan Rabbi and Other Stories.* New York: Dutton, 1983.

Paley, Grace. *Later the Same Day.* New York: Penguin, 1985.

Picard, Max. *The World of Silence.* Trans. Stanley Godman. South Bend, Ind.: Gateway Press, 1952.

Plaskow, Judith. *Standing Again at Sinai.* San Francisco: Harper and Row, 1990.

Plaut, W. Gunther, ed. *The Torah: A Modern Commentary.* New York: Union of American Hebrew Congregations, 1981.

Potok, Chaim. *The Gift of Asher Lev.* New York: Alfred A. Knopf, 1990.

Pool, David de Sola, ed. and trans. *The Traditional Prayer Book for Sabbath and Festivals.* New York: Behrman House, 1960.

Rich, Adrienne. *The Fact of a Doorframe: Poems Selected and New, 1950–1984.* New York: Norton, 1984.

Robert, Marthe. *As Lonely as Franz Kafka.* Trans. Ralph Manheim. New York: Schocken, 1986.

Rosen, Tova. "On Tongues Being Bound and Let Loose: Women in Medieval Hebrew Literature." *Prooftexts* 8 (1988): 67–87.

Rosenzweig, Franz. *The Star of Redemption.* Trans. William W. Hallo. New York: Holt, Rinehart, and Winston, 1971.

Roskies, David G. *Against the Apocalypse: Responses to Catastrophe in Modern Jewish Culture.* Cambridge: Harvard Univ. Press, 1984.

Roth, Henry. *Call It Sleep.* New York: Farrar, Straus, Giroux, 1991.

Roth, Philip. *Goodbye, Columbus and Five Short Stories.* Boston: Houghton Mifflin, 1959.

Rothenberg, Jerome, with Harris Lenowitz and Charles Doria, ed. *A Big Jewish Book: Poems and Other Visions of the Jews from Tribal Times to the Present.* Garden City, N.Y.: Anchor, 1978. Revised ed. titled: *Exiled in the Word.* Port Townsend, Wash.: Copper Canyon Press, 1989.

Rukeyser, Muriel. *Out of Silence*, ed. Kate Daniels. Evanston, Ill.: TriQuarterly Books / Northwestern University Press, 1992.

Scholem, Gershom. *On the Mystical Shape of the Godhead: Basic Concepts in the Kabbalah*. Trans. Joachim Neugroschel. New York: Schocken, 1991.

Shakespeare, William. *The Riverside Shakespeare*. Ed. G. Blakemore Evans. Boston: Houghton Mifflin, 1974.

Silverman, Morris, ed. *Maḥzor / High Holiday Prayer Book*. New York: Prayer Book Press, 1978.

Soloveitchik, Joseph B. *The Lonely Man of Faith*. New York: Doubleday, 1992.

Steiner, George. *Language and Silence*. New York: Atheneum, 1967.

Steinsalz, Adin. *The Essential Talmud*. Trans. Chaya Galai. New York: Basic Books, 1976.

——. *The Talmud: The Steinsalz Edition, a Reference Guide*. Trans. Israel V. Berman. New York: Random House, 1989.

Stern, Gerald. *Leaving Another Kingdom: Selected Poems*. New York: Harper and Row, 1990.

Tate, Alan. *Collected Poems: 1917–1976*. New York: Farrar, Straus, Giroux, 1977.

Trakl, Georg. *Dichtung und Briefe*. Ed. Walther Killy. Salzburg: Otto Müller Verlag, 1969.

Umansky, Ellen M., and Dianne Ashton, eds. *Four Centuries of Jewish Women's Spirituality: A Sourcebook*. Boston: Beacon Press, 1992.

Vercors [Jean Bruller]. *Les silences de la mer*. Ed. Jacques Schiffrin. New York: Pantheon, 1943.

Wiesel, Elie. *Somewhere a Master: Further Hasidic Portraits and Legends*. New York: Summit, 1982.

——. *Souls on Fire: Portraits and Legends of Hasidic Masters*. New York: Vintage, 1972.

——. *The Testament*. Trans. Marion Wiesel. New York: Summit Books, 1981.

Wirth-Nesher, Hana. "Between Native Tongue and Mother Language in *Call It Sleep*." *Prooftexts* 10 (1990): 297–312.

The Wisdom of the Zohar: An Anthology of Texts. Ed. Isaiah Tishby, trans. David Goldstein. Oxford: Oxford Univ. Press, 1989.

Wittgenstein, Ludwig. *Tractatus Logico-Philosophicus*. Introduction by Bertrand Russell. New York: Harcourt Brace, 1922.

Wolpe, David. *The Healer of Shattered Hearts: A Jewish View of God*. Harmondsworth: Penguin, 1990.

——. *In Speech and in Silence*. New York: Henry Holt, 1992.

Yovel, Yirmiyahu. *The Marrano of Reason*. Princeton, N.J.: Princeton Univ. Press, 1989.

The Zohar. Trans. Harry Sperling, Maurice Simon, and Paul P. Levertoff. London: Soncino Press, 1931–34.

Index